BEYOND THE MONOLITH

Published in cooperation with the Institute of
Central/East European and Russian-Area Studies,
Carlton University, Ottawa

BEYOND THE MONOLITH
The Emergence of Regionalism in Post-Soviet Russia

Edited by
Peter J. Stavrakis
Joan DeBardeleben
and Larry Black
with the assistance of Jodi Koehn

The Woodrow Wilson Center Press
Washington, D.C.

The Johns Hopkins University Press
Baltimore and London

Editorial offices:
The Woodrow Wilson Center Press
370 L'Enfant Promenade, S.W., Suite 704
Washington, D.C. 20024-2518
Telephone 202-287-3000, ext. 218

Order from:
The Johns Hopkins University Press
Hampden Station
Baltimore, Maryland 21211
Telephone 1-800-537-5487

© 1997 by the Woodrow Wilson International Center for Scholars
All rights reserved
Printed in the United States of America on acid-free paper ∞

2 4 6 8 9 7 5 3 1

Library of Congress Cataloging-in-Publication Data

Beyond the monolith: the emergence of regionalism in post-Soviet Russia
 / edited by Peter J. Stavrakis, Joan DeBardeleben, and Larry Black, with
 the assistance of Jodi Koehn.
    p.   cm.
  Includes bibliographical references and index.
  ISBN 0-8018-5617-5 (alk. paper)
  1. Regionalism—Russia (Federation) 2. Federal government—Russia
(Federation) 3. Post-communism—Russia (Federation) 4. Russia
(Federation)—Economic conditions—1991– 5. Russia (Federation)—
Social conditions—1991– 6. Russia (Federation)—Ethnic relations.
I. Stavrakis, Peter J., 1955–   . II. DeBardeleben, Joan. III. Black, J. L.
(Joseph Laurence), 1937–   .
JN6693.5.R43B49 1997
320.947—dc21   97-17749
                                                                          CIP

THE WOODROW WILSON INTERNATIONAL CENTER FOR SCHOLARS

BOARD OF TRUSTEES
Joseph H. Flom, Chair. Joseph A. Cari, Jr., Vice Chair. *Ex Officio Members:* Secretary of State, Secretary of Health and Human Services, Secretary of Education, Chair of the National Endowment for the Humanities, Secretary of the Smithsonian Institution, Librarian of Congress, Director of the U.S. Information Agency, Archivist of the United States.
Private Citizen Members: James A. Baker III, Steven Alan Bennett, Kathryn Walt Hall, Jean L. Hennessey, Eli Jacobs, Daniel L. Lamaute, Paul Hae Park, S. Dillon Ripley.
Designated Appointee of the President: Samuel R. Berger.

The Center is the living memorial of the United States of America to the nation's twenty-eighth president, Woodrow Wilson. Congress established the Woodrow Wilson Center in 1968 as an international institute for advanced study, "symbolizing and strengthening the fruitful relationship between the world of learning and the world of public affairs." The Center opened in 1970 under its own board of trustees.

In all its activities, the Woodrow Wilson Center is a nonprofit, nonpartisan organization, supported financially by annual appropriations from the Congress, and by the contributions of foundations, corporations, and individuals.

WOODROW WILSON CENTER PRESS
The Woodrow Wilson Center Press publishes books written in substantial part at the Center or otherwise prepared under its sponsorship by fellows, guest scholars, staff members, and other program participants. Conclusions or opinions expressed in Center publications and programs are those of the authors and speakers and do not necessarily reflect the views of the Center staff, fellows, trustees, advisory groups, or any individuals or organizations that provide financial support to the Center.

CONTENTS

Maps and Tables   ix

Acknowledgments   xi

Introduction: Russian Regionalism in Post-Soviet Society   1
Peter J. Stavrakis

I   THE HISTORICAL SETTING

1 Center-Periphery Relations in Historical Perspective: State Administration in Russia   11
Don K. Rowney

II   POLITICS

2 The Development of Federalism in Russia   35
Joan DeBardeleben

3 Electoral Behavior and Attitudes in Russia: Do Regions Make a Difference or Do Regions Just Differ?   57
Joan DeBardeleben and Aleksander A. Galkin

4 At the Bottom of the Heap: Local Self-government and Regional Politics in the Russian Federation   81
John F. Young

III   ECONOMIC REFORM AND SOCIAL CHANGE

5 Regional Aspects of Privatization in Russia   105
Darrell Slider

6 Labor Institutions in Post-Communist Russia: The Rise of Regionalism   118
Carol Clark

7 The Regionalization of Russia's Economy and Its Impact
on the Environment and Natural Resources   145
D. J. Peterson

8 Health in Russia: The Regional and National Dimensions   165
Mark G. Field

IV ETHNIC PERSPECTIVES

9 From the Outside Looking In: Armenians
in Western Siberia   183
Cynthia Buckley

10 A Tale of Two Villages: A Comparative Study
of Aboriginal-State Relations in Russia and Canada   195
Greg Poelzer

11 The Tatarstan Model: A Situational Dynamic   213
Nail Midkhatovich Moukhariamov

Conclusion: Democracy and Federalism in the
Former Soviet Union and the Russian Federation   233
Robert V. Daniels

Editors and Contributors   245

Index   249

MAPS AND TABLES

MAPS

2.1 Constituent Units of the Russian Federation   41

3.1 Economic Regions of Russia   59

TABLES

1.1 Comparison of Direct Taxes and Rents, 1726–1796   20

1.2 Change in the Cost of the Military as a Factor in State Budgets: Pintner's Data for the Imperial Period   23

2.1 Constituent Units of the Russian Federation   42

3.1 December 1993 Voting Results for the Largest Parties/Blocs in Type I Regions   63

3.2 December 1993 Voting Results for the Largest Parties/Blocs in Type II Regions   65

3.3 December 1993 Voting Results for the Largest Parties/Blocs in Type III Regions   68

3.4 December 1993 Voting Results for the Largest Parties/Blocs in Type IV Regions   69

3.5 Voting Behavior and Party Identification in Four Regions of Russia, 1993–1996   72

3.6 Expected Change in the Standard of Living in the Next Three to Four Years: Russian Postelection Survey, 1995–1996   74

3.7 Support for Introducing Democracy in Russia, 1995–1996   74

3.8 Satisfaction with Standard of Living, by Region, 1995–1996   75

3.9 Satisfaction with Level of Democracy in Russia, by Region, 1995–1996   75

3.10 Respondents' Feeling about Zyuganov, by Region   76

3.11 Predictors of Positive Attitude toward Zyuganov: Russian Postelection Survey, 1995–1996   78

7.1 Decline in Level of Physical Output of Selected Sectors in 1994 as Percent of 1990 Output   147

7.2 Increase in Selected Exports by Volume, 1992–1994   148

7.3 The Impact of Restructuring on Agriculture, 1986–1993   160

8.1 Atmospheric Discharge from Stationary Sources, Atmospheric Discharge per Capita (Urban Population), and Death Rates Due to Lung Cancer (Population 0–64), 1992, by Administrative Region   172

11.1 Political Evolution of the "Tatarstan Model"   217

11.2 Russian Federation Republic Budget Figures for the First Half of 1995   226

11.3 Subjects of the Federation Budget Figures of Regional Status in 1995   227

ACKNOWLEDGMENTS

Although the idea for this book originated from conversations in early 1994 between Blair Ruble, director of the Kennan Institute for Advanced Russian Studies, and Larry Black, director of the Centre for Research on Canadian-Russian Relations (CRCR) at Carleton University, its success is due to the generous support of several institutions and to the hard work of several key individuals who were essential in sustaining the academic research project. In particular, the authors are grateful to the CRCR and the Institute of Central/East European and Russian-Area Studies (CERAS) of Carleton University for cohosting the May 1995 conference "Regions in Russia," which formed the basis for most of the contributions to the book.

Thanks are due the Woodrow Wilson International Center for Scholars, which made federal conference funds available to the Kennan Institute to support the project, and the advisory board of the Centre for Research on Canadian-Russian Relations, which graciously allocated substantial support for conference activities and this book. A grant from the University of Calgary–Gorbachev Foundation facilitated Aleksander Galkin's participation in the conference, as well as the inclusion of his work here. Other Russian participants in the conference were in Ottawa in connection with a training program in survey research methods sponsored by the Canadian International Development Agency (CIDA) of the government of Canada, in cooperation with the Institute for Complex Social Studies (Moscow) and the CERAS's East-West Project at Carleton University.

On an individual level, Peter Konecny deserves thanks for his efforts to find funding on behalf of CRCR, for initiating a speakers' program, and for serving as a cordial host to the conference participants. Andrea Gardner, CRCR's administrator, also performed the vital logistical tasks associated with a highly successful conference. Finally, the editors and contributors owe an enormous debt of gratitude to Jodi Koehn, assistant editor of the Kennan Institute, who single-handedly undertook the daunting task of editorial revision. Without her tireless effort, efficiency, and patience in tolerating traditional scholarly chaos, this book simply could not have been completed.

Peter J. Stavrakis
Joan Debardeleben
Larry Black

BEYOND THE MONOLITH

Introduction

Russian Regionalism in Post-Soviet Society

Peter J. Stavrakis

> *Sovietologists need to study the Russian provinces today . . . for the future of Russia will be determined not in Moscow, but in the provinces and small towns.*
>
> Stepan Sulakshin, former representative of the Russian president in Tomsk oblast, October 9, 1992

The collapse of the Soviet Union in 1991 created the chance for Russia's provinces to loosen the bonds that held together one of history's most tightly centralized regimes. Although the Russian Federation avoided the disintegration that befell the USSR, by 1995 the eighty-nine "subjects" of the federation had clearly achieved a substantial decentralization of political and economic power. Moscow became enmeshed in a series of crises, culminating in the bloody civil war in Chechnya, and as world attention focused on power struggles in the Kremlin, many regional leaders exploited the center's distraction and seized the initiative in key areas of provincial life. Tax policy, foreign investment, privatization, municipal government, and other areas of public life increasingly bear the mark of regional governments struggling to articulate their own policies in the wake of Moscow's retreat from the provinces. Russia's central government was not absent from regional developments for long, however, and centralizing pressures have reappeared to challenge newfound regional authority. The resolution of these contradictory political tendencies, as well as the growing economic disparity between center and periphery, will determine whether Russia discards an authoritarian heritage in favor of a decentralized polity. Whichever path Russia chooses, the more than fifty regional elections in the latter part of 1996 ruled out a return to the Communist past. But electoral institutions will provide only part of the answer, for the consolidation of center-regional relations in Russia—whether through a renewed unitary state, an asymmetrical federation, or an unpredictable feudalism—entails legal, administrative, and social changes requiring more than a generation to complete.

Presidential and parliamentary elections in 1995 and 1996, paralleled by landmark federal legislation, have underscored the importance of regionalism in Russia and compelled analysts to reach beyond Moscow's city limits to understand the dynamics of post-Soviet reality.[1] Russian regions, previously subordinated to Moscow via autocratic institutions, have used the ballot box to register their unwillingness to tolerate the historic primacy of Muscovy. Democracy has given voice to a regional sentiment of opposition to the pro-Western and proreform policies of the central government. This is an important development, for it indicates that the still-unresolved regional issue will take us beyond "transition" and "reform," as these have been understood in the West, and into the next stage of Russia's troubled political future. This prompts tantalizing questions: If regional parties and elites retain their popularity, how will a truly national politics emerge that unites provinces and Russian metropole? What will a postreform Russia look like, especially given the increased prominence of regional elites?

This new regional assertiveness is not restricted to politics but draws its strength from the growing economic gulf that separates a prosperous center from increasingly impoverished provinces. The average income in Moscow in 1995 was more than three times higher than that of Russians living outside of Moscow's Ring Road.[2] More significant, average per capita income was *below* what the Russian President's Analytical Center deemed necessary to maintain a "subsistence" income in sixty-eight of Russia's eighty-nine component jurisdictions. And whereas only eleven regions—a bare 12 percent of the federation—had an individual per capita monthly income that exceeded a "subsistence" level, Muscovites' earnings exceeded the subsistence level by 243 percent. A March 1996 study commissioned by the European Union's TACIS Program confirmed that in terms of living standards and official unemployment Moscow retained—and to some extent increased—its privileged position relative to other regions.[3] In addition, the disparity between the richest and the poorest provinces in the Russian Federation has increased more than fivefold between 1992 and 1994, and more than three-quarters of all financial transactions occur in Moscow, a reflection of the extreme concentration of Russia's capital assets.[4]

Reform in Russia relegated regional issues to a lower priority; thus the ironic result of the country's transition was the substitution of the Communist-era imperative of building socialism in one country with a newer—and inherently problematic—goal of building capitalism in one city. Analysts who have concluded that Russia is now a "normal" society fail to appreciate that normality and stability are elusive in a society in which prosperity is not spreading beyond one city. The status of Moscow, with less than 6 percent of the Russian population, as an enclave of affluence in a landscape of despair was negatively reflected in the ballots cast by Russia's overwhelmingly regional electorate.

The emerging gap between Moscow and the provinces provides the West with important lessons for understanding the regional complexion of a future Russia. The recent popularity of non-Moscow-based political parties and personalities in Russian elections, for example, reflects a rejection of Moscow's success at the expense of the regional electorate. The Communist Party of the Russian Federation is perhaps the only truly organized political force outside of Moscow, and a massive pro-Yeltsin media blitz and the diversion of state funds to his campaign were required to ensure the president's reelection in 1996. Even so, assigning responsibility for the subsequent regional campaigns to Anatoly Chubais, Boris Yeltsin's chief of staff, testifies to the residual Communist strength in the regions. Much of the support for Alexander Lebed derives from beyond the Ring Road and from the former lieutenant-general's appealing image as an outsider capable of saving Russia from Moscow. By contrast, Yegor Gaidar, Boris Fyodorov, and most of the other once-prominent reformers—nearly all of whom know London, Paris, New York, and Washington better than Yekaterinburg, Krasnodar, Karelia, or Khabarovsk—have disappeared from view.

The electoral results in Russia's regions reflect profound disappointment over Western assistance. This is understandable, for the narrow Muscovite vision of Western aid agencies reinforced the historic role of Moscow in undermining the independence and economic promise of the regions—for its own gain. Until Western aid officials leave the comfortable environs of Moscow's luxury hotels and develop regional contacts to reduce the capital's stranglehold on economic wealth, Russian regionalism will likely promote a society that is deeply distrustful of the West, making constructive collaboration increasingly difficult.

Finally, the regional perspective should sensitize us to the fact that post-Soviet Russia has embarked on a course that leads neither to an eager embrace of Western-style democracy nor to a rejection of capitalism. Moscow has expropriated much of the economic benefits from the transition to capitalism, whereas Russia's regions have confronted the stark realities of unemployment, declining standards of living, minimal foreign investment, and a vanishing public revenue base. This distorted legacy of Russian history and Western reform exercises relentless pressure on regional elites to join with Moscow in finding a political solution that liberates their economic resources and mollifies a population skeptical of the promise of Western institutions.

The importance of regionalism in Russia's future has emerged only recently in Western scholarship. Post-Soviet Russia has been viewed predominantly through the prisms of ethnic conflict or rigid macroeconomic analysis.[5] Ethnicity remains central to comprehending Russia, but the task must now be to integrate the study of communal conflict with the regional variations present in Russia. Similarly, the arid theoretical determinism of the macroeconomic approach preferred by many policymakers and multilateral institutions must be modified in light of regional differences. Here too, the fundamental economic disparity between Moscow and the provinces is emerging as the defining characteristic of post-Soviet society, a characteristic that economists would be remiss to ignore. Refracting these dimensions of analysis through the lens of regionalism produces a variety of new, intriguing questions about the post-Communist era: How will regions respond to the need to integrate their economies into the global economy? What impact will administrative divisions designed to fulfill the demands of a Stalinist system have on regional behavior in the post-Soviet world? Do regional governments have the resources to respond to the daunting social and environmental problems they now confront? Have personal leadership styles among regional elites, now freed from central control, affected regional development? Will regional elites possess the skills and institutions to resist or modify the inevitable return of Moscow's demands on the provinces?

These questions reflect the emergence of a complex regionalism in Russia, unprecedented in its degree of decentralization yet ambiguous and unstable due to political and economic forces that have reanimated Moscow's acquisitive impulse. The objective of this book, based on the proceedings of a May 1995 conference held at Carleton University and cosponsored by the Kennan Institute for Advanced Russian Studies of the Woodrow Wilson International Center for Scholars, is to elucidate the principal factors that underlie the development of regionalism in post-Soviet Russia. As such, the contributions to this volume fill a gap in our understanding of contemporary Russian politics and society and challenge scholars to reconsider the traditional paradigms through which Soviet Russia has been understood: if Russia's future depends on the provinces, then we must seek to understand the challenges of socio-economic transformation from the perspectives that lie outside Moscow.

Collectively, the contributors to this volume have endeavored to identify the factors responsible for the pronounced variations that have become the hallmark of Russian regionalism. Some regions have moved aggressively forward with economic reform policies while others have stagnated; still other regions have been trendsetters in political reform even as they have languished in adapting to new economic realities. Pervading all of these regions is the intriguing question of the likely role of provincial Communists—the backbone of parliamentary successes in 1995—in the regions: will they resist or embrace the return of central authority? Once again, Russia's future appears bound to the fate of the Communist Party organization, but one wonders whether regional loyalties are not now strong enough to defeat party discipline.

President Yeltsin's reelection, the desire of Western policymakers to the contrary, has not excluded the likelihood that Russia's transformation may move in an unanticipated direction, but the chapters that follow make a strong case that no electoral outcome will be able to eradicate the new regionalism that has forever altered the development of Russian politics and society. No Russian state, whether federal or centralized, democratic or authoritarian, can avoid confronting the problem of regional relations. Even if substantial recentralization occurs, the developments of the last five years make it unlikely that Moscow's new rulers will be able easily to suppress the new regionalism. The darkening economic picture for many key provinces, moreover, indicates that serious regional disparities and instabilities lie ahead for any regime intent on turning back the clock. In such circumstances, regions will be inclined to cling to their autonomy, ultimately leading to a distinctively Russian brand of decentralized authoritarianism. Regardless of the outcome, there is little doubt that in the wake of the Communist monolith, the provinces have come to occupy a decisive role in determining Russia's future.

Even though the diversity of Russian regionalism makes it desirable to retain the rich detail of case studies, each contributor has made a conscious effort to present his or her analysis in a broader regional perspective that permits the reader to make sense of the heterogeneity of post-Soviet Russia. Don Rowney's study of the role of Russian central elites provides valuable historical perspective on the center-periphery relationship. Although he states that Moscow will return to its central role in Russian political life, Rowney tempers this conclusion with an intriguing historical analysis revealing that the reach of the Russian central elites has traditionally exceeded their grasp. This suggests that the new regionalism might survive in Russia, even if a substantial centralization of power recurs.

The section on politics is devoted to considering the broader constraints that operate on the development of Russian regionalism. Of particular interest in North America has been the extent to which federalism might suit post-Soviet conditions, a topic that Joan DeBardeleben takes up in her chapter. She documents the emergence of a uniquely Russian type of federal system, one reflecting many of the asymmetries that characterized its Soviet predecessor, and she reflects briefly on the larger implications, for Russian federalism, of the war in Chechnya. Next, DeBardeleben and Aleksander Galkin turn their attention to developing a classification of regions. They derive a typology with four distinct classes of regions, each class a product of the differential impact of the Stalinist command administrative structure. Electoral results are then used to reveal interesting differences between, as well as similarities across, regions while simultaneously suggesting further research directions that will enhance the explanatory value of their typology. Finally, John Young examines the other end of the regional political hierarchy through his study of the impact of local politics on regional elites in Omsk oblast. Young demonstrates how regional governments, like the central government, are engaged in struggles with the localities, over the same fiscal and political issues that characterize center-provincial relations. The indeterminate nature of local politics suggests that here too Russia will exhibit considerable variation.

The chapters in the third part focus on key socioeconomic sectors, revealing regional differentiation along several axes. Indeed, the marked variations in environmental, resource, and health factors suggest the troubling conclusion that Russia's asymmetries will prove intractable for a unitary government to manage successfully. In his examination of privatization policy, Darrell Slider reveals differences in the incentives and objectives of the center and the regional governments in Russia. His analysis points to the important conclusion that regional elites have been able to successfully resist, undermine, or defeat the economic and sociopolitical objectives of Moscow's privatization program. Changes in the Russian labor market are examined by Carol Clark in her study of the metallurgical sector. Clark concludes that regional factors have been central to the breakdown of the Soviet-era labor market, indicating that this area of economic activity will, in time, acquire a greater regional character. In assessing the status of Russia's environment and natural resources, D. J. Peterson demonstrates how the regionalization of the Russian landmass gives resource-rich provinces an advantage over their counterparts. His analysis indicates that uneven resource distribution will significantly affect the conditions under which various regions will succeed in entering the global economy. Finally, Mark Field assesses the daunting challenges confronted by Russia in the area of health care and reveals that the impact of this crisis has varied widely. As a result, provincial governments have adapted in various ways, creating a diversity of regional approaches to the problem of health care.

A separate section is devoted to the examination of the relationship between ethnicity and the new regionalism. Cynthia Buckley considers the relationship between the Armenian diaspora and the ethnic Russian population in Siberian regions far from the center. Greg Poelzer contributes a fascinating comparative study of the indigenous peoples of Russia and Canada in the more remote areas of each country—and finds surprising parallels. Finally, Nail Moukhariamov assesses the circumstances underlying the success of the "Tatarstan model," in which Moscow took the unprecedented step of negotiating a bilateral agreement with one subject of the federation. Moukhariamov identifies several factors that account for this success, which, in the long run, will likely prove more important for Russian regions than the debacle in Chechnya.

In the conclusion, Robert Daniels examines whether the Soviet past and the Russian present provide any hope for the development of federalism in Russia, which he deems as the political centerpiece of Russia's regional dilemma. Daniels is especially concerned about the likely fate of democracy in a society that may be torn between the simultaneous and irreconcilable temptations for too much and too little centralization of authority.

The chapters in this volume make a strong case for complementing our traditional Moscow-centric view of the former Soviet Union with a regional-level perspective. Russia will remain a top-heavy society and polity, so studies based on Moscow are unlikely ever to fall out of favor. But if we are to reach a fuller understanding of Russia's future (and perhaps its past as well), scholars must come to grips with the reality of regionalism in the post-Soviet era. In this respect, this book—along with others like it—begins the difficult process of adapting post-Soviet scholarship to the factors that will define Russian politics, economy, and society in the next century.

NOTES

1. One of the defining events of this period came with the Russian Federation's August 12, 1995, law: "General Principles of Organizing Local Self Government," *Rossiiskaya gazeta,* September 1, 1995; this law moved Moscow beyond bilateral agreements between the center and individual regions.
2. *Rossiiskie regioni nakanune vyborov—95,* Analiticheskoe upravlenie Prezidenta Rossiiskoi Federatsii (Moscow: Yuridicheskaya Literatura, 1995). Data are for the month of July 1995 and do not include statistics on the ten autonomous okrugs or the autonomous oblast.
3. *Analiz tendentsii razvitiia regionov Rossii v 1992–1995 gg.* (Moscow: TACIS

Program, European Union, March 1996), Appendices 2-1, 3-1: 84–95. A fuller assessment of the implications of the 1995 parliamentary elections on Russian politics is in Peter J. Stavrakis, "Russia after the Elections: Democracy or Parliamentary Byzantium?" *Problems of Post-Communism* 43, no. 2 (March/April 1996): 13–20.

4. Stefan Hedlund and Niclas Sundstrom, "The Russian Economy after Systemic Change," working paper #22, Department of East European Studies, Uppsala University, Uppsala, Sweden, November 1995, p. 17.

5. This is in the process of being redressed, even as decreased funding for Eurasian studies narrows the research horizon. In addition to the contributors to this volume, the work of Jo Andrews, M. Steven Fish, Susan Lehmann, Blair Ruble, Steven Solnick, Kathryn Stoner-Weiss, Michael Urban, and others will soon provide us with a richer base for understanding regional dynamics in Russia. Issues in local politics have received even greater attention than regional questions; see, for example, Theodore H. Friedgut and Jeffrey W. Hahn, eds., *Local Power and Post-Soviet Politics* (Armonk, N.Y.: M. E. Sharpe, 1994). European scholars focused on Russian regions somewhat earlier. See, for example, *Revue d'Etudes Comparative Est-Ouest* 24 (March 1993); the entire issue was devoted to regionalism and appeared as *Les Regions en Russie: Decomposition ou Recomposition?* The most unprecedented development, however, is the emergence of a generation of Russian scholars studying the phenomenon of regionalism. Western perspectives on Russia have been greatly enriched by the opportunity to work with Russian colleagues such as Sergei Shishkin, Nikolai Petrov, Vladimir Gel'man, and Nail Moukhariamov.

I
THE HISTORICAL SETTING

1

Center-Periphery Relations in Historical Perspective: State Administration in Russia

Don K. Rowney

INTRODUCTION: DEFINITIONS AND INTERPRETIVE PERSPECTIVES

The objective of this study is to identify and characterize key elements in the relationship between state organizations of the center and economic and social activities in the Russian periphery in the nineteenth and twentieth centuries. For our purposes, "center" will be taken to mean those organizations and institutions (1) created by state power, (2) located either in St. Petersburg or Moscow, and (3) whose span of authority encompassed all, or practically all, of the area ruled by the state. This definition would include, for example, organizations such as the Imperial Ministries of Finances, Education, and Internal Affairs, the Soviet-era Commissariats of Communications and of Posts and Telegraphs, the State Planning Commission, the Supreme Council of the National Economy and its successor commissariats, and the administrative organs of the Central Committee of the Communist Party. "Periphery," on the other hand, means those organizations, institutions, and informal groups that are distributed in geographic areas apart from the center. These would include regional and local administrative bodies for health and education, economic organizations such as commercial and manufacturing enterprises, and social entities such as clubs and households.

Central to my interpretation is the fact that during the period I am outlining here, the Russian national economy underwent two rapid growth spurts in manufacturing capacity and, as a consequence that I shall try to explain, an epochal transformation in the bases of power accessible to the state. Obviously, I cannot attempt to narrate in detail the changing nature of each of these relationships. Instead, I shall identify and describe specific cases that I believe demonstrate important aspects of the center-periphery linkage, at the end synthesizing a set of characteristics that these cases appear to illustrate.

I shall address two questions in this chapter. First, what are the key characteristics of state administration considered from the viewpoint of how administration bears on center-periphery linkages? Second, how do specific policy programs and the creation of specific organizational entities illustrate the nature of these linkages in the nineteenth and twentieth centuries?

No one will question, presumably, that the state, as a centralized collection of organizations, as a field of action for elites, or as a power arena, has played a dominant role in virtually every aspect of modern Russian national development. It has also been shown that the state's role in the formation of center-periphery relations, as measured, for example, by policy development or by organizational growth, expanded enormously in the period considered here.[1]

The historical sociologist Michael Mann defines the state in terms of autonomy, political geography, and two major types of power that the state projects into a given territory. In his view, states are complex social organizations that have historically tried to enhance their autonomy from other, nonstate entities while extending their authority, or sovereignty, over a specific geographic location.[2] States have done this through varying degrees of intensity and arbitrariness (despotic power) or through control of social resources (infrastructural power).[3] Particularly important for our purposes is Mann's vision of the beginning of the industrial era as a watershed for the development of state power because technology extended the projection of power across geographic space "exponentially."[4] "Power infrastructures leaped forward with the industrial revolution. Industrial capitalism destroyed 'territorially federal' societies, replacing them with nation states across whose territories unitary control and surveillance structures could penetrate.... Logistical penetration of territory has increased exponentially over the last century and a half."[5]

In Mann's view, state organizations have self-interestedly extended and deepened their control over geographic areas in a way that depended on the available supporting technology. With the onset of industrialization, states amplified their power not only by engaging international competitors (e.g., England vs. France, vs. Germany) but also by increasingly using new technology to project sovereignty within their own borders. "If we add together the necessity, multiplicity and territorial-centrality of the state, we can in principle explain its autonomous power. By these means the state elite possesses an independence from civil society which, though not absolute, is no less absolute in principle than the power of any other major group. As a consequence *we can treat states as actors in the person of state elites with a will to power.*"[6] To put the argument in its simplest terms, then, Mann asserts that we need to see that the state's role in industrial development, a particularly important example of the development of infrastructural power, mainly served interests within the state apparatus.

The view that there was a state self-interest in economic development, in the case of Russia, offers considerable interpretive strengths. State servitors (both military and civilian, both individually and in formal organizations) may be seen as exponents of infrastructural development. Such development is meant to preserve and promote the servitors' career interests, to enhance the survival of their organizational turf, and to serve the interests of their organizations and of the entire state apparatus.

THE STATE AND THE PROBLEM OF INSTITUTIONS IN TIME

The role of institutions ("perfectly analogous to the rules of the game in a competitive team sport")[7] in economic development is the primary focus of the economic historian Douglass C. North.[8] In his view, "History . . . is largely a story of institutional evolution in which the historical performance of economies can only be understood as part of a sequential story."[9] For our purposes, the crucial term here is "evolution." At several different points in various works, North explains why institutions are important, why they endure, and more important, why they change only incrementally. In North's view, institutions do not "collapse" or "dissolve."[10] As North explains the role of institutions: "Economic history is overwhelmingly the story of economies that failed to produce a set of economic rules of the game (with enforcement) that induce sustained economic growth. The central issue of economic history and of economic development is to account for the evolution of political and economic institutions that create an economic environment that induces increasing productivity." With a degree of sophistication not available in the work of other students of state development, such as Theda Skocpol, North's view helps us to focus on the crucial significance of the interaction among social and economic factors as they bear on state development. In establishing this perspective, North offers a much expanded understanding of the role of "legacies" from the past in constraining the present and the future of any given society.[11]

A critical point is that since institutions are more or less impossible to modify intentionally, especially within a short period of time, organizations—whether those of the state, of private enterprise, of the church, or of groups of private individuals—are formed so as to function within a given institutional framework, with little realistic expectation of changing that frame except marginally. The cumulative, structured interaction among individuals, organizations, and institutions, enduring in time, is an example of the phenomenon that North refers to as "path dependence."[12] Certain patterns of behavior by individuals or organizations are reinforced by success within a given institutional framework; thus these behaviors tend to be repeated, socializing all participants and creating a limited set of options for them. According to North and others, such path dependence tends to structure most exchanges in society.

Apart from the obvious broad applicability of the concepts of path dependence and transaction costs to state organizations, there is a specific role, in North's view, for the state and its organizations in social exchange. Although institutions provide the framework or the formal and informal rules of the game for social exchanges, there is no guarantee, in a given case, that the rules will be obeyed. This raises the problem of rule (law, custom) enforcement. In relatively simple societies or in relatively simple exchanges, enforcement is not a serious problem. But as societies and their exchanges grow more complex, evenhanded enforcement becomes more necessary, providing a greater role for the most usual and most cost-effective third-party enforcer, the state.[13]

To summarize the perspectives of Mann and North, we note Mann's view that state development of resources, including physical infrastructure, information systems, and organizations, enhances state power vis-à-vis other segments of society. The resulting state autonomy from other social organizations and individuals is not necessarily impersonal; on the contrary, it may be exercised by state elites "with a will to power" in their own self-interest. In North's view, the enhancement of infrastructure in the process of economic modernization, even if achieved through independent private development, will also elicit a self-interested state role. In addition, however, North argues that such a role consists in paths of behavior that are formed, or structured, through institutions that have emerged over time and that can be changed only incrementally, or marginally, at any given point. Finally, he emphasizes that even in cases in which exchanges are limited to nonstate individuals (for example, in trade or in civil organizations), the state, as "honest" broker, will have a role to play. In the view of both Mann and North, the extension of infrastructure based on new technology may expand the autonomous state's ability to play this role in self-interested ways.

PATTERNS FROM RUSSIAN HISTORY

In the following pages I shall trace, in very broad terms, the tidal rises and falls of four principal patterns of state behavior affecting center-periphery relations. The first is the reliance of Russian state authorities on the administrative option to centralize authority, denying both resources and control to the periphery. The second pattern is the enduring roles of self-interested state elites, expressed both in their control over the selection of succeeding generations of officials and in their policies that tend to protect their preemptive intervention in center-periphery relations. The third pattern is a lack of congruence between the intentions, or policy ambitions, of policymakers and their actual achievements as measured by outcomes in Russian society, the economy, or state roles in international relations. The fourth is the importance of exogenous factors that impose limits on policy choices and that, at certain moments, even change policymakers' agendas. These are controlling events, which Skocpol and others have noted.[14] What makes them important for our purposes is that they are events that policymakers have little control over and that nevertheless have had, at certain historic moments, profound consequences for center-periphery relations.

As opportunity allows, I shall indicate how the theoretical insights of Mann and North are useful for understanding the patterns that I shall describe. My method for achieving this ambitious task will be to focus on three case studies, chosen less for their suitability as samples than for their capacity to illuminate the problem of the nature of center-periphery relations. The center-periphery linkage characteristics that are common to the cases cited will be summarized in a conclusion, which will also attempt to identify those aspects that seem to have meaning for the roles of the state in Russia's future.

CASE I: ENDURANCE OF PREINDUSTRIAL ADMINISTRATIVE STRUCTURES AND ELITE ROLES

Rationalization and State Administration

During the eighteenth century, several attempts were made, at the highest levels of state authority, to enhance and rationalize central administrative control over the imperial periphery.[15] These attempts at increasing central state control included not only the reform of civil and military territorial administration but also the extension of elite servitors' social and economic authority over enserfed peasants. When Alexander I came to the throne in 1801, his reign inaugurated a host of activities—on both the international and the domestic fronts—that aimed to enhance and rationalize state power. For our purposes, the most significant results of this work were the reforms that created Russia's ministerial administrative system.

Reforms and Path Dependence

The ministerial government reforms of Alexander I were marked by two characteristics that are important to this narrative. First, these structures, introduced in the preindustrial era, when Russia was still an overwhelmingly traditional agrarian state in which serfdom marked lord and peasant relations, have endured to the present time. As an alternative to a federal, decentralized structure (generally unknown in Russian administrative history), or to a regional military dictatorship, or to a hypercentralized single administrative dictatorship (generally impractical given the physical size and the economic and cultural diversity of the empire), a center-provincial civil administration was created. This system was imposed on the geographic regions (in European Russia, fifty provinces) created by Catherine the Great in 1775; a hierarchy of civil administrators reported both to the ministers in St. Petersburg and to the empress. Second, this reformation of state organizations was entirely consonant with the self-interest of state elites, as N. M. Karamzin (1766–1826), an articulate critic of the reforms, tirelessly noted.[16] It systematized the access of senior officials, the ministers, to the emperor while aiming to enhance their control over subordinate organizations in the provinces.

*Enhancement and Continuation of the Status
of "State-Certified" Landed Elites*

During the generation preceding the creation of these administrative structures, the landed elites' authority over the provincial peasantry, the majority of the population, was extended to its historic maximum.[17] The legislation underlying these measures is usually described only as aiming to enhance the status and economic benefit of the gentry, a move that is regarded as increasing peripheral independence. As an enhancement to peripheral authority, however, the extension of noble privilege is ambiguous at best. It should be seen also as a measure to extend the administrative authority of the state through an elite whose reliability as managers of local economy and as participants in such state-enhancing activities as tax collection could be taken for granted or, at any rate, sanctioned.[18] Thus the administrative structures created in the early nineteenth century were grafted over the already established social-economic administration of estates by a "state-certified" landed elite, reinforcing central control over the peasant periphery.

The new organizations created under Alexander I were incapable of discharging their assigned responsibilities. The small number of people actually available to carry out state operations and the low level of their administrative expertise combined to validate the characterization of "undergoverned" provinces.[19] Why, then, should the underlying organizational structure have been sufficiently robust, as a template for centralizing administration, to survive through a series of profound economic and political transformations and an enormous population increase until the end of the Soviet regime and possibly beyond? This ministerial model was designed to rationalize central authority and power over a territorially dispersed economy and population while ensuring close contact between ministers and other senior officials and the emperor (or first secretary). As a device to serve the ends of a territorially expanding, autonomous state—before, during, and after industrialization—this administrative model was potent. Its survival through the Great Reforms, the onset of industrialization, the Revolution of 1917, the New Economic Policy, the creation of the command economy, and the transformation of the USSR into a superpower testifies to the enduring strength of the model of rational authority. Of course, structural rationality is not the same as the ability to achieve a broad range of administrative outcomes. Clearly, however, state administration in Russia was rarely judged by this criterion. The criteria of rationality and autonomy were evidently far more important.

The survival of the preindustrial ministerial model reveals the tendency of the state's agents to pursue autonomous administrative roles in a path-dependent fashion—as Mann, explicitly, and North, in general, predict they should have done.[20] Nevertheless, the objective of central control by state elites, the objective that the structure was designed to achieve, was consistently frustrated by the scale of centralizing ambition, by the size of the task of control, and by the very real limitations of staff training and of the information to which elites had access.

CASE II: THE TRANSITION FROM DESPOTIC TO INFRASTRUCTURAL POWER AND ITS IMPLICATIONS FOR CENTRAL CONTROL OF THE RUSSIAN PERIPHERY, 1885–1914

Russia as a Despotic Autonomous State:
A Revision of Mann's View

Mann describes the preindustrial state's military organizations as perhaps its most important structural resource. In the case of Russia, however, this relationship contributed more to state autonomy than Mann's analysis suggests. The close connection between the military and the state sharply defined one important aspect of the "despotic" state's relationship to the society and its control over the periphery.[21] The autonomous power of the preindustrial Russian state in fact rested on a broader range of power than the restricted band of control implied by fiscal monopolies such as seigniorage and a military that physically controlled territory. In Russia, despotic state power already included important infrastructural resources that increased, or were enhanced, when they were restructured during the modernization of state organizations. From at least the time of Peter the Great (1689–1725) until well into the nineteenth century, the central state's power over peripheral territory and society was concentrated along four channels in Russia: taxation policy, manipulation of the money supply, rents collected by serf owners and especially by the greatest serf owner (the state), and military conscription.

Elements of Preindustrial State Power: Taxes Taxes were the most obvious means by which the preindustrial Russian state guaranteed its control of a powerful armed force and thus autonomous control of the geographic periphery. From 1722, one of the most potent sources of revenue for the state was a direct tax that was explicitly and exclusively designed to pay for the cost of the army. This so-called poll or "soul" tax *(podat' podushnaia)* was imposed on the lower classes, including millions of enserfed peasants, at a level calculated to pay for the ongoing maintenance of the state's military formations.[22]

But although the poll tax was specifically intended to support the army, it cannot be considered the only way in which the state transferred the cost of its armed forces to the population. Military costs dominated the entire state budget. During the reign of Catherine the Great (1762–96), for example, economic restructuring and the development of civilian provincial infrastructure were explicit objectives of Jacob Sievers, Catherine, and other participants in her administration.[23] Nevertheless, military expenditure, as a proportion of net state revenues, *averaged* 66 percent and never fell below 44 percent.[24] As the military burden mounted with particular ferocity during the major wars of the era, the budget deficit—the state debt—also grew. Inflation, primarily the result of state fiscal policies, was especially pronounced during the Great Northern War (1700–1721), the Seven Years' War (1756–63), and the years of Catherine's military and diplomatic adventures—a point that did not escape Karamzin's attention: "Two ill-fated wars with the French, the war with Turkey, and especially the war with Sweden (in the late 18th century) had compelled the treasury to multiply assignats. The inevitable result followed: the price of things went up, while the value of the currency went down."[25]

As the state debt mounted, pressure rose to maximize revenues of all kinds. The poll tax alone was obviously not capable of sustaining the burden. State organizations, moreover, were placing an increasing burden on the budget and the tax system. As the state succeeded in using its military to extend the empire, state organizations increased in size and number. Because of changing bases on which the definition of state offices and the calculation of revenues rested in the eighteenth century, it has been notoriously difficult for historians to specify how much expansion occurred.[26] But it is clear that the growth that did occur enhanced the independence of state organizations from nonstate society, differentiated state elites from everyone else, and consequently sharpened the distinction between center and periphery. Writing about the later eighteenth century, Arcadius Kahan summarized this change: "The growth of expenditures can be explained in part at least by the numerical growth of the reigning elite, by the growth of the various formal occasions at which the top bureaucrats, and also members of the aristocracy and gentry, had to conduct business and participate in ceremonial affairs. It was also a manifestation of the rising international prestige of Russia and its relations with foreign countries. The growth of expenditures increased with the spread of tastes for sophisticated Western-type consumption and life-style. Last but not least, expenditures increased as a result of price inflation."[27]

The state used all of the established forms of taxation—the direct poll tax, excises, and indirect taxes on items such as salt and alcohol—as devices to "conscript" not manpower but the entire nonstate periphery. It effectively requisitioned the national economy to sustain its increasingly opulent autonomy, to support its military organizations, and to moderate the debt that supporting the military had produced.

Elements of Preindustrial State Power: Rents and Conscription Thus far this discussion makes Russia seem only slightly different from absolutist states elsewhere in Europe. The story of struggles by statesmen to find reliable revenues to pay for current costs of the military and to fund the debt that wars had produced is familiar in France, England, and Prussia.[28] But a discussion that includes the Russian Empire as but one of several growing state powers risks missing a highly crucial difference between Russia and the other great absolutist monarchies: the increasing degree to which Russia, even in those early days, relied on a particular form of infrastructure control. The human infrastructure of a vast population of enserfed peasants formed a particularly important economic resource for autonomous state power in Russia. As Kahan has argued, taxes were

Table 1.1
COMPARISON OF DIRECT TAXES AND RENTS,
1726–1796 (in current rubles)

Year	Tax	Rents (obrok)
1726	4,005,634	694,979
1744	4,688,187	807,137
1784	6,739,283	13,567,665
1796	10,369,351	14,256,285

Source: Arcadius Kahan, *The Plow, the Hammer, and the Knout: An Economic History of Eighteenth-Century Russia* (Chicago: University of Chicago Press, 1985), tables 8.13 and 8.14, p. 334.

high, but across the entire century they rose in real terms relatively little, due to the state's inability to control price inflation. On the other hand, revenues from rents imposed on the serfs, bound by law to state lands, increased enormously. He summarized this pattern in the data presented here in table 1.1.

There was a second channel through which the state exploited its control of the nonstate periphery: the Russian system of military conscription. Before the state responded to the demands of new technology by restructuring the military system in 1874, the Russian army relied on the state's power to conscript the army and navy rank and file for life. Indeed, from the most intense state-building years of Peter the Great's reign until 1762, even the nobility was obliged to serve, effectively participating in the conscription system.[29] In the case of the peasantry, however, the system was far more rapacious and long-lived. Thus it is reasonable to calculate, as Kahan does, the annual average cost to the peasantry of the manpower that was lost by conscription. It is also reasonable to regard this especially greedy form of manpower supply as an arbitrary use of autonomous state power over human infrastructure. Human lives were consumed by this system at a prodigious rate in the eighteenth century. Kahan estimates the size of the armed forces as ranging from 200,000 in 1720–44 to more than 480,000 in 1796–99. He estimates war losses from battle and disease as ranging from 7,000 dead during Alexander Suvorov's expedition in Italy and Switzerland (1799) to 215,000 dead during the Russo-Turkish War (1768–74). For the entire century, he estimates 679,000 wartime deaths.[30] Exclusive of war loss, Kahan estimates "normal" mortality as 4 percent of the total population per year, probably a conservative figure. Calculating the cost of labor commandeered by the state's armed forces over the century, Kahan isolated the charges for war years, determining that they rose from 12.5

kopecks per taxpayer in the 1760s to 42.7 in 1767–69, 109 in 1770–73, and 228 in 1787–89.[31]

Wartime crises affected the eighteenth-century Russian state and, through it, the larger society. But tax and fiscal policies, together with the systems that were established to exploit human infrastructure, structured the long-term relationship between the state, on the one hand, and the Russian social periphery and its resources on the other. This structure —embodied in laws on serfdom, traditions of elite privilege, and nearly unquestioned state authority—confirmed the state's power internationally and domestically. As we shall see, the changing economic and social environments in which the state operated in the nineteenth century were associated with gradual and enormously important changes to this institutional structure.

Transition from Fiscal Extraction to Material Extraction

The consolidation of state roles between 1801 and 1815, the first half of the reign of Alexander I, and the attempts to rationalize them were important. They included the creation of the ministerial form of government that would endure to modern times and that would prove to be flexible enough to allow for a spectacular expansion of state functions beginning in the second half of the nineteenth century. The changes also included additional functions that had little or no counterpart in previous eras, such as medical inspection (1828), a postal system, and a form of public education administration. The first major expansion of state roles into the economy would come in the later nineteenth century. But until then, the preindustrial elites exercised firm control over essential fiscal, tax, and human resources. Given the successes of the Russian state in wielding its military power early in the nineteenth century, it is small wonder that there was little incentive to change the basis of the relationship between the state and the economy until technological change elsewhere in Europe obliged the state to do so.

Certainly there were those who realized that reliance on the traditional channels of control and state support constrained state behavior. The relation between the health of the national economy and the strength of the state was long recognized in Russia, as it was elsewhere in Europe. Karamzin demonstrated considerable insight into the nature of the problem: "I can become richer by raising the rent of my peasants, but the government cannot, because its taxes are general, and always result in high prices. The exchequer can enrich itself in two ways only: by increasing the quantity of things, or by reducing expenditures, by industry or by thrift. If we produce each year greater quantities of bread, cloth, leather, and linen, then the upkeep of the army will be cheaper. A carefully run economy yields more riches than do gold mines."[32]

But until well into the nineteenth century, the most powerful state elites saw the road to such riches as paved with unacceptable risk. Walter M. Pintner detailed senior state officials' intense interest in the problem of industrialization in the 1830s. In the end, the policy that emerged was conservative: to quash further growth in manufacturing. Some of their reasons stemmed from a fear of the modern: movement of people, education of the ignorant, introduction of foreign technology, loss of control over society owing to erosion of traditional structures.[33] The tsar thought that workers needed "energetic and paternal supervision of their morals; without it this mass of people will gradually be corrupted and eventually turn into a class as miserable as they are dangerous for their masters."[34]

In addition, however, there were concerns over the state's inability to control or manage industrial growth. For example, too much success in manufacturing might produce what we would today call a recession. Pintner quotes Nicholas I's minister of finances, Yegor Kankrin: "In recent years machines have greatly increased here. The government promotes this, but a forced and steep increase of factory production is also bad, for production and sales must increase together, and this requires time."[35]

Table 1.2 shows Pintner's version of the relation between military expenditures in Russia and everything else in the state budget during the imperial period. Overall, until well into the nineteenth century, state finances did little more than support the armed forces and the organizations and activities associated with the imperial court.

I have added annotations that relate these data to specific episodes in the history of the military, episodes that may reasonably be supposed to have affected the size of the budget. The systematic decline in the ratio of allocations for the military to those for the rest of the state activities caused Pintner to ask whether Russia was becoming less militaristic by the turn of the twentieth century.[36] In the light of other data that describe the growth of the state in the nineteenth century, we can answer "yes" to this question. But the "yes" is provisional. The military's role continued to be central to the power of the state in spite of its decline as the dominant consumer of state resources. Even though other state roles were introduced and even though many of them grew very rapidly, *the military continued to acquire additional resources from an expanding economic base.*[37] Taken together, these findings support the argument that whether or not militarism was on the decline in Russia, the power of the state over society continued to grow.

Table 1.2
CHANGE IN THE COST OF THE MILITARY AS A FACTOR IN STATE BUDGETS: PINTNER'S DATA FOR THE IMPERIAL PERIOD

Period	Defense State Year	Army %	Navy %	Total %	Residual %
Wars of the	1804–9	40.1	9.6	49.7	50.3
Napoleonic Era	1810–14	55.2	6.0	61.2	38.8
	1815–19	46.1	5.0	51.1	48.9
	1820–24	40.3	5.5	45.8	54.2
	1825–29	37.8	6.6	44.4	55.6
	1830–34	35.1	6.8	41.9	58.1
	1835–39	34.4	6.7	41.1	58.9
	1840–44	33.8	6.6	40.4	59.6
	1845–49	33.1	5.9	39.0	61.0
Crimean War	1850–54	31.2	6.2	37.4	62.6
	1855–59	35.6	5.4	41.0	59.0
	1860–64	30.6	5.5	36.1	63.9
	1865–69	29.0	4.3	33.3	66.7
Army Reform	1870–74	28.0	4.0	32.0	68.0
Russo-Turkish War	1875–79	28.8	4.2	33.0	67.0
	1880–84	26.8	3.9	30.7	69.3
	1885–89	22.8	4.4	27.2	72.8
Franco-Russian	1890–94	23.8	4.3	28.1	71.9
Alliance	1895–99	18.7	5.5	24.2	75.8
	1900–4	17.3	5.2	22.4	77.6
Russo-Japanese War	1905–9	18.9	4.4	23.3	76.7
Balkan Wars & Modernization	1910–14	19.0	6.2	25.2	74.8

Source: Walter M. Pintner, "The Burden of Defense in Imperial Russia, 1725–1914," *Russian Review* 43 (1984).

Note: Differences in totals are due to rounding.

Each of the eighteenth-century channels of state access to the national economy was decisively altered within one generation after 1861. As these channels changed, they transformed the nature of the state's autonomy—especially of the state's capacity to extract resources arbitrarily from the rest of society—reducing it in some respects but enhancing it in many others. The poll or soul tax was abolished between 1881 and 1887. The state's arbitrary capacity to inflate the money supply was severely curtailed by new fiscal discipline standards that were being increasingly imposed from abroad at approximately the same time.[38] Control over human infrastructure was fundamentally altered with the legal abolition of the institution of serfdom (1861) and the introduction of a "professional" military system that aimed to rely on universal short-term service and a reserve (1874). Local administration was changed extensively with the introduction of the *zemstvo* assemblies and associated administrations.

Taken together, these changes certainly curtailed the autonomy of the traditional despotic state and its control of social and economic peripheries. Rather than constituting a permanent withdrawal of the state as an autonomous, controlling force in society, however, these changes represented milestones in the transformation of the state's relation to the national economy—from "despotic-fiscal" to "infrastructural-material," in Mann's terms. Between 1861 and 1900, state organizations for oversight and control of the economy, for example, grew enormously.[39] As the principal engine behind industrialization, the state not only monitored investment but also aggressively structured the terms of both domestic and foreign investment.[40] This meant that the state was in a position to change the historically "normal" pattern of industrial development—the one established by the experience of Great Britain—from a consumer-driven model to a capital goods-driven model. As a consequence of policies designed to monitor the industrial labor force, the state created special police and judicial administrations for industrial oversight. It handled the "accreditation" of participants in manufacturing and trade.[41] And the state tightly controlled the procedures for incorporation of manufacturing and commercial enterprises.[42] Finally, in numerous areas of manufacturing and trade—for example, alcohol, salt, and railways—the state was a monopolist, a monopsonist, or at least the principal corporate client. Between 1885 and 1914, state expenditures for defense, as a percentage of net national product, remained approximately flat on average—that is, they increased at approximately the same rate as the national income. State expenditures on health and education increased by approximately ten times. Meanwhile, state expenditures on enterprises increased twentyfold.[43]

CASE III: WORLD WAR I AND ITS IMPLICATIONS FOR CENTRAL CONTROL

Even as the economy industrialized and the state focused more intently on acquiring control of burgeoning infrastructures such as roads, harbors, and an educated, healthier urban workforce, Russia grew less into a budding social welfare system than into a society whose expanding resources were harvested, as they were in the eighteenth century, by a growing state.

But the traditionally autonomous behavior of state elites was increasingly constrained by external circumstances. In modern times, Russia had relied on foreigners to provide some military technology; but the rapidly changing technology base of the industrial era meant that this reliance was now constant, inevitably demanding close strategic relations with technologically advanced allies. Such alliances—first with Imperial Germany and subsequently with the Third French Republic—were fundamentally different from those Russia had joined in the eighteenth or early nineteenth century. Rebuilding the fleet and reequipping the army after the Russo-Japanese War were costly programs. They also demanded even closer Russian reliance on other European states for both finance and technology.[44] Thus, Russia's ability to formulate and pursue an autonomous foreign policy, and even an independent domestic policy in some respects, was much weaker at the turn of the twentieth century than at the turn of the nineteenth.

Early in the course of World War I, the State Council adopted unprecedented measures to enhance control of manufacturing and transport in the name of supporting the war effort. The creation of Special Councils, the first supraministerial organizations of their type in Russian state history, marked a fresh organizational departure in the history of state-economy relations and a new level of ambition in central government efforts to control the now semi-industrial social periphery.[45]

Of equal importance in the course of industrialization was the fact that the restructuring of autonomy meant that traditional elites who had managed and benefited from autonomy in the past were increasingly incapable of doing so. If noble military elites had been the ideal expediters of state autonomy in the eighteenth century, university-trained engineers, lawyers, physicians, and teachers increasingly took over the role under industrialization.

State administration changed, but it did so slowly, even grudgingly, when it came to the modernization of elites.[46] Underlying all efforts to impose significant change in central organizations were, as always, the institutional and organizational structures of a historically autonomous state and of the deeply etched pathways of power that habitually enforced the values and perspectives of one generation of elites on the next. The destruction of the Russian army in World War I, however, demonstrated that even extensive changes to the structure of state central administration were inadequate and that the financial, organizational, and technological demands of industrialized military force would undermine, rather than sustain, the state's ability to remake the world arbitrarily, as it had been used to doing from the time of Peter the Great. In most domestic policy programs, administrative outcomes were sufficiently vague and hard to measure so as to leave the self-assurance of a self-interested state elite intact. But from the mid–nineteenth century forward, military confrontations with technologically superior foes provided unmistakable proof of the inadequacy of Russia's "rational" administrative institutions and of the ineptness of its administrative elites.

Losses to state autonomy and the increasing independence of peripheral society focused on the declining ability of the state to act independently of nonstate individuals and groups. These losses included erosion through the creation of the State Duma and the Constitutional Statutes following the Russo-Japanese War and also through the occupation of territory by foreign powers after the Treaty of Portsmouth. But these losses were dwarfed by the reductions in sovereignty and autonomy after the beginning of World War I in 1914. The dramatic erosion of state sovereignty was caused by the intervention of foreigners (wartime friend and foe alike) and of revolutionary groups including, especially, the Soviets, by the spontaneous seizure of rural and urban economic resources, and by military forces operating against the central government in the Civil War. Losses also included a rapidly growing fiscal paralysis brought on by hyperinflation and a revolutionary ideology that was essentially hostile to state power and that condoned challenges to this power.

CONCLUSION

At this point we should trace the reemergence of the hypercentralized autonomous state at the expense of peripheral independence beginning in the early 1920s. We have discussed elsewhere aspects of the extension of Soviet state power through economic administration.[47] Additional examples of reemerging state and elite autonomy would include the restructuring and increased centralization of the growing Communist Party of the USSR, the enhanced size and role of the police and security apparatus, and of course, collectivization. We judge that it will be more helpful to a clarification of our argument, however, if we proceed instead to a summary and conclusion. Not only is this approach mandated by limits of space, but it is made possible by the fact that each of the principal elements of Russian state-periphery relations has now been illustrated.

First, we recognize that state autonomy and, within that, exercise of the option to centralize state administrative control are fixed objectives for Russian state servitors in the nineteenth and twentieth centuries. The state consistently adopted policies and created organizations that aimed to gain and enhance its control of the rest of society while avoiding social control over its own operations. Moments during which this tendency was reversed, such as early in the era of the Great Reforms and during

World War I, were comparatively brief. Second, we argue that autonomy and centralization at the expense of peripheral independence have tended to serve the interests of state elites, enhancing their status vis-à-vis the rest of society and their power over the admission and socialization of new generations of elites. Third, we recognize that centralization has tended to be "extreme" if we measure it by what the administrative system could actually have expected to achieve or by what the society could sustain. This extreme centralization is manifested in a lack of congruence between the intentions of policymakers and their actual achievements as measured by outcomes. In this typical contrast between elites' ambitions and their administrative achievements, we see the enduring weight of institutions—those "rules of the game" that, in this case, are being played by state elites in such a way as to enhance their standing in Russian society, without consistent regard for the quality or meaning of the social outcomes of their professional activity. Fourth, we recognize that whatever may have been the scale of elite ambitions and administrative autonomy, the Russian state frequently has been obliged to react to exogenous forces including, throughout the period under consideration, technological and military factors and, during the industrial era, fiscal factors.

What are the patterns of peripheral attempts at independence from the state? First, we see that there have been some (very few) efforts by the state itself to decentralize. These efforts include, paradoxically, the introduction of ministerial government. Although the ministerial model was itself a system that allowed for extreme centralization, in 1801 it represented an effort to relax and rationalize the centralization of the *kollegia* model introduced in the eighteenth century. The Great Reforms of the first half of Alexander II's reign once more included efforts both to rationalize and to decentralize the control of property by what I referred to earlier as "state-certified elites," the landed gentry. These reforms also began a redistribution and mobilization for investment of the wealth that previously had been concentrated in the hands of that elite and of state organizations. The best-known decentralizing moves of this era created new, locally funded and staffed administrative organizations (the *zemstva*). In fairly short order, however, most of these decentralizing initiatives were reduced in their effectiveness by the creation of new state organizations for economic administration, by systematic reduction in the local political roles of the peasantry (through the Land Captain statutes of 1889, for example), by reorganization and redefinition of elite administrative roles, and by unprecedented expansion of administrative organizations.

It is true that economic development in the nineteenth century and, especially, the onset of industrialization created new, decentralized, peripheral organizations and informal groups. These included corporations, cooperative credit associations, merchants' and manufacturers' associations, and professional associations such as the Pirogov physicians' society, as well as massive additions—via education and new career opportunities—to a previously narrow social elite. Each of these developments was limited or even reversed by the state's institutionalized and path-dependent need to resolve administrative issues centrally and with maximal autonomy from nonstate society. These patterns were realized through measures such as the excessive oversight of corporations, banks, and the labor force and the centralized funding of very large portions of industrial development.

The moment of greatest peripheral independence occurred in 1917–18 with the emergence of soviets and spontaneous land reform, the expropriation of manufacturing and commercial enterprises, and the success of Bolshevism, a revolutionary political movement that, in its Marxist origins, was deeply hostile to the state. But following the Revolution of 1917, the old patterns reemerged, to such an extent that the revolutionary political leadership, in a dramatic shift of its basic strategy, became a major proponent of state autonomy, centralization, and elite power. The new autonomy reached its apogee during the early Five-Year Plans, resulting once more in overcentralization and extreme state autonomy.

NOTES

1. For the critically important turn-of-the-century period, when large-scale manufacturing corporations and foreign investment might have shifted the balance of power and initiative away from the state, see R. W. Davies, ed., *From Tsarism to the New Economic Policy: Continuity and Change in the Economy of the USSR* (Ithaca: Cornell University Press, 1990), especially the chapters by Davies, "Introduction: From Tsarism to NEP," pp. 4–28, and Peter Gatrell and Davies, "The Industrial Economy," pp. 127–59. See also Don K. Rowney, "The Autonomous State and Economic Development: Industrial Administration in Russia, 1880–1920," *Journal of Policy History* 7, no. 2 (1995): 226–61.
2. Mann puts it forcefully: "The territoriality of the state has created social forces with a life of their own." See Michael Mann, "The Autonomous Power of the State: Its Origins, Mechanisms, and Results," in John A. Hall, ed., *States in History* (New York: Blackwell, 1986), p. 134.
3. Ibid., p. 190.
4. Ibid., pp. 204–5.
5. Ibid., p. 205.
6. Ibid., p. 201 (emphasis added).
7. Douglass C. North, *Institutions, Institutional Change, and Economic Performance*

(New York: Cambridge University Press, 1990), p. 4.
8. In addition to North, *Institutions, Institutional Change,* see Douglass C. North, "A Transaction Cost Theory of Politics," *Journal of Theoretical Politics* 2, no. 4 (1990): 355–67, and "Institutions," *Journal of Economic Perspectives* 5 (winter 1991): 97–112.
9. North, "Institutions," p. 97.
10. North, *Institutions, Institutional Change,* p. 89. For an alternative view that sees institutions suddenly disappearing or coming into existence by social instrumentality, see Theda Skocpol: *States and Social Revolution: A Comparative Analysis of France, Russia, and China* (Cambridge: Cambridge University Press, 1979), pp. 161–235, and "France, Russia, China: A Structural Analysis of Social Revolutions," *Comparative Studies in Society and History* 18 (1976): 175–210.
11. North, *Institutions, Institutional Change,* pp. 100 ff.
12. See, for example, North, "Transaction Cost Theory," pp. 355–67; E. L. Jones, *The European Miracle: Environments, Economies, and Geopolitics in the History of Europe and Asia,* 2d ed. (Cambridge: Cambridge University Press, 1987); David Stark, "Path Dependence and Privatization Strategies in East Central Europe," *East European Politics and Societies* 6, no. 6 (winter 1992): 17–54; Paul A. David, "Clio and the Economics of QWERTY," *American Economic Review* (May 1985): 332–37.
13. North, *Institutions, Institutional Change,* pp. 58–59.
14. Skocpol, *States and Social Revolution,* pp. 19–24, 185–95, 214–18; see also Teodor Shanin, *Russia as a "Developing Society,"* vol. 1 of *The Roots of Otherness: Russia's Turn of the Century* (London: Macmillan, 1985), pp. 196–206, and Alexander Gerschenkron, *Economic Backwardness in Historical Perspective* (Cambridge: Harvard University Press, 1962), especially pp. 28–29.
15. Iu. Got'e, *Istoriia oblastnogo upravleniia v Rossii ot Petra I do Ekateriny II:* vol. 1, *Reforma 1727 goda. Oblastnoe deleniie i oblastnyia uchrezhdeniia 1727–1775 gg* (Moscow: Lissner and Sovko, 1913); vol. 2, *Organy nadzora. Chrezvychainye i vremennye oblastnye uchrezhdeniia. Razvitiie mysli o preobrazovanii oblastnogo upravleniia. Uprazdneniie uchrezhdenii 1727 g* (Moscow: Nauka, 1941).
16. Richard Pipes, ed., *Karamzin's Memoir on Ancient and Modern Russia: A Translation and Analysis* (New York: Atheneum, 1966), p. 150.
17. Robert E. Jones, *The Emancipation of the Russian Nobility, 1762–85* (Princeton: Princeton University Press, 1973).
18. David L. Ransel, *The Politics of Catherinian Russia: The Panin Party* (New Haven: Yale University Press, 1975), pp. 150–60.
19. S. Frederick Starr, *Decentralization and Self-Government in Russia, 1830–70* (Princeton: Princeton University Press, 1972), pp. 3–50.
20. Mann, "Autonomous Power," pp. 210–11; North, "Institutions," pp. 97–112.
21. Walter M. Pintner, "The Burden of Defense in Imperial Russia, 1725–1914," *Russian Review* 43 (1984): 231–59. See also S. M. Troitsky: *Finansovaia politika russkogo absoliutizma v XVIII veke* (Moscow: Nauka, 1966) and *Russkii absoliutizm i dvorianstvo XVIII v.* (Moscow: Nauka, 1974), pp. 3–46.
22. Arcadius Kahan, *The Plow, the Hammer, and the Knout: An Economic History of*

Eighteenth-Century Russia (Chicago: University of Chicago Press, 1985), pp. 319, 320.
23. S. M. Troitsky, "Finansovaia politika russkogo absoliutizma vo vtoroi polovine XVII-XVIII vv.," in N. M. Druzhinin et al., eds., *Absoliutizm v Rossii XVII-XVIII vv. Sbornik statei* (Moscow: Nauka, 1964); Troitsky, *Russkii absoliutizm*.
24. Kahan, *The Plow*, table 8.16; Pintner, "Burden of Defense," table 4, p. 248.
25. Pipes, *Karamzin's Memoir*, p. 167.
26. Troitsky, *Russkii absoliutizm*, pp. 119–294, makes a creditable effort.
27. Kahan, *The Plow*, p. 337.
28. Fernand Braudel, *Civilization and Capitalism, Fifteenth-Eighteenth Century*, vol. 2, *The Wheels of Commerce*, translated from the French by Sian Reynolds (New York: Harper, 1986), pp. 519–55; Paul Kennedy, *Rise and Fall of the Great Powers: Economic Change and Military Conflict from 1500 to 2000* (New York: Random House, 1987), pp. 73–139.
29. Troitsky, *Russkii absoliutizm*. See especially the discussion of the evolution of obligatory state service for nobility and the genesis of the manifesto of February 18, 1762: pp. 119–54.
30. Kahan, *The Plow*, p. 9 and table 1.4.
31. Ibid., p. 348.
32. Pipes, *Karamzin's Memoir*, p. 168.
33. Walter M. Pintner, *Russian Economic Policy under Nicholas I* (Ithaca: Cornell University Press, 1978), pp. 97–104.
34. Ibid., p. 100.
35. Ibid., pp. 93–94.
36. Pintner, "Burden of Defense," pp. 258–59; William C. Fuller Jr., *Civil-Military Conflict in Imperial Russia, 1881–1914* (Princeton: Princeton University Press, 1985), pp. 47–74.
37. This view is at odds with the one in Fuller, *Civil-Military Conflict*, pp. 47–58, in the sense that he focuses on the military's share of a rapidly rising state budget and finds, correctly, that the *percentage* declined.
38. Ian Drummond, "The Russian Gold Standard," *Journal of Economic History* 36 (1976): 663–88; Haim Barkai, "The Macro-Economics of Tsarist Russia in the Industrialization Era: Monetary Developments, the Balance of Payments, and the Gold Standard," *Journal of Economic History* 33 (1973): 339–71; Paul R. Gregory, "Economic Growth and Structural Change in Tsarist Russia: A Case of Modern Economic Growth?" *Soviet Studies* 23 (1972): 135–64; Arcadius Kahan, "Government Policies and the Industrialization of Russia," *Journal of Economic History* 27, no 4 (December 1967): 460–77.
39. Rowney, "Autonomous State," pp. 246–58.
40. Arcadius Kahan, "Capital Formation during the Period of Early Industrialization in Russia, 1890–1913," vol. 7 of M. M. Postan and H. J. Habakkuk, eds., *The Cambridge Economic History of Europe* (Cambridge: Cambridge University Press, 1966–), pt. 2, pp. 265–307; Kahan, "Government Policies"; Gregory, "Economic Growth and Structural Change."
41. Alfred J. Rieber, *Merchants and Entrepreneurs in Imperial Russia* (Chapel Hill: University of North Carolina Press, 1982), pp. 3–129; Thomas C. Owen, *The*

Corporation under Russian Law, 1800–1917: A Study in Tsarist Economic Policy (Cambridge: Cambridge University Press, 1991), pp. 198–219 and passim.
42. Owen, *The Corporation,* pp. 79–115.
43. Paul R. Gregory, *Russian National Income, 1885–1913* (New York: Cambridge University Press, 1982), Tables G 1–3, pp. 261–63.
44. Peter Gatrell, *Government, Industry, and Rearmament in Russia, 1900–1914: The Last Argument of Tsarism* (Cambridge: Cambridge University Press, 1994), pp. 271–77.
45. "O nekotorykh merakh k obezpecheniiu toplivom uchrezhdenii armii i flota i putei soobshcheniia a ravno chastnykh predpriiatii, rabotaiushchikh dlia tselei gosudarstvennoi oborony," *Sobranie uzakonenii,* st. 865 (March 31, 1915); "O rasprostranenii polnomochii, prisvoennykh Ministru Putei Soobshcheniia Imennym Vysochaishim Ukazom 4ogo Marta 1915 goda, na dela po obezpecheniiu toplivom gosudarstvennykh i obshchestvennykh uchrezhdenii," *Sobranie uzakonenii,* st. 1091 (May 2, 1915); "O Predostavlenii Ministru Torgovli i Promyshlennosti Osobykh Polnomochii po Obshchemy Rukovodstvu Prodovol'stvennym Delom v Imperii," *Sobranie uzakoneniia,* st. 1169 (May 19, 1915); "Ob"utverzhdenii pravil o Poriadke i usloviiakh raspredeleniia tverdago mineral'nago topliva mezhdu potrebiteliami," *Sobranie uzakonenii,* st. 1215 (May 29, 1915); "Ob utverzhdenii polozheniia ob Osobom Soveshchanii dlia ob"edineniia meropriiatii po obezpecheniiu deistvuiushchei armii predmetami boevogo i material'nago snabzheniia," *Sobranie uzakonenii,* st. 1280 (June 7, 1915). A summary appears in *Pravitel'svennyi Vestnik,* no. 181 (August 19–September 1, 1915), p. 1, cols. 2, 3. See also Lewis Siegelbaum, *The Politics of Industrial Mobilization in Russia, 1914–17: A Study of the War-Industries Committees* (New York: St. Martin's, 1983).
46. Don K. Rowney, *Transition to Technocracy: The Structural Origins of the Soviet Administrative State* (Ithaca: Cornell University Press, 1989), ch. 2.
47. Don K. Rowney, "The Scope, Authority, and Personnel of the New Industrial Commissariats in Historical Context," in William G. Rosenberg and Lewis H. Siegelbaum, eds., *Social Dimensions of Soviet Industrialization* (Bloomington: Indiana University Press, 1993), pp. 124–45.

II
POLITICS

2

The Development of Federalism in Russia

Joan DeBardeleben

Since Russia stepped out as a newly independent state in December 1991, a rapid transformation of political institutions has been under way. An important component of this transformation has been a redefinition of relations between the central government in Moscow and Russia's diverse regions, a process that has taken shape under the shadow of the Soviet legacy. Although the USSR proclaimed itself to be a federal state, in practice it was a highly centralized polity. Now, in Russia, it appears that a specifically Russian type of federalism may be emerging.

THE LEGACY OF SOVIET "FEDERALISM"

The USSR was formally a federal system. According to the Soviet constitution, certain powers lay within the jurisdiction of the central government, and others lay within the jurisdiction of the fifteen *union republics*, which have since become independent states (including the Russian Federation). However, this was a type of "phony federalism" in that all major aspects of life were overseen by the apparatus of the Communist Party of the Soviet Union, a highly centralized structure despite the existence of regional party organs. Although the constitution and ideology asserted the rights of nations and ethnic groups to develop freely, in practice central policy encouraged political and economic integration and a considerable degree of cultural assimilation.

The administrative-political structures of the USSR form the foundation for the new federal structures emerging in Russia. In most cases the terminology used to describe those units has been carried over from the Soviet period with only minor changes. The administrative-political structures of the USSR were based on two principles: the national (ethnic) principle and the territorial principle.

In the Soviet period, both the union republics and some of the units subordinate to them were defined according to a national (ethnic) principle. Other than the union republics, most important were the *autonomous republics*, which were constituent units of the union republics in which they were located and were populated by a significant national (ethnic) group. In many cases, however, the titular nationality formed only a small portion of the actual population of the autonomous republic. Under Soviet rule, these units were initially conceived as providing a basis for the national self-determination of a titular nationality that occupied a territory not on an external border of the USSR (in contrast to the union republics, which were on an external border).

Other regional units defined according to this "national principle" were the *autonomous oblast* and the *autonomous okrug*. In the Soviet period there were five autonomous oblasts in the Russian Soviet Federated Socialist Republic (RSFSR, now the Russian Federation). These units did not have the same stature as the autonomous republics but were proclaimed to facilitate national self-determination of the titular nationality. They had a status roughly equivalent to that of the oblast, discussed below. An autonomous okrug, on the other hand, was subordinate to the larger administrative unit (the oblast or the krai) within which it was located.

The criteria for setting the borders of these units were often arbitrary, but for the most part these borders have been maintained in the present period, although some border disputes do exist. In most cases the titular national group does not make up a majority of the population in the autonomous region. Historically, these so-called regions have enjoyed some leeway in implementing cultural policy, but under Soviet rule they were politically and economically subordinate to the administrative region within which they lay. Most of the autonomous republics, oblasts, and okrugs were located within the Russian republic of the USSR, so they now form the basis for several of the new federal units of the Russian Federation.

In addition to the national-ethnic regions were units that were defined on a territorial rather than a national basis. The oblast was the most important of these territorial administrative units and generally did not have a non-Russian national-ethnic basis. The krai, another important territorial administrative delineation, was similar to the oblast except that a part of each krai's border was on an external border of the country and/or the krai included a mixture of diverse ethnic territories. Most often krais were initially less industrialized, sparsely populated, and geographically large. Two cities in the Russian Federation, Moscow and St. Petersburg, were also given a separate administrative status within the

USSR. These federal cities are located within the geographic boundaries of Moscow oblast and Leningrad oblast, respectively, but do not form parts of those oblasts.

Under Soviet rule, the autonomous republics were constituent parts of the union republics within which they were located, but like the union republics, they had their own constitutions and were formally given independence in certain jurisdictions. Unlike the union republics, they were not described in the Soviet constitution as "sovereign," nor were they given the right to secede from the Soviet Union. The oblasts and krais were strictly territorial administrative units. The autonomous oblasts and autonomous okrugs were also administrative units, though defined on a national basis.

THE EVOLUTION OF FEDERALISM IN RUSSIA

In 1991, Mikhail Gorbachev tried to hammer out a new Union Treaty that would redefine relations between the union republics and the Soviet state and thus prevent the disintegration of the USSR itself. In this process, Gorbachev invited the leaders of the autonomous republics to take part in the negotiations as well, presumably to counterbalance the demands of the union republics. This elevated the political status of the autonomous republics, as did Boris Yeltsin's support for their claims, as he sought to weaken the central Soviet structures following the failed coup d'état of August 1991. Both before and after the breakup of the Soviet Union in December 1991, demands for increased regional autonomy emerged from regions within Russia itself. In response to such demands from the autonomous republics located within Russia's borders, the government of Russia upgraded their status to that of full republics. In July 1991, four of the autonomous oblasts within Russia (all except the Jewish autonomous oblast) were also made republics.

The division of powers between the various levels of government remains one of the major points of contest within the Russian Federation. Two aspects of this controversy have concerned whether the national-ethnic units, particularly the republics, should have more autonomy and rights than do the territorially based units (oblasts, krais), and whether the autonomous okrugs should have a status equal to that of the oblasts and krais.[1] A first effort in trying to resolve these disputes was the conclusion of the Federal Treaty in March 1992. This document proved, however, to be only a stepping-stone to adoption of a new constitution, which laid the basic ground rules for Russian federalism, in December 1993.

The Federal Treaty

The Federal Treaty was signed on March 13, 1992, by the head of the Supreme Soviet of the Russian Federation and the heads of eighteen of the (at that time) twenty republics.[2] (It was subsequently ratified by the Supreme Soviet of the Russian Federation.) Tatarstan and Checheno-Ingushetia (the latter subsequently divided into two separate republics) refused to sign it. Also in March 1992, the Supreme Soviet adopted a "Law on Krai and Oblast Soviets of People's Deputies and Krai and Oblast Administrations," laying the legal foundation for those units. Rights granted to the oblasts and krais in this document were more limited than those given to the republics in the Federal Treaty. For example, republics were to have their own constitutions and to establish their own regional governmental structures, whereas the structure of local organs was set out for the oblasts and krais.

The Federal Treaty defined the division of powers between the federal government and the republics, and the treaty was formally made part of the constitution of the federation.[3] It should be emphasized that the twenty-one republics of the Russian Federation comprise only 28.6 percent of the territory of the Russian Federation and only 15.2 percent of its population. The major urban and industrial regions of the country are not located in the republics but are in oblasts or constitute cities of federal status (units equivalent to oblasts). Although some of the republics (e.g., Sakha, Komi) have rich deposits of natural resources and significant urban settlements, in general the republics are geographically peripheral areas. It is therefore understandable that the oblasts, krais, and cities of federal status found it inequitable that they were given few rights and a narrower range of autonomy than the republics.[4]

The Federal Treaty granted the republics the rights and powers of a state with the exception of those powers that were transferred to the federal government. Republics were explicitly granted the rights to conduct an independent foreign policy and foreign economic policy and to conclude agreements with other republics, krais, oblasts, and autonomous okrugs of the Russian Federation; these agreements, however, could not contradict the constitution, the laws of the Russian Federation, or current agreements. The coordination of international relations and international economic relations of the republics was given to the federal government together with republican governments. Other advantages the republics received included the right to autonomously determine governmental structures and to formulate tax and budget policy. Bilateral agreements were to be worked out regarding the distribution of natural resources between the center and the republics.

With the adoption of a new constitution for the Russian Federation in

December 1993, the status of the Federal Treaty was left unclear. The Federal Treaty was not defined to be a part of the new Russian constitution. Indeed, some provisions of the Federal Treaty contradicted aspects of the new constitution. In general, the new constitution reduced some of the privileges of the republics. Furthermore, both the method of adoption of the new constitution and the unclarity of some of its provisions left open wide areas of negotiation and conflict between the central government and the regions of Russia. Another key event that cast a shadow over center-periphery relations in Russia was the war that erupted in the Russian republic of Chechnya in late 1994 as a result of the latter's declaration of independence.

Adoption of a New Constitution

The constitutional referendum of December 1993 was a controversial political event and represented the culmination of an extended period of tension between the executive and the legislative branches of the government of the Russian Federation in 1992 and 1993. The constitution was adopted in a highly charged political environment, and the mechanism of its adoption was also controversial. One of the most contentious issues surrounding the debate over adoption of a new Russian constitution in 1992–93 was the definition of federal relations. Preceding the crisis of October 1993, several drafts for the new constitution were under discussion. No method was found for resolving disputes either over the content of the new constitution or over the appropriate mechanism for its adoption. Yeltsin's approach, namely the unilateral calling of a referendum, left in his hands the decision about the exact content of the draft to be voted on. The procedure elicited broad criticism because it allowed Yeltsin to define the political agenda and influence the referendum's outcome. The constitution that was put to a vote weakened the legislative body and gave great power to the president himself. Allegations of unfair media coverage and dishonest electoral reporting further increased skepticism toward the process.

Apart from the broader dispute surrounding the adoption of the constitution, two specific issues of controversy related to the construction of the federal system. First, the draft constitution that was put to a vote in December 1993 deviated, in its contents, from compromises that had been reached between the center and the units of the federation during 1992 and 1993. Second, in addition to dissolving the federal parliament, in October 1993 Yeltsin ordered the dissolution of elected local councils at the city level and below throughout the country. He also encouraged elected councils at the regional and republic levels to disband themselves and depicted these bodies as holdovers from the Soviet period that were blocking the reform process. Thus, in the period preceding the December 1993 vote, local councils and some regional councils did not exist throughout many parts of Russia. This served to strengthen the executive branch in the regions and to create an uncertain political environment for the exercise of governance on the regional level. In most parts of Russia, elections for new regional and local councils did not occur until 1994. At that time no federal law was in place to provide a framework for these elections or for the operation of the new bodies. All of these factors introduced uncertainty and tension into center-regional relations in Russia during this period.

THE CONSTITUTION OF DECEMBER 1993

The Units of the Federation: Basic Terminology

The 1993 Russian constitution defines 89 constituent units of the federation. This includes 21 republics, 49 oblasts, 2 cities of federal status, 6 krais, 1 autonomous oblast, and 10 autonomous okrugs. (See map 2.1 and table 2.1 for a list of these units.) Republics, oblasts, and krais do not overlap with one another territorially. In contrast, most of the autonomous okrugs had, at least initially, the dual status of being units of the Russian Federation and, simultaneously, constituent parts of the oblasts or krais within which they are located. (The clearest exception is the Chukotka autonomous okrug, which is not a part of any other krai or oblast.)[5] The definition of federalism, as laid out in the 1993 constitution, shows considerable continuity with federal relations as defined in the Federal Treaty. Most important, the eighty-nine constituent units of the federation were retained in the new constitution (although their relative status within the federation was redefined). Thus, the units of the federation, as defined in the new constitution, are derived from territorial divisions established in the Soviet period and adapted in the immediate post-Soviet period.

An important change, however, was introduced with the new constitution. The constitution defines all eighty-nine units of the country to have an equal status within the federation. In other words, each of these units, regardless of whether it is a republic, an oblast, a krai, or an autonomous okrug or oblast, is considered to be an equal member of the federation. This represents a break from past approaches, when the republics were granted a higher status than other regional divisions (oblasts, krais, okrugs). Even in the Soviet period, the republics (formerly called autonomous republics) were considered to be constituent units of the Russian republic

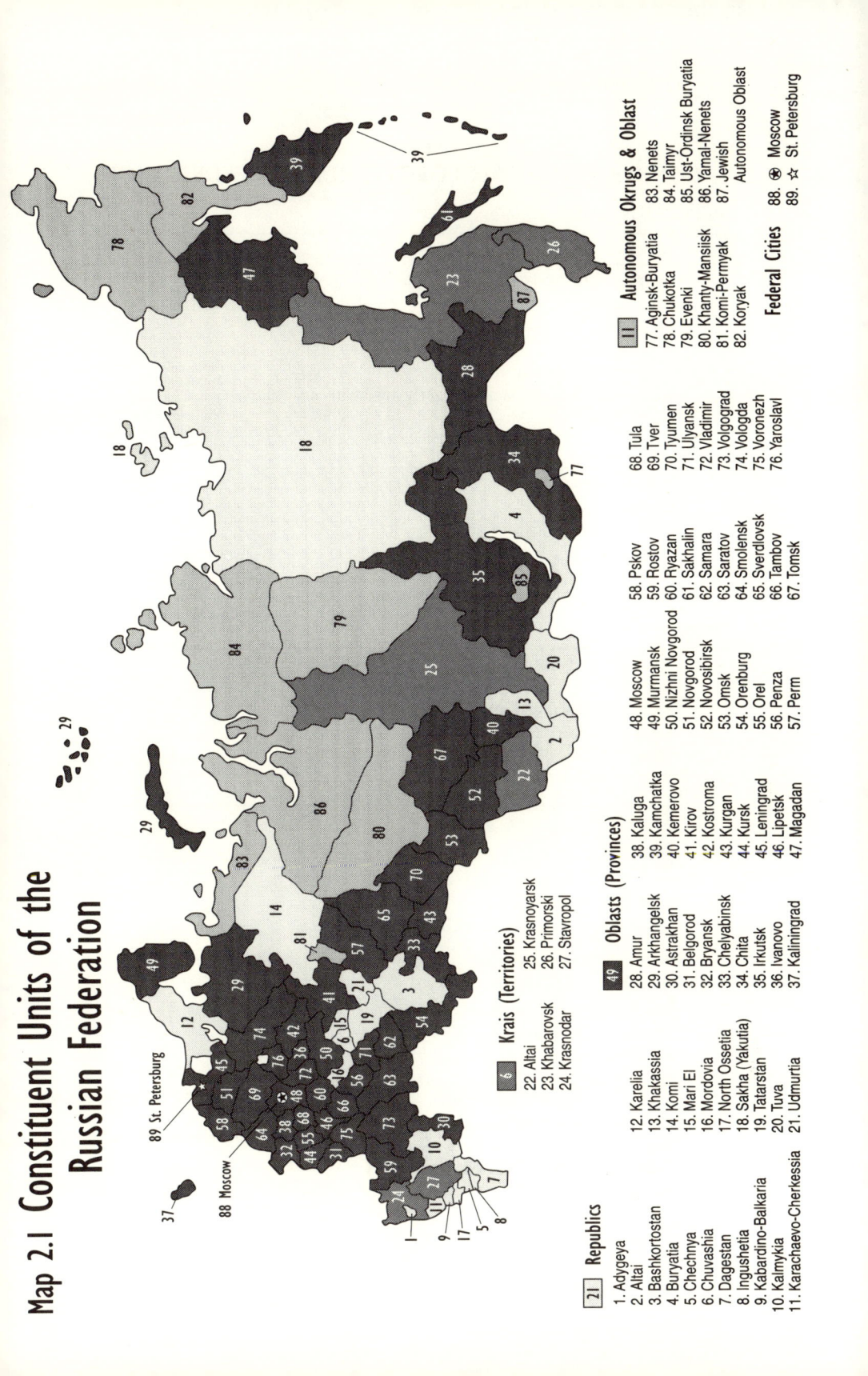

Map 2.1 Constituent Units of the Russian Federation

Republics

1. Adygeya
2. Altai
3. Bashkortostan
4. Buryatia
5. Chechnya
6. Chuvashia
7. Dagestan
8. Ingushetia
9. Kabardino-Balkaria
10. Kalmykia
11. Karachaevo-Cherkessia
12. Karelia
13. Khakassia
14. Komi
15. Mari El
16. Mordovia
17. North Ossetia
18. Sakha (Yakutia)
19. Tatarstan
20. Tuva
21. Udmurtia

Krais (Territories)

22. Altai
23. Khabarovsk
24. Krasnodar
25. Krasnoyarsk
26. Primorski
27. Stavropol

Oblasts (Provinces)

28. Amur
29. Arkhangelsk
30. Astrakhan
31. Belgorod
32. Bryansk
33. Chelyabinsk
34. Chita
35. Irkutsk
36. Ivanovo
37. Kaliningrad
38. Kaluga
39. Kamchatka
40. Kemerovo
41. Kirov
42. Kostroma
43. Kurgan
44. Kursk
45. Leningrad
46. Lipetsk
47. Magadan
48. Moscow
49. Murmansk
50. Nizhni Novgorod
51. Novgorod
52. Novosibirsk
53. Omsk
54. Orenburg
55. Orel
56. Penza
57. Perm
58. Pskov
59. Rostov
60. Ryazan
61. Sakhalin
62. Samara
63. Saratov
64. Smolensk
65. Sverdlovsk
66. Tambov
67. Tomsk
68. Tula
69. Tver
70. Tyumen
71. Ulyansk
72. Vladimir
73. Volgograd
74. Vologda
75. Voronezh
76. Yaroslavl

Autonomous Okrugs & Oblast

77. Aginsk-Buryatia
78. Nenets
79. Evenki
80. Khanty-Mansiisk
81. Komi-Permyak
82. Koryak
83. Nenets
84. Taimyr
85. Ust-Ordinsk Buryatia
86. Yamal-Nenets
87. Jewish Autonomous Oblast

Federal Cities

88. ⊛ Moscow
89. ☆ St. Petersburg

Table 2.1
CONSTITUENT UNITS OF THE RUSSIAN FEDERATION

REPUBLICS (21)

North Caucasus Area

    Adygeya (formerly autonomous oblast)
    Chechnya*
    Dagestan
    Ingushetia
    Kabardino-Balkaria
    Karachaevo-Cherkessia (formerly autonomous oblast)
    North Ossetia

Volga/Urals Region

    Bashkortostan
    Chuvashia
    Mari El
    Mordovia
    Tatarstan
    Udmurtia

Siberia

    Altai (formerly autonomous oblast called Gornyi Altai)
    Buryatia
    Khakassia (formerly autonomous oblast)
    Sakha (formerly Yakutia)
    Tuva

Others

    Kalmykia
    Karelia
    Komi

AUTONOMOUS OBLAST (1)
    Jewish autonomous oblast (in Khabarovsk krai)

AUTONOMOUS OKRUGS (10)
    Aginsk-Buryatia (in Chita oblast)
    Chukotka
    Evenki (in Krasnoyarsk krai)
    Khanty-Mansiisk (in Tyumen oblast)
    Komi-Permyak (in Perm oblast)
    Koryak (in Kamchatka oblast)
    Nenets (in Arkhangelsk oblast)
    Taimyr (in Krasnoyarsk krai)
    Ust-Ordinsk Buryat (in Irkutsk oblast)
    Yamal-Nenets (in Tyumen oblast)

Table 2.1 *continued*

Table 2.1 *continued*

OBLASTS (49)
    Amur
    Arkhangelsk
    Astrakhan
    Belgorod
    Bryansk
    Chelyabinsk
    Chita
    Irkutsk
    Ivanovo
    Kaliningrad
    Kaluga
    Kamchatka
    Kemerovo
    Kirov
    Kostroma
    Kurgan
    Kursk
    Leningrad
    Lipetsk
    Magadan
    Moscow
    Murmansk
    Nizhni Novgorod (formerly Gorki)
    Novgorod
    Novosibirsk
    Omsk
    Orel
    Orenburg
    Penza
    Perm
    Pskov
    Rostov
    Ryazan
    Sakhalin
    Samara (formerly Kuibyshev)
    Saratov
    Smolensk
    Sverdlovsk
    Tambov
    Tomsk
    Tula
    Tver (formerly Kalinin)
    Tyumen
    Ulyansk

Table 2.1 *continued*

Table 2.1 *continued*

Vladimir
Volgograd
Vologda
Voronezh
Yaroslavl

CITIES OF FEDERAL STATUS (2)
Moscow
St. Petersburg

KRAIS (6)
Altai
Khabarovsk
Krasnodar
Krasnoyarsk
Primorsky
Stavropol

* Declared independence, but declaration not recognized by the government of the Russian Federation.

whereas the oblasts and krais were considered to be strictly administrative units. The Federal Treaty, signed by Russia's central government and eighteen of the (then) twenty republics in 1992, reaffirmed the special status of the republics. Thus, the new constitution represented a break from past policy and bowed to the demands made by the oblasts and krais to be granted a legal status equal to that of the republics.

Despite their formal equality, the constitution still recognizes some differences between the various types of constituent units. Thus, the eighty-nine units of federation are considered to be different but equal. Republics are to adopt constitutions of their own; these constitutions, along with the constitution of the Russian Federation, define the status of the republics. In recognition of the national principle upon which they were originally formed, republics are also granted the right to establish their own state languages, to be used alongside the Russian language, which is defined as the state language of the Russian Federation. Other members of the federation (oblasts, krais, okrugs, cities of federal status) are to adopt charters or statutes that, along with the federal constitution, define their status.[6]

Finally, autonomous districts may have varying types of relationships with the krais or oblasts within which they are located. For example, the Chukotka autonomous okrug stands solely as a member of the Russian Federation in its own right. In most cases, however, the okrug is simultaneously a member of the Russian Federation in its own right and a constituent unit of an oblast or krai. Therefore, in principle, citizens of such okrugs can vote in elections both at the okrug level and at the oblast or krai level. At times, this ambiguous status has led to political conflict and stalemate. For example, the leadership of the Yamal-Nenets autonomous okrug, which is located within the borders of Tyumen oblast, asserted its right to a status independent of Tyumen oblast by boycotting the Tyumen gubernatorial elections in December 1996. The Khanty-Mansiisk autonomous okrug, also located within the borders of Tyumen oblast, participated in the first round of the Tyumen gubernatorial election but boycotted the second round, since the okrug's law specified that a voter turnout of 25 percent was needed to make an election valid; turnout in the first round was below 15 percent in the okrug. Because the two okrugs have rich deposits of oil and gas resources, the leadership of Tyumen oblast is resistant to their claims for complete autonomy. Another contested case relates to the Taimyr autonomous okrug, which has sought to establish its independence of Krasnoyarsk krai, where it is located, and to bring the rich nickel combine located at Norilsk, in northern Krasnoyarsk krai, into its jurisdiction as well. [7] Here again, this case of contested jurisdiction (and thus of constitutional interpretation) has an important economic foundation.

The status of the Federal Treaty was left ambiguous by the new constitution. Although the Federal Treaty was not formally abrogated, the failure to define it as part of the constitution (as was the initial expectation) left the status of the document in limbo. Thus republics can appeal to provisions of the Federal Treaty (which grants them certain privileges), even though others point out that some provisions of the Federal Treaty (those very privileges) have been overridden by the constitution, which is the supreme law of the land. Over time, however, references to the Federal Treaty have declining legitimacy. The fact that Yeltsin's constitutional draft omitted reference to the Federal Treaty is a sore point for the leaders of some republics. It is significant that in twelve of the twenty republics of Russia that participated in the 1993 referendum vote (Chechnya did not participate), either the constitution did not win a majority or turnout was less than the 50 percent needed for ratification, possibly indicating dissatisfaction with the powers of the republics as defined in the new constitution.

Provisions of the Constitution

The provisions of the constitution do conform to generally accepted norms for federal systems, that is, they define jurisdictions for the federal government and for the members of the federation. Certain powers are reserved for the federal government; certain powers are to be exercised jointly with the governments of the republics and regions; and certain powers reside with the members of the federation. But in many spheres, the powers are shared by the federal government and the members of the federation, and the constitution fails to make clear exactly how this joint authority should be exercised, creating room for jurisdictional disputes between the parties.

Powers specifically reserved for the central government include the following: jurisdiction over the continental shelf (Article 67); responsibility for guaranteeing the rights of indigenous minorities (Article 69); protection of human rights; establishment of citizenship; establishment of federal state institutions; development of the legal basis for a single market (money, federal banks, pricing policy, taxation policy) (Articles 71, 75); the federal budget; a federal energy system; foreign policy and international relations; defense and security; border control; and organization of the court system (Article 71).

Other spheres are defined as within the joint authority of the federal government and the members of the federation. Some of these seem to overlap with areas defined as within the federal jurisdiction. For example, the protection of human rights and the establishment of general principles of taxation are placed in both categories. Other functions are more clearly defined as joint: ensuring of law and order; possession and use of natural resources; environmental protection; education; public health; social protection and social security; dealing with natural disasters; labor, housing, and family policy; court personnel; and coordination of international and external economic relations of members of the federation.

Finally, some powers are reserved for the members of the federation. Members may, for example, establish their own state institutions, within the framework of the constitutional system and federal laws. This provision allows considerable diversity of state structures at the republic and regional levels, including diverse electoral systems and varying degrees of power granted to the legislative and executive branches. This represents a sharp break from the Soviet period, when uniform structures were mandated throughout the country. It also opens the possibility of disputes over the permissible degree of variation, particularly because Article 77 (par. 2), states, "Federal executive bodies and bodies of the executive authority of the members of the Russian Federation shall form a single system of executive authority." As discussed below, the procedure for selecting the head of the executive branch in the regions was an issue of controversy in 1995 and 1996. Furthermore, the constitution gives the president of the Russian Federation broad powers of decree (Article 90) as well as the power to "suspend acts of executive bodies of Russian Federation members if they contradict the Constitution, federal laws or international obligations of the Russian Federation or constitute a breach of human and civil rights and freedoms, until the matter is decided by the appropriate court" (Article 85, par. 2). Such powers have been utilized by the president to suspend actions of the republics and regions. The efficacy of the court system in adjudicating these disputes is not well established. The constitution clearly states that where federal or joint jurisdiction is not established, "the members of the Russian Federation shall enjoy full state power" (Article 73) and "shall exercise their own legal control, including the adoption of laws and other normative legal acts" (Article 73, par. 4). However, laws of member units of the Russian Federation may not contradict federal laws, and in cases of conflict, the federal law shall prevail, presuming the latter is adopted in accordance with other provisions of the constitution.

Interpretation

The new constitution lays out a basic framework for the Russian federal structure, a framework that differs significantly from that of the Soviet past. However, many problems have emerged from that constitution or have been left unresolved:

- Not all members of the federation accept the principle of the equality of the eighty-nine units of the federation.
- In practice, the eighty-nine units do not have equal rights. Because equality between the units is enshrined in the constitution, this provides a basis of protest.
- In practice, the republics and regions have appropriated many powers to themselves, even when those powers are not specifically granted to them by the constitution.
- The president is given broad powers of decree that can be utilized to try to counteract such appropriations of power. However, enforcement of decrees is not always effective and, as the Chechnya case indicates, reversion to force remains a possibility.

Debate continues over the basic nature of the federal structure. At least one important political figure, Sergei Shakhrai, has proposed radical changes in the regional organization of power, including devolution of power to local governments but amalgamation of some existing federal units.

DISPUTES ABOUT FEDERALISM IN RUSSIA

Ad Hoc and Asymmetrical Federalism

Despite the legal equality of the eighty-nine units of the federation, the republics generally have a greater scope of authority than do most of the regions (oblasts) and territories (krais). The power of the autonomous okrugs varies from case to case. Generally, richer areas have managed to appropriate more privileges for themselves than have poorer regions because the former have more bargaining power. This widens the gap between the "haves" and the "have-nots" and creates problems for the federal government in trying to enforce any system of regional redistribution.

Most of the republics have now adopted their own constitutions (some had already adopted constitutions in the Soviet period), and several regions and territories have adopted or are in the process of formulating charters. Some regional charters and several of the republic constitutions have provisions that are deemed to contradict aspects of the federal constitution or of federal law.[8] Examples would be provisions for secession from the federation, declarations of state sovereignty, special rights for particular nationality groups, jurisdiction over subsoil resources, and possible usurpations of federal rights of appointment in the judiciary or other agencies. In some cases, the federal constitutional court has declared several provisions of regional charters unconstitutional.[9] Some of the republics (most notably Tatarstan, Sakha, and Bashkortostan), at various times, have used single-track tax-collection systems (all taxes collected by republic authorities) or have refused to turn over tax revenues to federal authorities.

Since adoption of the 1993 constitution, one mechanism used to try to reduce tensions between the center and some of the more recalcitrant republics has been a series of bilateral treaties between the federal government and individual republics, beginning with Tatarstan.[10] Such treaties have been concluded also with Bashkortostan,[11] Kabardino-Balkaria, Sakha,[12] Buryatia,[13] Udmurtia,[14] Komi,[15] and Chuvashia.[16] It seems likely that most of the other republics of the federation will eventually conclude similar treaties. The signing of such treaties gives the appearance of granting the republics a special status within the federation. It continues the earlier approach of ad hoc federalism, in which special agreements are concluded on an individual basis with specific units of the federation. The result is asymmetrical federalism, with some of the "equal" members of the federation enjoying distinctive privileges.

The first treaty signed, that with Tatarstan in February 1994, seems to have been quite successful in ameliorating tension between that republic and the central authorities. (The treaty is entitled "The Treaty of the Demarcation of Objects of Jurisdiction and the Mutual Delegation of Powers between the Bodies of State Power of the Russian Federation and the Republic of Tatarstan.") The treaty affirms that Tatarstan is a state united with the Russian Federation, and references to Tatar state sovereignty are absent. Although the constitution of the republic has not been altered to eliminate all provisions deemed to contradict the federal constitution, the provisions of the bilateral treaty are considered to be in accord with the federal constitution. The republic agrees to transfer to the federal government a share of tax revenues. At the same time, the republic is granted considerable autonomy in several areas, including taxation.

The treaty with Bashkortostan was signed in August 1994 and does include a reference to the state sovereignty of that republic within the Russian Federation. The treaty gives Bashkortostan rights in conducting its own foreign policy, in ownership of natural resources, and in establishing taxation principles for the republic. Despite the treaty, conflicts over accounting and taxation relationships continue between the federal government and Bashkortostan.[17] The treaty with Sakha (signed in June 1995) was important in establishing rights of ownership and use of the rich natural resource base of that republic.

These treaties have elicited criticism from the leaders of some of Russia's regions (oblasts or krais), for these treaties seem to imply a special status for the republics, despite the formal equality provided for in the constitution.[18] For example, following the conclusion of the bilateral treaty with neighboring Bashkortostan, the leadership of Perm oblast demanded equal rights and presented to the federal authorities a long list of grievances relating to tax payments, use of natural resources, and federal programs in the region.[19] A December 1995 agreement between Orenburg oblast and the federal government defined the division of powers between the two levels of government; this was the first such agreement with an oblast or krai. Further such agreements, each with its own unique characteristics, were subsequently signed with other regions, including Kaliningrad oblast,[20] Sverdlovsk oblast,[21] Nizhni Novgorod oblast,[22] and the city of St. Petersburg.[23] In May 1996, the first trilateral treaty was signed, between the federal government of Russia, on the one hand, and Irkutsk oblast and the Ust-Ordinsk Buryat autonomous okrug, on the other.[24]

Even though federal authorities have attempted to respond to some of the specific grievances in this way, the more general policy line is a subject of dispute. Prime Minister Viktor Chernomyrdin and others frequently express their high regard and support for the bilateral treaties;

at the same time, there seems to be a recognition that establishing such special arrangements with particular republics may represent a deviation from the norms of equal treatment laid out in the constitution. This approach involves a continued reliance on an individualized, ad hoc mechanism to construct federalism, a process likely to evoke continuing perceptions of favoritism and discrimination. Granting concessions in response to demands from particular regions is likely to engender an escalation of demands for regional privileges and a drop in the perceived fairness of central policy. The asymmetrical features of Russian federalism have their proponents and detractors within Russia and abroad. Although this arrangement may seem to provide a mechanism for ameliorating immediate problems, in the long term it may reinforce perceptions of discrimination and produce a cascade of pleas for special treatment.

Selection of Governors

The heads of the executive branch in the republics have generally not been appointed by the president and in some cases have been directly elected. This gives them considerable autonomy. An issue of dispute, however, has involved the method of selecting the governors of the regions (oblasts, krais). Since 1991, the president has appointed his own representative to each unit of the federation. Subsequently, the power to appoint the governors of the regions was also placed in his hands. Legislation passed by the federal parliament provided for the popular election of governors of the regions. President Yeltsin blocked these elections through his power of decree, presumably part of the effort to realize the idea of a unified executive structure. These appointments strengthened the president's hand in dealing with regional self-assertion. Some observers feel that the system of appointed governors allowed Yeltsin to maintain a regional personnel network similar to that which existed under Communist Party rule. No doubt, the levers of control are much more limited than previously; nonetheless, the president's power of appointment may have encouraged a more conciliatory stance on the part of these officials.

In May 1995, the federal parliament (the Federal Assembly) again passed a resolution supporting the popular elections of heads of the regions and districts, elections to be held simultaneously with the December 1995 parliamentary elections.[25] Although the president overrode this decision, he did grant special permission to some oblasts to allow the direct elections of governors. An election was approved and carried out in Sverdlovsk oblast in August 1995. Requests from other regional assemblies resulted in approval for gubernatorial elections to be carried out in conjunction with the December 1995 parliamentary elections in Orenburg oblast, Tambov oblast, Tomsk oblast, Nizhni Novgorod oblast, Primorsky krai, Belgorod oblast, Novosibirsk oblast, Tver oblast, and Yaroslavl oblast. Following a long dispute regarding the formation of a new Federal Assembly, a more general compromise was reached, providing for the popular elections of the remaining governors by December 1996. Between September 1996 and January 1997, elections for governor were carried out in forty-four units of the Russian Federation; seven republic presidential elections were also held.

Federal Institutions and Elections

The 1993 constitution established a bicameral legislature. The upper house, the Federation Council, represents the regions, although the principles of its selection were not fully specified in the constitution itself. Because some regional councils had been disbanded after the events of October 1993, it was decided that in December 1993, members would be popularly elected to the Federation Council, two from each unit of the federation (with the exception of Chechnya, which did not participate in the elections). It was presumed, however, that the system might later be changed so that the two representatives would be appointed by the regional legislative and executive organs.

A long dispute unfolded between the president and the two houses of the parliament regarding the selection of a new Federation Council after the term of office of the body elected in December 1993 expired, in December 1995. The parliament supported popular election of the deputies, but the president opposed this idea and favored an appointment procedure. Elements in the Federation Council suggested extending the term of the existing body if a compromise could not be reached about the direct election of a successor. The Constitutional Court was not prepared to issue a judgment on the conflict, since there were no clear constitutional grounds for doing so. A conciliation commission met in late August 1995, but resolution of the dispute did not take place until November 1995. The compromise provided for ex officio membership in the Federation Council, including the head of the regional administration (the governor or president, for republics) and the head of the representative council from each unit of the federation. However, regional governors appointed by the president were required, under the compromise, to undergo popular elections in their regions before December 1996.

With the formation of the Federation Council, the Council of Heads of Republics, established in 1992, ceased to function. However, in the face of the Chechnya crisis, leaders of some republics proposed that it be reactivated as a forum to allow direct interaction between the president and the republic heads. The inability of republic or regional heads to influence the president's policy in Chechnya seems to have evoked considerable discontent over the lack of representation of regional interests in the executive branch.

REGIONAL, ETHNIC, AND CULTURAL AUTONOMY

In light of the patterns described above, the autonomy of any given region depends to a large extent on the initiative of its leaders and the degree to which they are willing to assert their authority vis-à-vis the federal authorities. Regions with a rich natural resource base or other important economic resources have an advantage here, whereas regions heavily dependent on federal subsidies are in a weaker position.

In broad stroke, central executive authorities seem to be pursuing the following goals regarding regional autonomy: (1) to pass to the regions as many responsibilities in the social sphere as possible, for example, responsibility for handling social problems arising from the economic reform and development of the regional infrastructure (e.g., transportation, recreational facilities, service and retail outlet structures, health care facilities); (2) to retain powers related to the control and redistribution of particularly valuable enterprises and assets; and (3) to maintain control over personnel appointments in regional executive structures.

At the same time, regional authorities have pursued the following goals: (1) to gain as much autonomy as possible, depending on the availability of local economic resources, but at the same time to retain federal subsidies; (2) to gain maximum control over the privatization process, particularly where it relates to potentially lucrative assets;[26] (3) to create associations joining economic or national regions in order to replace certain coordinative functions of the center;[27] and (4) to honor only those central directives that are based on recent mutual agreements or that correspond to the interests of the region.

To describe the level of regional autonomy, one currently has to make a distinction between republics, on the one hand, and oblasts and krais, on the other. As a general rule, republics have the highest level of autonomy with regard to all spheres of life. The degree of actual autonomy of the autonomous okrugs varies greatly from case to case.

The regions have received a relatively high degree of autonomy regarding ethnic and cultural affairs. The major question in this sphere is funding, which is now the responsibility of the republic, oblast, or krai.

Differing regional capabilities and the likelihood of serious ethnic unrest or clashes determine the extent to which the federal government becomes involved with this issue. Areas with mixed ethnic composition and regions in the Transcaucasian area (bordering other unstable states) are particularly volatile.

CHECHNYA: IMPLICATIONS FOR RUSSIAN FEDERALISM

Chechnya has long been a trouble spot for Russia and later the USSR.[28] Before Chechnya's incorporation into the Russian Empire in 1859 and again after the Bolshevik revolution in 1917, local forces fought to maintain Chechnya's independence. In 1924 Chechnya was made part of the USSR and in 1934 was joined with an adjacent region, Ingushetia, to form a single autonomous republic within the Soviet Union. During World War II, following an anti-Soviet uprising, hundreds of thousands of Chechens (along with other peoples from the Caucasus region) were deported by Stalin to Soviet Central Asia.

In October 1991 the newly elected president of the republic, Dzhokhar Dudaev, declared independence from Russia; the Russian president and the federal government have never recognized the validity of this declaration. Checheno-Ingushetia did not sign the Federal Treaty in March 1992. Later that year Chechnya and Ingushetia were officially recognized as two separate republics. The government of Chechnya maintained its independence stance, and the republic's leaders did not permit participation by the republic in the 1993 parliamentary elections and referendum. Ingushetia, on the other hand, did not claim independence.

Chechnya is a small republic; according to the latest census (1989), the population of Checheno-Ingushetia was 1.27 million. At that time, 58 percent were Chechen, 13 percent Ingush, and 23 percent Russian. The population of Chechnya alone was estimated at about 600,000 in 1994. Despite its small size, Chechnya holds an important position on the southern border of Russia. Chechnya is also widely perceived to be a kind of "safe haven" for the mafia and criminal elements that operate in Russia. This and the (probably unfounded) fears that Chechnya's example might embolden other recalcitrant republics to pursue outright independence were likely motives for the Russian attack on Chechnya in December 1994.

After the split from Ingushetia in 1992, the leadership of the Chechen republic continued to pursue its claim to independence, despite its rejection by the Russian government. Internal political conflicts within Chechnya also emerged. In 1993 the Chechen parliament voted to impeach Dudaev, who proceeded to dissolve the parliament. An opposition

Provisional Council was formed in August 1994. Fighting broke out between government and opposition forces in 1994, but forces of the Russian Federation did not become openly involved until December 1994.

The Russian intervention in Chechnya evoked widespread opposition within the Russian Federation and its leadership circles, extending even to former Yeltsin allies, such as Yegor Gaidar and other reform figures. The leaders of several other republics also protested the invasion, seeing it as an expression of the government's willingness to take unilateral and forcible action against recalcitrant republics. In early January 1995, the leaders of several of the republics of the Urals-Volga area met in Cheboksary to express their discontent regarding their lack of influence on the president's policy and their desire for the revitalization of the Council of Heads of Republics.[29] A decree of the Chuvash republic established the right of its residents to decline service in Chechnya,[30] and attempts were made by the governments of other regions to recall their soldiers from the conflict. The leadership of the oblasts and krais were generally more restrained in their criticism, but there was considerable regional variation in the response to the Chechnya war. Some opposed the military intervention completely and pressed for a political solution; others were primarily critical of the ineffective manner in which the war effort was carried out.

The Chechnya crisis demonstrates the lack of agreement on how to resolve fundamental disputes between the federal government and rebellious regions. To some extent, Chechnya appears to be a special case, since other republics have not, in fact, demanded outright independence. Furthermore, the Chechnya crisis does not seem to have called into question the fundamental federal structure of the country. Methods of negotiation and diplomacy have continued to prevail in relations between the federal government and the other members of the federation. Most demands emanating from the republics and regions have an economic character, rather than being unconditional demands for independence.[31] Economic goods, unlike separatist demands, are divisible and thus are subject to negotiation and compromise. It therefore seems unlikely that other republics will follow in the footsteps of Chechnya and demand outright independence. A more likely scenario is that growing economic autonomy and economic linkages with regions outside Russia (particularly in the Russian Far East) will gradually produce even stronger pressures for weakened federal ties.

NOTES

1. See Vladimir Yefimov, *Rossiiskaya gazeta,* July 14, 1992, p. 5, translated in *FBIS-USR-92–096* (July 31, 1992), p. 71.

2. For an English translation of the Federal Treaty, see *FBIS-SOV-92-051* (March 16, 1992), p. 67.
3. See Article 84 of the amended constitution, as translated in *FBIS-USR-92-091* (July 12, 1992), p. 12, translated from *Vedemosti s"ezda-narodnykh deputatov Rossiiskoi Federatisii i Verkhovnogo Soveta Rossiiskoi federatsii,* no. 20 (May 21, 1992), pp. 1417-40.
4. One might draw an analogy to a hypothetical situation in which highly developed and populated provinces such as Ontario and Quebec were treated as administrative subdivisions of Canada, whereas the territories were given the degree of autonomy presently enjoyed by the Canadian provinces.
5. See the decree of the Russian Federation Supreme Soviet of July 15, 1992, in *Rossiiskaya gazeta,* August 20, 1992, p. 6, translated in *FBIS-USR-92-124* (September 27, 1992), p. 20. This decision was apparently taken on appeal to the Constitutional Court but was ruled valid in the summer of 1993.
6. Vladimir Lysenko, *Rossiiskie vesti,* April 18, 1995, translated (condensed) in *Current Digest of the Soviet Press* (hereafter, *CDSP*) 47, no. 16 (1995): 8-9.
7. See Alexei Tarasov, in *Izvestiya,* September 7, 1995, p. 5, translated (excerpts) in *CDSP* 47, no. 36 (1995): 15-16; and *Izvestiya,* November 10, 1995, translated (condensed) in *CDSP* 47, no. 45 (1995): 11.
8. Yelena Tregubova, *Segodnya,* October 21, 1994, p. 2, translated in *CDSP* 46, no. 42 (1994): 16-17; and *Segodnya,* January 19, 1995, p. 1, translated in *CDSP* 47, no. 3 (1995): 15.
9. For example, relating to the charter of Chita oblast. See Alexei Kirpichnikov, *Segodnya,* February 3, 1996, p. 2.
10. Radik Batyrshin, *Nezavisimaya gazeta,* February 16, 1994, p. 1, translated (condensed) in *CDSP* 46, no. 7 (1994): 11.
11. Radik Batyrshin, *Nezavisimaya gazeta,* August 4, 1994, p. 2, translated in *CDSP* 46, no. 31 (1994): 14-15.
12. Vladimir Yemelyanenko, *Moskovskie novosti,* no. 44 (June 25-July 2, 1995), p. 10.
13. Yelena Tregubova, *Segodnya,* July 12, 1995, p. 2.
14. Badezhda Bannikova and Dmitry Kamyshev, *Kommersant-Daily,* October 18, 1995, p. 3, translated (condensed) in *CDSP* 47, no. 42 (1995): 16-17.
15. Tatyana Borisevich, *Rossiiskie vesti,* March 21, 1996, p. 1, translated (condensed) in *CDSP* 47, no. 12 (1995): 16.
16. *Kommersant-Daily,* May 28, 1996, p. 3.
17. See Vladimir Todres, *Segodnya,* February 7, 1995, p. 3, translated (condensed) in *CDSP* 47, no. 6 (1995): 8; and Alexandra Lugovskaya, *Rossiiskie vesti,* January 27, 1995, p. 1, translated (condensed) in *CDSP* 47, no. 6 (1995): 8-9.
18. For example, the legislative assembly of St. Petersburg drafted its own treaty for presentation to the president; this treaty provided that the city should get the same preferential treatment that was granted to any other unit of the federation through such treaties. See Alexander Pozdyiakov, *Segodnya,* October 31, 1995, p. 3, translated (excerpts) in *CDSP* 47, no. 44 (1995): 16.
19. Igor Lobanov, *Segodnya,* August 31, 1994, p. 2.

20. See Dmitry Orlov, *Rossiiskie vesti*, January 17, 1996, p. 2, translated (condensed) in *CDSP*, no. 3 (1996), p. 21.
21. See the interview with Eduard Rossel in *Rossiiskie vesti*, January 19, 1996, p. 2, translated (condensed) in *CDSP*, no. 3 (1996), p. 21.
22. Andrei Chugunov, *Kommersant-Daily*, January 18, 1996, p. 2, translated (condensed) in *CDSP*, no. 3 (1996), pp. 21–22.
23. See Andrei Sinitsyn, *Kommersant-Daily*, June 15, 1996, p. 2, translated (condensed) in *CDSP*, no. 24 (1996), p. 17. This agreement was signed after the victory of Vladimir Yakovlev over Anatoly Sobchak in the mayoral election in St. Petersburg and represented somewhat of a reversal from the more critical stance previously endorsed by the St. Petersburg legislative assembly and by Sobchak himself. In the fall of 1995, the St. Petersburg assembly had proposed a draft treaty that would give St. Petersburg all of the same rights as those given to *any* federal unit by *any* federal law, normative act, or treaty. This proposal represented a de facto challenge to the very premise of ad hoc treaties. The treaty actually signed by Yakovlev, on the other hand, accorded to St. Petersburg specific rights and powers but did not contain any such all-encompassing provision. On the earlier proposal, see Alexander Pozdnyakov, *Segodnya*, October 31, 1995, p. 3.
24. *Kommersant-Daily*, May 28, 1996, p. 3. Ust-Ordinsk Buryat autonomous okrug is located within the borders of Irkutsk oblast. This treaty provides an example of the close links that can still exist between an oblast and an okrug that was previously a subunit of the oblast but is now an independent subject of the federation.
25. Resolution of the State Duma and Council of the Federation of the Russian Federation, "O vyborakh glav administratsii kraev, oblastei, gorodov federal'nogo znacheniia, avtonomnoi oblasti, avtonomnykh okrugov," May 26, 1995, published in *Sobranie zakonodatel'stva Rossiiskoi Federatsii*, no. 24 (June 12, 1994), p. 4311.
26. An example is the efforts of Eduard Rossel, the influential governor of Sverdlovsk oblast. See Viktor Smirnov, *Kommersant-Daily*, December 16, 1995, p. 2.
27. Examples would be the attempts to form (1) a Urals republic under the leadership of Eduard Rossel and (2) a Siberian republic. Apparently the federal authorities offered Orenburg oblast special benefits as a reward for shunning efforts to form the Urals republic. See Vladimir Yemelyanenko, *Moskovskie novosti*, December 10–17, 1995, p. 9.
28. Portions of this section are reprinted from Joan DeBardeleben, *Russian Politics in Transition* (Boston: Houghton-Mifflin Co., 1997), pp. 146–47, by permission of Houghton-Mifflin Co.
29. See Lyubov Tsukanova, *Rossiiskie vesti*, January 10, 1995, p. 1, translated (condensed) in *CDSP* 47, no. 2 (1995): 22; and *Kommersant-Daily*, January 13, 1995, p. 3, translated in *CDSP* 47, no. 3 (1995): 13–14.
30. Yelena Tregubova, *Segodnya*, January 13, 1995, p. 2, translated in *CDSP* 47, no. 2 (1995): 23.
31. See Dmitry Oreshkin and Vladimir Kozlov's comment relating to the decline in concerns with sovereignty in *Segodnya*, July 10, 1996, p. 5.

3

Electoral Behavior and Attitudes in Russia: Do Regions Make a Difference or Do Regions Just Differ?

Joan DeBardeleben and Aleksander A. Galkin

Just as regional governments have become increasingly important political actors within the context of emerging Russian federalism, so too has a clear regional dimension been discerned in mass political attitudes and behavior in Russia.[1] Previous scholarship on regional electoral behavior in Russia has identified fairly clear and consistent patterns of regional voting.[2] But does the region in which people reside have an independent impact on how people think about basic political issues? Or do people who share similar characteristics but live in different regions tend to think alike? Our hypothesis is that political consciousness and electoral behavior are determined to a significant degree by the region in which the respondent resides. In this chapter we develop a typology for understanding regional differences in mass political behavior and attitudes. We then select four distinctive Russian regions that represent each of the types in our typology. Although the distribution of votes and attitudes varies across our four regions, in our analysis we examine the question of whether region itself acts as an independent predictor of attitudes or whether the regional differences are more likely explained by the characteristics of the population in the four regions.

TOWARD A TYPOLOGY OF RUSSIA'S REGIONS

Because of the wide diversity of Russia's regions, it is important, for analytical purposes, to identify a conceptual basis for analyzing their similarities and differences. Although case studies of particular regions generate useful insights, this approach does not easily allow generalizable conclusions. On the other hand, it would be difficult to collect sufficient statistical or survey data from all of Russia's eighty-nine federal units. There are, furthermore, not only differences between the regions but also similarities among their separate groups. This fact underlies the importance of developing typologies of regions. The typology presented in this chapter is exploratory and simple in conception but captures at least one of the underlying dynamics of regional differentiation in Russia.

During the Soviet period, the regional administrative units reflected, to an important degree, the political goals and pragmatic concerns of the political leadership. These administrative units (republics, oblasts, okrugs, krais) have endured (although their exact legal status has changed) to form the basis for an administrative model of regionalization in Russia. The eighty-nine regional units are incommensurate with one another in terms of their positions and contributions to national wealth; in many cases their formation and the determination of their boundaries were only weakly linked to geopolitical, economic, or other imperatives.

Traditionally, in addition to Moscow, eleven economic regions have been identified in Russia: North, Northwest, Central, Central Chernozem ("Black Earth"), North Caucasus, Povolzh'e, Volga-Vyatka, Ural, Western Siberia, Eastern Siberia, and the Far East (see map 3.1). Each economic region includes several units of the federation that share some basic economic features. These economic divisions (or variations on them) are still used by several leading survey research organizations in Russia to construct representative samples of the Russian population. In developing a typology of Russia's regions, one should take into account both the political factors that led to the definition of the eighty-nine federal units and the economic factors that underlie the definition of these economic regions. An important consideration is that statistical data, both economic and sociopolitical, are generally aggregated on the basis of the separate subjects of the federation, reflecting the situation in these units.

A typology of regions could be based on various criteria: *geographic* (the availability or lack of natural resources, the advantages or disadvantages of physical location); *economic* (sectoral mix, development of the infrastructure, the level and characteristics of the productive forces, the availability and quality of labor resources); *sociopolitical* (the nature of social relations, the dominant political orientations, the existence and influence of political parties, elite structures, and orientations of local governments); *ethnopolitical* (the presence of ethnic diversity, refugees, and minority ethnic groups); and *ecological* (environmental) conditions. Some of the above-mentioned criteria correlate with one other. For example, geographic location and resource endowment are likely to be associated with certain patterns of (sectoral) economic development as well as with

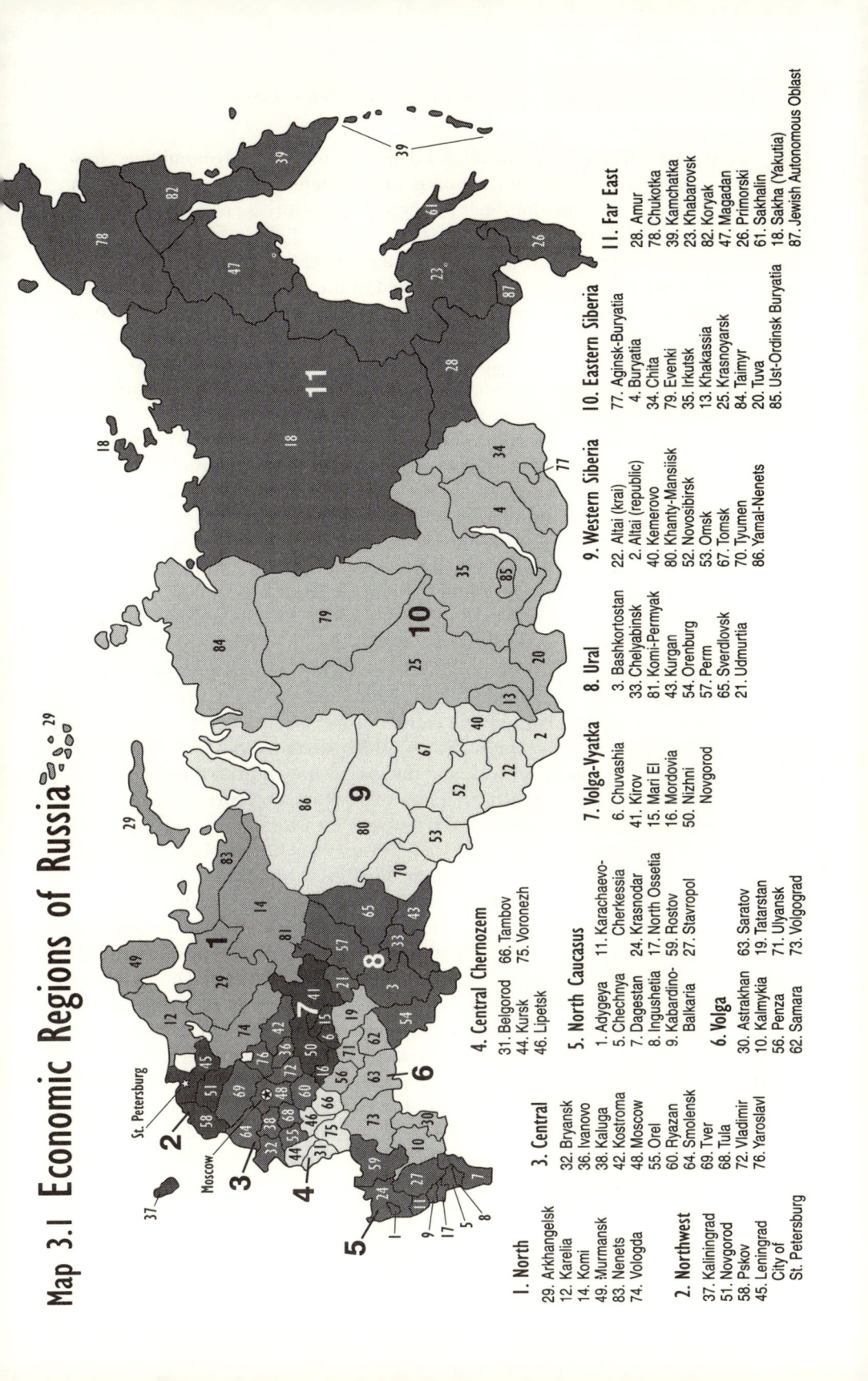

Map 3.1 Economic Regions of Russia

1. North
29. Arkhangelsk
12. Karelia
14. Komi
49. Murmansk
83. Nenets
74. Vologda

2. Northwest
37. Kaliningrad
51. Novgorod
58. Pskov
45. Leningrad
City of St. Petersburg

3. Central
32. Bryansk
36. Ivanovo
38. Kaluga
42. Kostroma
48. Moscow
55. Orel
60. Ryazan
64. Smolensk
69. Tver
68. Tula
72. Vladimir
76. Yaroslavl

4. Central Chernozem
31. Belgorod
44. Kursk
46. Lipetsk
66. Tambov
75. Voronezh

5. North Caucasus
1. Adygeya
5. Chechnya
7. Dagestan
8. Ingushetia
9. Kabardino-Balkaria
11. Karachaevo-Cherkessia
24. Krasnodar
17. North Ossetia
59. Rostov
27. Stavropol

6. Volga
30. Astrakhan
10. Kalmykia
56. Penza
62. Samara
63. Saratov
19. Tatarstan
71. Ulyansk
73. Volgograd

7. Volga-Vyatka
6. Chuvashia
41. Kirov
15. Mari El
16. Mordovia
50. Nizhni Novgorod

8. Ural
3. Bashkortostan
33. Chelyabinsk
81. Komi-Permyak
43. Kurgan
54. Orenburg
57. Perm
65. Sverdlovsk
21. Udmurtia

9. Western Siberia
22. Altai (krai)
2. Altai (republic)
40. Kemerovo
80. Khanty-Mansiisk
52. Novosibirsk
53. Omsk
67. Tomsk
70. Tyumen
86. Yamal-Nenets

10. Eastern Siberia
77. Aginsk-Buryatia
4. Buryatia
34. Chita
79. Evenki
35. Irkutsk
13. Khakassia
25. Krasnoyarsk
84. Taimyr
20. Tuva
85. Ust-Ordinsk Buryatia

11. Far East
28. Amur
78. Chukotka
39. Kamchatka
23. Khabarovsk
82. Koryak
47. Magadan
26. Primorski
61. Sakhalin
18. Sakha (Yakutia)
87. Jewish Autonomous Oblast

typical environmental profiles. Likewise, patterns of economic development determine the socioprofessional structure of the population. In other cases, correlations may not be so apparent (e.g., regarding the ethnopolitical situation).

The selection of criteria (or a set of criteria) for developing a typology depends primarily on the task defined by the researcher. Criteria may be selected solely for prognostic purposes (to determine the characteristics of the consumer market or structural characteristics of the electorate), or the goal may be broader or more scholarly in orientation (e.g., to understand long-term trends of social development). This explains the multiplicity of possible typologies that may be proposed.

The typology set forth in this chapter is based on an effort to address a "middle-range" task, namely, clarifying the transformation of the sociopsychological orientations and the societal behavior (above all, political behavior) of the population of the various regions as they undergo a process of fundamental economic change. In other words, our goal is to develop a typology that will help to explain regional differences in mass attitudes toward the reform process, as well as electoral behavior. Thus the first two types of criteria mentioned above (geographic and economic) will be viewed as primary defining features of our typology. This view is based on our assumption that economic and geographic features crucially shape the way in which a region undergoes the transformation from a centrally planned to a market or quasi-market economic formation. Resource endowment, geographic proximity to different types of markets and supply sources, and the preexisting industrial profile of the region are key factors affecting how regions and enterprises within those regions weather the period of economic transformation. Our hypothesis is that a typology based on these features will be useful for explaining sociopolitical attitudes and political behavior of the population. Since our typology is based on economic and geographic conditions of the regions, it will be less adequate for dealing with differences between regions that have a national-ethnic basis or are rooted in more or less idiosyncratic characteristics of particular regional leaders. These types of factors can be used to "correct" the typology at a later stage of analysis.

On the basis of the defining criteria we have selected, four types of regions, which share essential characteristics, may be delineated:

- Type I: regions rich in natural resources, with developed extractive industries and relatively poor agricultural sectors (mainly northern Russia including northern Siberia, Povolzh'e, parts of Kuzbass, and to a lesser degree, parts of North Caucasus)
- Type II: regions with a developed transportation infrastructure, and

a high concentration of primary industries, including transport and machine-building (the Urals, southern parts of the Western Siberia and Eastern Siberia regions, greater Moscow and St. Petersburg)
- Type III: regions with an average level of industrial production and with a relatively developed agricultural sector (Central Chernozem, parts of the Northwest and Povolzh'e regions)
- Type IV: regions and parts of regions in which agriculture predominates (Krasnodar and Stavropol krais, specific parts of Volgograd and Saratov oblasts, Altai krai)

Even though the defining features of our typology are geographic and economic features, certain distinctive patterns of social and economic development are associated with each type of region. These form the basis for the hypothesized linkages between economic-geographic bases and mass attitudes. We present first an overview of the foundation of these linkages and then proceed to examine electoral and attitudinal data from a representative region of each type.

Type I (Extractive) Regions

During the first years of the economic reform process, this group of regions enjoyed a privileged position. Oil, gas, and nonferrous metals that were extracted in these regions formed—and still do form—the most important part of Russia's exports. The weakening of the regulatory role of the central government meant that these regions received a significant portion of export revenue. This, in turn, had a positive effect on the standard of living of those portions of the population that worked in the extractive sector or in the transportation of natural resources. To some extent coal miners were the exception, due to the high cost and relative uncompetitiveness of the coal they were mining.

In general the social situation in this group of regions remained relatively stable in the first years of the post-Communist period. The level of satisfaction with the policies carried out after August 1991 was visibly higher than the average in the country. From time to time this stability was interrupted by outbreaks of protest by miners who demanded raises and regular payment of wages. Some manifestations of dissatisfaction were registered among oil industry workers. However, local and central authorities were usually able to engineer compromises to control discontent.

It is no coincidence that during the April 1993 referendum, which was in fact a referendum "for" or "against" the policy of President Boris Yeltsin and his government, voters in these regions (above all in the Northwest, the North, and Povolzh'e) affirmed their trust in the government more strongly than did voters in other regions. The loyalty index, calculated by a group of researchers from the Institute of Geography of RAN (Russian Academy of Science) was highly favorable in these areas, and the index of oppositionism was one of the lowest.[3]

The situation began to change in 1994. By this time the advantages enjoyed by the extractive regions had started to disappear. The crisis in the mining industry became more severe. On the one hand, this crisis was caused by the slump in demand for coal because of the recession throughout the country. On the other hand, it was a result of cuts in government subsidies. The decline of investment activity in the oil industry also caused a drop in oil extraction and generated initial problems in the gas industry. These problems became more serious in 1995 after the "currency corridor"—a fixed range for fluctuation of the dollar-ruble exchange rate—was established. This policy artificially lowered the dollar-ruble exchange rate, making it harder to export oil and gas. Consequently the sources of hard currency revenue began to contract.

The general economic crisis affecting the country brought a reduction of financial support from the central government to all northern regions, which for a long time had depended on centralized injections for development and maintenance of the infrastructure. In addition, an enormous increase in nonpayments became a chronic illness of the Russian economy, seriously damaging the extraction industry. The growth in nominal earnings of the people living in these regions was absorbed by galloping inflation.

As a result of these economic strains, social tensions have developed in Type I regions, despite the advantageous economic base of these areas. Expectations rose in the early phases of *perestroika;* thus a gap between reality and expectations is likely to take on greater political significance here than in other areas of the country, where the costs of the economic transition were recognized much earlier. Consequently the social and political atmosphere has begun to change in the Type I regions. Dissatisfaction has manifested itself in more frequent strikes, involving political as well as economic demands, and in the acuteness and duration of labor conflicts.

Although support for liberal and radical-democratic ideas in these areas remains higher than the average levels for Russia, support for oppositional ideas has also begun to rise. For example, during the Federal Assembly elections in December 1993, Russia's Choice and the Yabloko bloc (liberal-reform formations) received more votes than the average in the country. At the same time an appreciable number of the voters abandoned these groupings to support the extreme, nationalistically oriented Liberal Democratic Party of Russia (LDPR), headed by Vladimir

Table 3.1
DECEMBER 1993 VOTING RESULTS FOR THE LARGEST PARTIES/BLOCS IN TYPE I REGIONS (in percent)

Region	Russia's Choice	Yabloko	LDPR	CPRF	Agrarian Party
Arkhangelsk oblast	21.83	8.20	22.22	6.44	6.39
Kemerovo oblast	13.74	6.83	29.42	9.57	5.61
Komi republic	21.83	7.09	24.31	7.05	5.57
Murmansk oblast	23.47	14.25	24.26	5.67	1.30
Taimyr autonomous okrug	27.99	7.85	17.37	4.67	1.04
Tyumen oblast	13.44	5.90	21.03	11.03	10.57
Khanty-Mansiisk autonomous okrug	23.66	8.24	21.25	4.63	1.04
All-Russian vote	15.51	7.86	22.92	12.40	7.99

Data for tables 3.1–3.4 were taken from *Bulletin of the Central Electoral Commission of the Russian Federation* 12, no. 1 (Moscow, 1994): 52–66.

Zhirinovsky. Supporters of this party were in large part citizens who had earlier distanced themselves sharply from the Communists and therefore were not ready to vote for the CPRF (Communist Party of the Russian Federation); at the same time they wanted to demonstrate their rejection of the present situation and policy. The low level of support for the Agrarian Party reflected the extremely small proportion of agrarian population in these regions, except in the southern part of Tyumen oblast (see table 3.1).

Ethnic factors complicate efforts to construct a workable typology of Russia's regions. However, for Type I regions, the economic factors (the rich natural resource base, in particular) that fuel the urge to regional economic autonomy are reinforced by ethnic factors in republics such as Tatarstan and Bashkortostan. These Volga republics occupy a special place in this group due to their heterogeneous ethnic composition and the existence of interethnic tensions. But whereas the configuration of political forces in 1993 in Tatarstan differed only insignificantly from that in other Type I regions, the situation seemed quite different in Bashkortostan, where Russia's Choice enjoyed lesser support and the CPRF and the Agrarian Party garnered more support. The specific character of the situation in both republics is also determined by the increasing activity of regional parties that have an ethnonationalist orientation.

The ecological situation in this group of regions is very complex. The level of crime is high, based on two factors. First, there is a wide differentiation in the standard of living in these regions. Second, the structure of the population in a number of these regions has been affected by the release of criminals from detention centers situated there.

Type II (Highly Industrialized) Regions

In these regions is concentrated a large proportion of the economically and politically active population of the country, including highly qualified workers, technicians, and engineers. In the earlier stages of the reform process, these groups, with their highly critical potential, played a very important role in movements for radical economic and political change. Political movements that proclaimed themselves democratic and put forth slogans of radical reform have found their most active support in this group of regions. The index of loyalty to the president and the government, as measured on the basis of the data from the April 1993 referendum, was above average; the indicator of oppositionism was well below average.

The 1993 elections for the Federal Assembly showed some weakening of the influence of the liberals and radical democrats in this group (see table 3.2). A swing in favor of the nationalistically oriented LDPR was recorded everywhere, providing convincing evidence of the growing dissatisfaction of voters with the results produced by the governing forces that had come to power in August 1991. Nevertheless, a backbone of support for the liberal and reform-democratic parties was preserved. Despite the scattered character of the data relating to specific oblasts and krais, common trends in the arrangement of political forces are evident. These regions evidenced disproportionably stronger support for the liberal-reform parties, as well as significant influence by the LDPR. As in Type I regions, voting for the LDPR indicated the withdrawal of support, on the part of some voters, from the forces that had come to power in August 1991.

Since December 1993, erosion of support for the liberal-radical forces has continued. The reason lies in the progressive decline in the machine-building industry, above all in weapons production. The first blow came when energy prices were freed from state control, causing skyrocketing production costs. The second blow involved abrupt cutbacks in govern-

Table 3.2
DECEMBER 1993 VOTING RESULTS FOR THE LARGEST PARTIES/BLOCS IN TYPE II REGIONS (in percent)

Region	Russia's Choice	Yabloko	LDPR	CPRF	Agrarian Party
Kirov oblast	12.48	7.54	27.53	8.74	15.27
Krasnoyarsk krai	13.96	7.29	31.17	9.06	7.84
Moscow oblast	19.82	9.75	26.64	10.82	3.99
Nizhni Novgorod oblast	13.96	12.29	19.91	11.58	9.11
Novosibirsk oblast	12.06	12.23	25.64	11.44	8.69
Perm oblast	27.12	8.24	14.81	6.91	4.86
Samara oblast	16.26	8.75	19.67	16.44	6.33
Sverdlovsk oblast	25.20	8.17	17.72	5.79	3.97
Chelyabinsk oblast	23.58	11.34	20.38	7.49	4.06
City of Moscow	34.73	12.08	12.82	11.03	1.43
All-Russian vote	15.51	7.86	22.92	12.40	7.99

ment contracts for the sector's industrial output and the cessation of government subsidies. By the beginning of 1995, according to various estimates, monthly industrial production fell to 45–50 percent of January 1992 levels; in the machine-building industry, in some sectors, the drop reached 80 percent. As a result, unemployment rose rapidly. Applying methods of the International Labor Organization, we see that at the beginning of 1995, 6.5 million people (7.6 percent of the economically active population) were unemployed.[4] A significant part of the loss in production and, along with it, the increase in unemployment occurred in Type II regions.[5]

Within this group, the economic situation varies from relatively acceptable to disastrous. Additional factors explain this variation: employment opportunities in the intermediary sector exist in megalopolises such as Moscow and St. Petersburg; some enterprises have managed to find a new production niche or to gain access to international markets. Metallurgical plants (above all nonferrous metallurgy) and some branches of the chemical industry that work for export are surviving and even growing. However, in general, the recession in this group of regions is quite severe, and the social and political environment is characterized by growing tension and shifts from earlier political loyalties.

In terms of public attitudes toward the reform process, in 1991–92 the situation in Type II regions was fairly similar to that in Type I regions. Beginning in 1994, however, differences between the two became more noticeable as the variations in the economic structure of the two regions produced different outcomes. Negative attitudes toward government policy are significantly stronger in most Type II regions, where the negative effects of the economic transition have been more marked.

The ecological situation in Type II regions is very complex. The level of crime is high, connected with the generally critical situation in these regions.

Type III (Mixed Economic) Regions

The particular character of this group of regions is strongly conditioned by the harmonic combination of massive industrial production and agricultural production. Large industrial centers exist, but they do not take the shape of megalopolises; rather, they are interspersed with vast agricultural territories. In the past (in the Soviet period), for various reasons, living conditions here were better than in Type II regions, nourishing conformist orientations among a significant part of the population; the high proportion of the population employed in agriculture encouraged support for fundamentalist values.

A significant part of the population in Type III regions expressed reserved apprehension toward the events of August 1991 and viewed the reforms undertaken since 1992 with aloof distrust. At first, the signs of crisis in the country were not as acutely evident in these regions as they were elsewhere in the country. In these areas, the consequences of the fall in industrial production, which affected the manufacturing centers, were softened; this occurred, in part, due to the migration of people to rural areas as they combined industrial labor with work on the land. In this way, the cities could be fed.

Nevertheless, from the very beginning, dissatisfaction with the general course of events was quite strong. However, this dissatisfaction was not directed primarily at the regional or local authorities but rather at the center and its policies. The reforms that were being implemented were, as a rule, perceived negatively. As the crisis intensified, the attachment to traditional values grew.

The index of loyalty, calculated on the basis of the April 1993 referendum, was either low or extremely low in this group of regions; the indicator of oppositionism was high or extremely high. During the elections in December 1993 a significant portion of the population voted for the parties that opposed the president and the government. In general, due to high levels of adherence to the Communist Party of the Russian Federation and the Agrarian Party, the regions of this group have acquired the reputation of being "red" (see table 3.3).

The national republics of the northern Caucasus region stand somewhat apart within this group of regions. The situation in these republics has been acutely affected by ethnopolitical conflicts and heightened emigration of the Russian-speaking population from unstable areas. The military conflict in Chechnya has also had a negative impact on the economic and sociopolitical situation of these territories. The configuration of political forces here is defined by the particular national-ethnic orientation or conflicts in the region. In some cases this was manifested in particularly high levels of voting for the CPRF (in North Ossetia, Kabardino-Balkaria, Karachaevo-Cherkessia, Adygeya, Dagestan); in other cases, it was manifested in high levels of voting for smaller parties. (In Ingushetia, for example, 71 percent of voters supported the relatively uninfluential "Democratic Party of Russia.")

The ecological situation in the northwestern regions of this group (above all, Bryansk oblast) suffers increased radiation levels, the result of the Chernobyl disaster. The level of crime is average except in the territories bordering Chechnya and Dagestan.

Type IV (Agricultural) Regions

It is difficult to single out particular oblasts that belong unambiguously in this group. Parts of Krasnodar krai and Stavropol krai, as well as particular districts within Volgograd oblast, Saratov oblast, and Altai krai, among others, could be included here. This type of region is characterized above all by the high quality of the soil.

Overall, Russia's agricultural sector faces severe difficulties, and this is the primary source of social and political tension in Type IV territories. Peculiarities in the configuration of political forces in this group of regions include particularly high levels of support for the nationalist forces (the LDPR) and for the Agrarian Party (see table 3.4).

In most cases, agricultural regions are still able to support themselves on the basis of local food production, when combined with maximal cuts in nonfood consumption. However, a continuing rapid decline in the volume of agricultural production, in conjunction with its diminished marketability, could seriously complicate the food supply situation of large

Table 3.3
DECEMBER 1993 VOTING RESULTS FOR THE LARGEST PARTIES/BLOCS IN TYPE III REGIONS (in percent)

Region	Russia's Choice	Yabloko	LDPR	CPRF	Agrarian Party
Belgorod oblast	10.02	4.57	37.07	15.90	10.23
Bryansk oblast	12.57	4.46	27.23	20.18	10.80
Volgograd oblast	11.86	9.53	27.67	14.42	10.90
Voronezh oblast	11.91	7.84	30.63	14.54	11.99
Kursk oblast	10.64	4.79	33.48	20.03	11.46
Mordovia republic	7.65	5.39	35.34	18.74	12.46
Lipetsk oblast	12.93	5.89	31.70	14.27	12.24
Orel oblast	9.58	4.13	31.80	25.69	7.03
Penza oblast	8.56	6.95	32.56	19.49	10.40
Tambov oblast	9.27	5.32	35.32	16.86	9.83
Udmurtia republic	16.19	8.18	17.59	11.14	11.07
Ulyansk oblast	12.23	4.78	24.57	17.50	13.98
Chuvash republic	8.90	3.43	22.53	19.73	12.75
All-Russian vote	15.51	7.86	22.92	12.40	7.99

cities and industrial centers. Increased food imports pose threats to parts of Russia's agricultural sector, although these sources are unlikely to compensate for the decrease in agricultural production, given hard currency constraints and rising transport costs. In 1995 the agricultural situation in Russia worsened due to a more pronounced "scissors" effect, that is, a widening gap between prices for agricultural goods and industrial production, as well as by a bad harvest produced by drought. These factors intensified oppositional sentiments in agricultural regions. Ethnic and national tensions in the North Caucasus affect several of these agricultural districts. The majority of these agricultural regions border areas with difficult national-ethnic problems (the national republics of the

Table 3.4
DECEMBER 1993 VOTING RESULTS FOR THE LARGEST PARTIES/BLOCS IN TYPE IV REGIONS (in percent)

Region	Russia's Choice	Yabloko	LDPR	CPRF	Agrarian Party
Altai krai	10.81	3.19	27.75	9.86	23.40
Krasnodar krai	11.90	9.51	25.49	16.83	7.59
Stavropol krai	9.32	5.13	38.53	12.35	11.48
Rostov oblast	12.30	7.44	22.28	17.31	7.52
All-Russian vote	15.51	7.86	22.92	12.40	7.99

northern Caucasus region) and therefore serve as havens for large numbers of refugees and migrants from "hot spots." Regional wars in the North Caucasus (earlier in southern Ossetia and Abkhazia, now in Chechnya) have affected another important traditional sector of the local economy, tourism, since people from other parts of Russia or the Commonwealth of Independent States (CIS) may hesitate to vacation near war zones. Oppositionism in these regions, therefore, acquires a clearly national or even nationalistic character.

The ecological situation in the Type IV regions is more favorable than in regions with high levels of industrialization and with developed extractive sectors. Exceptions are the territories affected by the radioactive contamination caused by the Chernobyl explosion. The level of crime here is significantly lower than in large industrial centers, although perceptions of high crime and corruption result from the influx of refugees from the Caucasus.

Of course, the typology proposed in this section presents only a rough picture of the real situation. Far from all of the eighty-nine units of the federation can be clearly assigned to one of the four types discussed above. There are intermediary types, sharing features of more than one type. In addition, the dividing line between types does not always correspond to the administrative boundaries of the units of the federation. One should also consider that the aggravation of the crisis in the country in 1994–95 was accompanied by rising popular dissatisfaction with the economic and political situation, by growing alienation from power structures, and by a more obvious discrediting of those political forces that had taken the reins of power in August 1991. Consequently, this process has led to a softening of distinctions between the various types of regions. Nevertheless, these distinctions, which are rooted in objective causes, remain. Under certain circumstances, they could again be strengthened.

ELECTORAL ATTITUDES IN THE FOUR REGIONS

For the empirical analysis of differences between the four types of regions outlined above, we have selected one region from each type for in-depth study: Khanty-Mansiisk autonomous okrug (KMO) (Type I), Nizhni Novgorod oblast (Type II), Orel oblast (Type III), and Stavropol krai (Type IV). Following the December 1995 elections for the State Duma, an all-Russian survey on economic and political attitudes was carried out (based on a representative sample from nineteen of Russia's eighty-nine units), with oversampling in our four designated regions.[6] The analysis that follows is based on data from this survey as well as on official election results.

Examination of voting behavior in these four regions reveals significant differences, beginning with the 1993 elections for the State Duma and continuing into 1996. Table 3.5 summarizes support for three major categories of parties or electoral blocs—liberal-reform,[7] left,[8] and national-patriotic[9]—based on four periods: party list vote in the 1993 Duma elections, party list vote in the 1995 Duma elections, responses to a question on party identification following the December 1995 elections,[10] and vote in the first round of the presidential elections in 1996. One must exercise caution in comparing data for each category over time, since definitions of the terms "left," "national-patriotic" and "liberal-reform" have evolved. We have included, in parentheses, the category "centrist" for the 1993 elections;[11] by the time of the 1995 elections, several of the parties that were earlier considered centrist (most notably "Our Home Is Russia," arguably the successor to Civic Union) could now be categorized as liberal-reform, given the clearer definitions that were emerging for political orientations. Furthermore, for the presidential election, there were many fewer choices available to the voter than there were in the 1995 Duma elections, and the former was a winner-take-all situation. Thus voters were more likely to vote for one of the two or three most prominent candidates (Yeltsin, Zhirinovsky, Gennady Zyuganov, Alexander Lebed); in the 1993 and 1995 Duma elections, on the other hand, smaller parties or blocs had a chance of gaining representation through the party list (proportional representation) portion of the ballot.

Table 3.5 provides evidence of significant regional differences in voter orientation. Most notably, in our Type I and Type II regions (KMO and Nizhni Novgorod), support for the liberal-reform orientation has consistently been higher than the all-Russian average, and in our Type III and IV regions (Orel and Stavropol), it has been lower than average. On the other hand, the Communists have received above-average support in the latter two regions, whereas support in KMO has been below average. Only in Nizhni Novgorod has support for the Communist grouping fluctuated around the all-Russian level. Support for the Communists has strengthened over time in Stavropol and Orel. Communist support also increased in our other two regions, but starting from a lower level; it remained well below the national average in KMO over the whole period. The national-patriotic forces received the strongest support in Stavropol, but if both the moderate nationalists (e.g., supporters of Lebed's Congress of Russian Communities) and more extreme nationalists (supporters of Zhirinovsky's LDPR) are combined, there is significant support for this orientation in other regions as well.

Attitudinal differences are also visible between the regions. Table 3.6 suggests that there is significant regional variation in the respondents' assessment of future economic prospects. Over half of the respondents in Nizhni Novgorod, Orel, and Stavropol anticipated a worsening of their standard of living in the next three or four years, but only a little over one-third held this view in KMO. Somewhat surprisingly, those in Nizhni Novgorod were the most pessimistic.

Our data also show that residents of KMO assessed the past two years more positively. About half said they had experienced a worsening of their standard of living, compared with about two-thirds in each of the other three regions. On the other hand, nearly one-quarter of the KMO residents reported an improvement, compared with about 13 percent in Stavropol and Nizhni Novgorod and some 16 percent in Orel.

Attitudes toward democracy also differed across our regions. We asked our respondents: "If we're talking about the very idea of democracy, do you support the introduction of democracy in Russia?" This question followed a series of questions that allowed the respondent to express his or her own understanding of the idea of democracy. As table 3.7 indicates, support for the idea of democracy differed significantly across our four regions. Support was the weakest in Stavropol, with 40 percent of the respondents expressing disapproval; support was highest in Nizhni Novgorod, with 14 percent expressing disapproval, followed by KMO's 19 percent. Our results indicate that attitudes in our four regions differ on multiple dimensions.

Despite the regional differences in perceived material conditions and in levels of support for democracy, our data show no significant

Table 3.5
VOTING BEHAVIOR AND PARTY IDENTIFICATION IN FOUR REGIONS OF RUSSIA, 1993–1996 (in percent of those voting or indicating preference)

Political Force[a]	Region	1993 Duma Vote	1995 Duma Vote	1995–96 Party Ident.[b]	1996 1st Pres. Vote
Liberal-Reform (Centrist)	All-Russian	27 (22)	29	37	43
	KMO	40 (30)	37	44	60
	Nizhni Novgorod	31 (27)	33	53	43
	Orel	16 (17)	16	27	26
	Stavropol	18 (18)	17	24	26
Left	All-Russian	20	31	30	32
	KMO	6	11	14	13
	Nizhni Novgorod	21	27	27	33
	Orel	39	52	50	55
	Stavropol	24	38	49	44
National-Patriotic	All-Russian	23	18	12	21
	KMO	21	20	18	23
	Nizhni Novgorod	20	20	11	21
	Orel	26	16	15	16
	Stavropol	39	25	13	26

Note: Figures for particular regions and for Russia as a whole do not add up to 100% because some voters and respondents chose parties not falling into one of the three categories covered by the table. The survey results reported in the third data column have a valid N of 1598 for this question. The Cramer's v value for the regional comparison on this question is .21 with p < .01.

[a] The parties included in each group are defined in chapter notes 7, 8, and 9. For 1993, the centrist category includes voters for the following parties or blocs: Women of Russia, Democratic Party of Russia, Civic Union, and Party of Russian Unity and Concord.

Table 3.5 *continued*

Table 3.5 *continued*

ᵇThe survey question asked which electoral union was closest to the respondent on the issue that was most important to the respondent.

Source: Compiled by Joan DeBardeleben and Aleksander A. Galkin. Data on the 1993 vote are from Michael McFaul and Nikolai Petrov, *Previewing Russia's 1995 Parliamentary Elections* (Moscow: Carnegie Endowment for International Peace, 1995). Data on the 1995 elections are from Central Electoral Commission of the Russian Federation, *Vybory deputatov Gosudarstvennoi Dumy 1995. Elektoral'naia statistika* (Moscow, 1996). Presidential vote figures are from the results published by the Central Electoral Commission in *Rossiiskaya gazeta,* July 1 and July 16, 1996. Survey data reported here are based on the "Carleton 1995 Russian Post-Election Survey" (see note 6).

differences in levels of material and political satisfaction across our regions. As tables 3.8 and 3.9 indicate, dissatisfaction with the standard of living and with the level of democracy in Russia was widespread and present in nearly equal measure in all regions at the time the survey was undertaken. Over 80 percent of our Russian respondents indicated dissatisfaction with their standard of living. Although it appears that residents of Orel were somewhat less satisfied than respondents in Stavropol, Nizhni Novgorod, and KMO, these regional differences are not statistically significant. Likewise, dissatisfaction with the level of democracy in Russia was widespread. Only 10 percent of the all-Russian sample expressed satisfaction; in all four of our regions, levels were even lower than this average. General pessimism was also widespread and did not vary significantly across our four regions. About four of every five respondents indicated a belief that Russia would emerge from its crisis either never or only in the distant future.

Our data thus produce a mixed picture of regional differences. On the one hand, vote, political orientation, support for democracy as an idea, and economic expectations differed significantly across our four regions. On the other hand, levels of dissatisfaction with the state of affairs (both political and economic) in Russia were nearly uniformly negative in all four regions. This is because levels of satisfaction are conditioned by expectations as well as by objective circumstances. People in regions that were doing better early in the reform process but that have seen a subsequent decline may be just as dissatisfied as people in those regions that became accustomed earlier to even lower levels of material provision. Dissatisfaction takes on a particular political meaning only after passing through a set of individual psychological filters, related, for example, to the perceived causes, effects, and permanence of the situation as well as to individual preferences and values.

Table 3.6
EXPECTED CHANGE IN THE STANDARD OF LIVING IN THE NEXT THREE TO FOUR YEARS: RUSSIAN POSTELECTION SURVEY, 1995–1996 (column percent)

	All-Russia	KMO	Nizhni Novgorod	Orel	Stavropol
Likely improve	20%	25%	18%	14%	20%
Remain the same	30	39	21	30	21
Likely worsen	50	36	61	56	59
N	1321	64	117	134	133

Note: Cramer's $v = .13$, $p < .01$.

Table 3.7
SUPPORT FOR INTRODUCING DEMOCRACY IN RUSSIA, 1995–1996 (column percent)

	All-Russia	KMO	Nizhni Novgorod	Orel	Stavropol
Yes, definitely	42%	42%	41%	42%	36%
More yes than no	37	39	44	32	25
More no than yes	13	12	8	15	23
Definitely not	8	7	6	12	17
N	1570	83	144	164	146

Note: Cramer's $v = .14$, $p < .01$.

Weak regional differentiation in expressed levels of satisfaction with both political and economic conditions stands beside strong regional variations in attitudes toward the leading opposition politician in Russia at the time the survey was undertaken. Using a modified thermometer scale measure, we asked our respondents to indicate their positive or negative attitude toward Gennady Zyuganov, the leader of the Communist Party of the Russian Federation. Respondents were asked to give Zyuganov

Table 3.8
SATISFACTION WITH STANDARD OF LIVING, BY REGION, 1995–1996 (column percent)

	All-Russia	KMO	Nizhni Novgorod	Orel	Stavropol
Satisfied	4%	5%	1%	2%	2%
More satisfied than not	14	14	13	8	15
Less satisfied than not	32	38	37	33	27
Not satisfied	50	43	49	57	56
N	1750	86	163	191	172

Note: Cramer's $v = .09$, $p = .12$.

Table 3.9
SATISFACTION WITH LEVEL OF DEMOCRACY IN RUSSIA, BY REGION, 1995–1996 (column percent)

	All-Russia	KMO	Nizhni Novgorod	Orel	Stavropol
Satisfied	2%	0%	1%	1%	0%
More satisfied than not	8	9	3	6	6
Less satisfied than not	38	41	34	35	33
Not satisfied	52	51	62	58	61
N	1601	81	151	182	157

Note: Cramer's $v = .07$, $p = .47$.

a rating of 1 to 10, where 10 was the most positive and 1 the least positive. Table 3.10 shows the results, aggregated into four categories. Positive feeling about Zyuganov was strongest in Stavropol and Orel and weakest in KMO, replicating patterns observed in voting results and party identification cited above.

Overall, there is a clear distinction between our Type I and Type II regions on the one hand and our Type III and Type IV regions on the other, very much along the lines described in our typology. Despite the respondents' more positive assessments of future economic prospects in our Type I region, these respondents nonetheless expressed only slightly weaker levels of dissatisfaction with their standard of living when

Table 3.10
RESPONDENTS' FEELING ABOUT ZYUGANOV, BY REGION (column percent)

Reported Attitude[a]	All-Russia	KMO	Nizhni Novgorod	Orel	Stavropol
Very positive	26 %	15%	19%	42%	46%
Somewhat positive	17	12	21	17	15
Somewhat negative	27	32	27	23	22
Very negative	31	42	35	18	17
N	1607	69	151	179	162

Note: Cramer's $v = .18$, $p < .01$.

[a] Very positive aggregates scores of 9–10, somewhat positive aggregates scores of 6–8, somewhat negative aggregates scores of 3–5, and very negative aggregates scores of 1–2.

compared with respondents from our Type II, III, and IV regions, where the economic decline has been more severe. Likewise, levels of support for establishment (liberal-reform) political forces are stronger in our Type I and II regions, but dissatisfaction with the level of democracy in Russia is only slightly less than in our Type III and IV regions, where oppositionist political orientations are stronger. This likely reflects differing frames of reference, since satisfaction is conditioned by expectations; our Type I and II regions have witnessed a decline in both the political and the economic spheres since the early reform period. According to our expectations, support for the liberal-reform forces is stronger in Type I and II regions but showed less strength in the latter than in the former in the 1996 presidential elections, likely a result of the more intense situation of economic decline in the Type II region. However, in both of these two regions, support for opposition forces has grown since 1993. At the same time, support for democratic values is strongest in our Type II region, reflecting, most likely, the stronger position of the intelligentsia. Support for traditional (Communist) forces is strongest in our Type III and Type IV regions (somewhat stronger in our Type III region, overall), and support for national-patriotic forces shows the most strength in our Type IV region.

The next step in the analysis was to examine the extent to which region acts as an independent influence on positive orientation toward the leader of the CPRF. Using "attitude toward Zyuganov" as the dependent variable (rather than vote, which is a nonordinal variable) allowed us to undertake a regression analysis. We included in the regression as independent variables (1) sociodemographic factors; (2) measures of the respondent's satisfaction with his or her standard of living; (3) attitudinal factors; and (4) region (in the form of a dummy variable for each of our four regions).

The regression analysis shows that the strongest predictors of a positive attitude toward Zyuganov are attitudinal (see table 3.11). Those respondents who opposed the market transition, who opposed the very idea of privatization, and who were against state encouragement of foreign economic involvement were significantly more likely to feel positively about Zyuganov. The Communist leader appears to retain a strong ideological base of support in Russia. Second in importance were the sociodemographic variables of age and gender. Independent of attitudinal factors, women and older people were more likely to express positive attitudes toward Zyuganov. Level of education did not have an independent effect. Perception of material well-being also played a role, though family income did not.

In terms of regional differences, our data produced some intriguing results. Our analysis shows that in two cases (Stavropol and Orel), region did act independently as a predictor, even after other variables have been controlled for. Although the association is not strong, it is measurable and statistically significant. This suggests that simply residing in these two regions was likely to make a respondent more supportive of Zyuganov than if the respondent resided in another region. Reasons behind this finding require further examination. It may well be that there are other individual-level variables that we have not measured in our survey and that would wash out this effect. However, since we have included a variety of theoretically significant variables in our regression equation, it is equally likely that the ecological effect of living in a particular region may indeed be a predictor. This could be due to the influence of the regional political leadership, it could be a function of observing the effects of the reform policy on the region as a whole, or it could be due to the effectiveness or pervasiveness of Communist Party organizations or culture on the local and regional levels. The fact that living in our two regions with lower levels of Communist support (Nizhni Novgorod and KMO) was not significantly associated with more or less positive attitudes toward Zyuganov (once other variables were controlled for) suggests that the importance of region of residence, as such, varies from region to region and probably from attitude to attitude.

Table 3.11
PREDICTORS OF POSITIVE ATTITUDE TOWARD ZYUGANOV: RUSSIAN POSTELECTION SURVEY, 1995–1996
OLS Multiple Regression Analysis (pairwise deletion of missing cases)

Sociodemographic Variables	Beta
Being older	.10[a]
Being female	.12[a]
Having less education	.02

Material Well-Being	
Standard of living perceived to have worsened in last two years	.07[a]
Lower family income	.01

Attitudinal Variables	
Oppose market transition	.27[a]
Oppose state support for foreign economic involvement	.09[a]
Oppose very idea of privatization	.08[a]

Region[b]	
Live in Stavropol krai	.09[a]
Live in Orel oblast	.08[a]
Live in Khanty-Mansiisk autonomous okrug	-.04
Live in Nizhni Novgorod oblast	-.02

Adjusted R = .27; N = 1275.
[a] Statistically significant at the .01 level.
[b] These variables are entered as dummy variables.

CONCLUSION

Our research suggests that when we examine mass political orientations, regions do a make a difference, and regions also differ. First, region of residence may, in and of itself, be important in some cases. Particular regions may have their own mix of features that appear to have an independent influence in shaping the attitudes of the population. The fact that simply residing in Orel oblast or Stavropol krai generates positive attitudes toward Zyuganov offers an example. To the extent that region of residence in itself influences attitudes, a further and more in-depth study of the particular region in question is necessary.

More frequently, however, the configuration of attitudes in any given region results from the distribution of characteristics of the population residing there. In other words, regions differ (in their economic structure, geographic location, resource endowment); therefore the structure of the population differs, and a different aggregate attitudinal mix results. Our typology provides the basis for developing hypotheses about the manner in which certain types of regions differ from one another and about the attitudinal correlates of these differences. People in our four types of regions are variously affected by the process of economic and political change. These factors are, in turn, important in shaping the sociopsychological and political attitudes of a region's population. In this case, if one had data on a respondent's sociodemographic characteristics and attitudes, one could just as easily predict the respondent's political orientation without knowing region of residence. But this would not reduce the importance of focusing on the differences between the regions themselves.

NOTES

1. For analysis of popular attitudes toward regionalism in Russia, see Josephine Andrews and Kathryn Stoner-Weiss, "Regionalism and Reform in Provincial Russia," *Post-Soviet Affairs* 11, no. 4 (1995): 384–406.
2. Some of these studies rely on aggregate economic and sociological data to try to explain regional voting patterns. See, for example, Ralph S. Clem and Peter R. Craumer's analysis of the 1993 referendum results in *Post-Soviet Geography* 34, no. 8 (1993): 481–96. See also their analysis of the 1993 elections in "A Raion-Level Analysis of the Russian Election and Constitutional Plebiscite of December 1993," *Post-Soviet Geography* 36, no. 8 (1995): 459–75. Darrell Slider, Vladimir Gimpel'son, and Sergei Chugrov examine voting patterns in the 1993 parliamentary elections in "Political Tendencies in Russia's Regions: Evidence from the 1993 Parliamentary Election," *Slavic Review* 53, no. 3 (fall 1994): 711–32.
3. D. Oreshkin, "Regional Solitaire on the Eve of the Constitution Day," *Segodnya*, August 8, 1993, p. 3.
4. *Finansovye Izvestiya*, no. 52 (July 25, 1995).
5. These data describe the situation in Russia as a whole. However, taking into consideration the concentration of industrial enterprises in the regions of this group, the trends demonstrated are especially typical for this particular type of region.
6. Data in this section are taken from the "Carleton 1995 Russian Post-Election Survey." This survey was undertaken by Joan DeBardeleben and Jon H. Pammett (both of Carleton University, Ottawa), Vladimir Yadov (Institute of Sociology, Russian Academy of Sciences), and Andrei A. Kazakov (Institute for Complex Social Studies, Moscow). Kazakov directed the fieldwork. The survey involved a representative sample ($N = 2080$) from nineteen regions of Russia and was conducted in late December 1995 and early January 1996, following the 1995 parliamentary elections. The survey was funded by the

Social Sciences and Humanities Research Council of Canada (Grants 410-94-0963 and 804-92-0013) and the University of Calgary-Gorbachev Joint Trust Fund. Data from the survey are deposited at the Carleton University Library Data Archive.

7. For the 1993 election this category includes Russia's Choice, Yabloko, and the Russian Movement for Democratic Reform. For the 1995 parliamentary election and for the 1995 postelection survey, the category includes Our Home Is Russia, Russia's Democratic Choice, Yabloko, Forward Russia, Women of Russia, and the Republican Party; for the 1996 presidential election the category includes votes for B. Yeltsin and V. Yavlinsky.
8. For the 1993 election this includes voters for the Communist Party of the Russian Federation and the Agrarian Party. For the 1995 election and survey this also includes supporters of the Bloc of Communists—Laboring Russia. For the presidential election it includes voters for G. Zyuganov.
9. For the 1993 vote this includes voters for the Liberal Democratic Party of Russia. In the 1995 vote and survey it includes, in addition, supporters of the Congress of Russian Communities, and for the 1996 election it includes voters for A. Lebed and V. Zhirinovsky.
10. It should be noted that our survey asked the respondent "which of the electoral unions is closest to you" on the issue that was "most important to you personally" and that was discussed by candidates in the campaign for the State Duma election. This question allowed us to tap the party identification of nonvoters as well as voters; because of uneven turnout rates among party identifiers (turnout was lower among those identifying with the liberal-reform parties), party identification rates are bound to differ from voting results, even if the survey is completely representative of the voting population.
11. This includes voters for the Civic Union, Women of Russia, the Democratic Party of Russia, and the Party of Russian Unity and Concord.

4

At the Bottom of the Heap: Local Self-government and Regional Politics in the Russian Federation

John F. Young

The new regional dimension in post-Soviet Russian politics is not a temporary manifestation of the collapse of central power. The regions now play an integral role in the ongoing process of arranging power and authority within the Russian state.[1] Organizing the "vertical" dimension of the Russian state is a complex and messy problem. It is complicated by the multitude of regional leaders who demand a substantial share of state power, even though Russia has only just begun to forge an institutional framework premised upon the division of power. And it is messy because the division of power and authority is relevant not only to Moscow and the subjects of the federation: the hopes and aspirations for power and authority extend beyond the regions to the local level, to cities and villages throughout Russia. The definition and division of authority and power along the numerous axes that radiate outward from Moscow beyond the eighty-nine regions to the institutions of local government remains as the most difficult task of organizing power in the Russian state. In this sense, the organization of power should be construed less as a two-dimensional challenge than as a three-dimensional chess game.[2] That negotiations over the vertical organization of power in Russia have been dominated by two levels of government is a fair indication of the fate of the third level of the Russian Federation, local self-government.

    This chapter is a study of intergovernmental relations in post-Soviet Russia, with a primary focus on local governments. It begins with a brief account of center-regional relations and underscores the rise of regional power from 1992 to 1995. It then highlights the consequences of regional power for the development of local government in Russia. From a central perspective, regional politics involves the demarcation of power and authority between the center and the regions. But from the perspective of local governments, the regions themselves can be considered "centers" of political power. Although the primary objective of many regional leaders may be to overcome the diktat of Moscow, a critical objective of advocates of local government is to overcome the diktat of the region. This focus on regional-local relations is important for at least two reasons. First, these relations can help us better understand the role of regions in contemporary Russia. These regions are not just a supporting cast in the federal arena; they also have starring roles in local politics. Second, the dominance of regional governments is critical to the fate of local self-government in Russia. Local governments continue to struggle to emerge from the tutelage of regional control.

THE DIVISION OF POWER AND THE RISE OF THE REGIONS

To understand the nature of the problems inherent in the demarcation and allocation of power among different tiers of government, we need first to differentiate between *power* and *authority*. Power, particularly in the sense of intergovernmental relations, refers not to any right or claim a governmental institution may make to decide a particular matter but to the *ability* of that institution to actually do something. The legal right or claim to power (authority) can be quite distinct from this ability (power). Various levels of government, for example, may possess the authority to determine policy over specific issues, but unless these same institutions possess the capacity, or power, to implement policy, then authority alone is an ineffective tool of government.

Among different tiers of government, power is a relative commodity: particular levels of government have power in reverse proportion to their dependence on other levels of government. The relative autonomy of one level of government is measured both by its control over resources sufficient to resolve matters under its purview and by its ability to resist incursions from other tiers of government. Resources include, but are not limited to, control over personnel appointments, autonomous revenues, independence in budget formation, administrative coherence, and control over information.[3] In Russia, such resources are often referred to as *rychagi*, or "levers."

The distinction between authority and power is critical to understanding the task of the arrangement of power and authority in contemporary Russia. It is one thing, for example, for a constitution or act of legislation to declare that authority over a specific issue belongs to a particular level of government. This legal authority is little more than a liability, however, unless the constitution or other legislation also grants that level of government the power (in this case, sufficient resources) to deal with that issue. Governments, local ones in particular, do not require more responsibility over issues that they do not have the power to resolve.

Alternatively, if subordinate levels of government successfully resist policy implementation from a higher level of government, then the authority of the latter is undermined significantly. The ability to implement directives and decisions over subordinate levels of government is also critical to the notion of power. This is why the issue of power as something distinct from authority is critical to understanding contemporary Russian politics. The paradox of organizing power is such that, on the one hand, the central government must extend its reach throughout the territory it purports to govern but, on the other hand, regional and local governments must also possess sufficient power to resolve issues within their purview. Ascribing authority to various levels of government without the requisite amount of power only fuels the administrative chaos and *bezvlastie* ("power vacuum") that plagued Russia at the onset of political reforms.

Russian politicians, of course, have not been unaware of the great need to demarcate and allocate power among various tiers of government. Since the last years of *perestroika*, the regions throughout Russia have become much less dependent on Moscow. Initially, the regions were targeted by Boris Yeltsin as allies in his struggle against Mikhail Gorbachev and the Soviet Union. The devolution of power was part of Yeltsin's strategy to break the power of the Soviet government, and he encouraged the regions to "take as much power as they could swallow." As a consequence, after the Soviet collapse, Yeltsin was forced to confront stronger regional demands in the early years of Russian state-building. These demands for more regional power conflicted with the simultaneous assertion of central authority by Yeltsin's new government, and nascent Russian federalism was pulled in two opposite directions. Establishing a working relationship between Moscow and the regions has since been at the core of much of Russian politics.

Every federal arrangement of power is a complicated endeavor, and few such arrangements are static. Through the first four years after the collapse of the Soviet Union, the working relationship between Moscow and the regions was relatively fluid and unclear. Two main characteristics of Russian federalism help explain this fluidity and lack of clarity. The first was the asymmetry in the division of authority and power among different regions. Yeltsin's efforts at regional integration endorsed an asymmetrical federalism that allowed different regions various degrees of authority and power. Republics were often the most privileged lot, retaining through 1992–94 the right to elect their own heads of executives and receiving preferential control over their natural resources and budget revenue.[4] In fairness to Yeltsin, however, symmetrical federalism was a practical impossibility. Different designations in Russian federalism were a carryover from the previous regime, and the regions themselves lacked any consensus as to what type of new federalism should emerge. Some regions supported asymmetry; others expected strict equality. Some demanded that federalism be arranged according to territorial principles; others wanted nationalities to be the foundation for regional governments. Regardless of its origins, however, asymmetry provoked many oblasts and krais to demand the same rights as republics. Various bilateral negotiations and arrangements made between Moscow and particular regions only compounded this confusion over Russian federalism.

The second characteristic was the shaky legal status of the federal division of powers. In spite of the federal facade of the RSFSR, Russia began the functional division of powers essentially from scratch as the Soviet Union's government crumbled. The existing arrangement of power between the center and the regions was only vaguely defined by a collection of assorted documents that included the Federal Treaty of March 1992, the December 1993 constitution of the Russian Federation, and various decrees and legislation dating back to 1991.[5] Significantly, none of these documents established a clear division of power. The main purpose of the Federal Treaty, for example, was not to define and divide power between the center and the regions but to stabilize relations between the two and prevent any further unraveling of the Russian state. Although this treaty fulfilled an important role, it was a statement of principles that required much further legislation to provide the kind of details necessary for clarity among the different tiers of government. The constitution was only a marginal improvement in clarifying the federal division of powers, and there remain numerous gaps in clarity and much ambiguous language. Article 72, for example, has fourteen areas that fall under the joint authority *(sovmestnoe vedenie)* of federal and regional governments, including almost the entire gamut of government operations. One commentator pointed out that at least thirty-five new laws would be required to clarify this joint authority.[6]

In light of the asymmetry and in lieu of detailed legislation that will yet require many years to create, Russian federalism emerged in 1992–95 as a collection of ad hoc arrangements. This, of course, cannot be considered uncommon. Any federal system requires decades to achieve some measure of predictability and stability. But given this ad hoc system, it is not the formal but the informal aspects of power, or the "levers," that are critical to understanding center-regional relations. This was especially so in Russia between 1992 and 1995. One important lever was the presidential prerogative to appoint and dismiss the executives of oblast and krai regional governments, a prerogative established by presidential decree in 1991. The reform process, Yeltsin explained at the time, demanded that a unitary system of executive power be extended throughout all of Russia. Although Yeltsin's appointments were to be made "with the approval" of the corresponding regional legislature, this qualification was often ignored in practice. Another lever in favor of central control could be found in the center-regional negotiations that helped determine federal subsidies to each region. Subsidies were usually necessary to make up the shortfall between the minimal financial requirements of the region and the regional revenues. But even those regions with "surplus" revenues sought to supplement their revenue base with support from the center, and regional leaders routinely made periodic pilgrimages to Moscow to negotiate with officials in the central government for financial subsidies.[7] There appeared to be little rationale to the amount given to various regions, except that the president and the central government came to rely on the subsidies as a bargaining chip in negotiations with regions, as a means to encourage loyalty among regional leaders.[8]

The fate of these two levers by 1995 suggests an important shift in federal relations in Russia. The declining influence of these levers indicates a weakening of central prerogative and an increase in regional power. Yeltsin's regional governors, for example, were hardly the loyal clients suggested by their direct appointment. Concessions to regional governors in exchange for loyalty during the president's power struggle with parliament in 1993, the political costs of economic reform to the federal government, and the Chechen war at the end of 1994 provided governors with both opportunity and motive to ignore many of Yeltsin's directives and to engage in anti-Moscow political posturing. This posturing strengthened their local support, which often made it difficult and costly for Yeltsin to wield his "stick" and dismiss recalcitrant governors.[9] And governors who felt they possessed sufficient local support made arrangements for regional elections to both consolidate their regional position and loosen the influence of Moscow. Seeking to maintain some influence over regional executives, Yeltsin declared that his approval for such elections was required, and he affirmed—in a decree in October 1994—presidential prerogative over the appointment, dismissal, and election of all regional governors.[10] Additionally, multiregional conferences of governors and the supraregional conference in Cheboksary in January 1995 represent not only Moscow's inability to satisfy disparate regional interests but also the governors' willingness to assert their own demands and exert influence in the federal arena.[11]

The "carrot" of subsidies also declined in influence. With a finite amount of revenues, the center had limits to the support it could buy from the regions, and any preferential funding it gave to one region risked becoming the standard for the rest. A further brake on the use of subsidies for political purposes was that the regions themselves began to collect increased shares of tax revenues, which made them less dependent on federal transfers. The three largest revenue sources were the profit tax, the value-added tax (VAT), and the personal income tax (PIT). From 1992 to 1994, regional shares of the profit tax increased from 53 percent to 63–66 percent, and shares of the VAT increased from 0 percent (although ad hoc negotiations could allow a share) to 25 percent. The regional share of the PIT declined from 100 percent to 92–97 percent. In real terms, however, VAT and PIT revenues were relatively equal, whereas the profit tax contributed almost as much as the VAT and the PIT combined.[12] If regions felt shortchanged by federal transfers, they often responded by withholding federal money. In August 1993, for example, thirty-three of the eighty-nine regions unilaterally reduced payments to the center.[13] In the past, the center could have threatened to halt all federal expenditures in the region, to withhold export and import licenses, to deny central bank credit, or to halt delivery of materials. But the breakdown of central control over the economy made such measures less threatening. The impunity with which regions withheld funds from federal coffers represented the new limits to federal power. And the effect that such transfers may have had on loyalty to the center can be questioned if we notice that some of the most recalcitrant regions, such as Tatarstan, received some of the largest federal subsidies.

To reiterate, by 1995 the regions were less dependent on the central government. This is not to say, however, that the tail was now wagging the dog: regional budgets, for example, were still approved by the center. But the dog appeared to have little conscious control over what the tail did. Although the arrangement of power remained fluid, regional governments acted with impunity in a variety of areas. They often ignored federal authority on issues of price regulation, subsidies, and the registration of foreigners. They pursued disparate policies for such things as budgets, social matters, the judiciary, and banking. This led to significant variation among regions, something that can be expected in any federal arrangement of power. Sakha (Yakutia) republic and Primorsky krai, for example, were much more independent from Moscow than Belgorod and Bryansk oblasts. But in almost all instances, the levers of federal power were not nearly as strong as either Russian political traditions or the existing constitution would suggest. Regions thus emerged as key players in post-Soviet Russian politics.

There is, however, a further dimension to regional power, one that is ignored by a focus limited to center-regional relations. A different way to illustrate the growing importance of the regions in Russian politics is to sketch the relationship between regions and subordinate levels of local government. Regional governments possess power not only because they are increasingly independent from the center but also because they directly influence the affairs of local governments subordinate to them. In this sense, the weakness of the central government in relation to the regions is *not* replicated at the next level.

THE FATE OF LOCAL GOVERNMENT

In Russia, "local government" refers to the thousands of municipal and rural governments throughout the country and to their subordinate levels, such as municipal wards, towns and villages, and rural settlements.[14] The Russian term for local government is *mestnoe samoupravlenie* (local *self-government*), which makes a critical conceptual distinction between organs of state power and those of local government. Theoretically, local organs do not belong to the organization of state power. But this conceptual distinction is rarely realized in practice, particularly among executive organs.[15]

Local governments are asked to perform important functions in Russian society. They are responsible for the implementation or determination of policies affecting the most pressing issues in the daily lives of citizens, from housing to health services and from education to the distribution of garden plots. But aside from these functions, there are a number of reasons why local governments should be more than mere administrative tentacles of the state. One of the general arguments for local government is that the efficiency of community services and the recognition of specific community needs can be lost if local governments do not possess the capacity to resolve such matters. On a more theoretical level, local government is also the critical link between society and state, fostering the development of civil society and functioning as a forum for democratic values and practices. More important, local government might also serve as a balance against any abuse of power by the state, represented by either the center or the region.[16] Yet all of these justifications are premised on the notion that local governments possess real authority and real power. Without these, they can neither represent local interests nor resolve local matters.

There is little dispute in contemporary Russia that local governments have an important role to play in post-Soviet society.[17] Political and cultural leaders routinely declare the importance of establishing strong and effective organs of local government. Yet efforts to create such have met only limited success. Russian attempts to restructure and reform local government began immediately after the 1990 republic and local elections. The existing, "unitary" system of soviets, which was then the foundation for local government, was incapable of assuming a functional role in government and administration. The RSFSR Supreme Soviet Committee for Local Soviet Affairs and the Development of Local Self-Government thus began deliberations on a draft piece of legislation that would establish the structures and demarcate the authority necessary for local governments to play a more effective role in society. After a year of intense lobbying, conflict, and negotiation, legislation was finally passed by the Supreme Soviet in July 1991.[18] Although the law represented significant progress concerning the structural components of executive-legislative (horizontal) relations, the actual contribution to a division of power between state and local (vertical) government failed to make the necessary leap from theory to practice.

This failure can be explained in part by the difficulties of trying to construct new structures of both local government and central executive power upon the shifting sands of Russian federalism. Consequently, the law on local government left a vague and malleable organization of authority at the local level. Even though this malleability paralleled the new relationship between the center and the regions, its consequences were quite different. Whereas the regions were able to take advantage of much of the vagueness and ignore the center with relative impunity, local governments were much more beholden to the regional governments. In other words, the emergence of regional power became a greater obstacle to the development of local government. This is revealed by a closer look at the "levers" used by regional governments to influence and even dictate policy and personnel to local governments during these formative years of Russian state-building.

Some of these levers were wholly informal. In the Soviet period, regions controlled the distribution of materials to local enterprises and coordinated the delivery of foodstuffs to urban areas. If the city tried to ignore the authority of the region, usually the regional administration simply yanked on the food-delivery reins to let the city know who was in charge. In the post-Soviet period, the breakdown of the central economy did not carry over quite so quickly below the regional level. The distribution of foodstuffs and materials, for example, was still largely conducted by regional administrations. Local officials were convinced, rightly or wrongly, that the regions could deliberately sabotage municipal economies and restrict food supplies in urban areas.[19]

Other levers are less subtle. The power of executive appointment to local governments is one tool that regional executives have used to influence local affairs. Governors and the presidents of republics used the prerogative of executive appointment to create "integral," or unitary, systems of executive power within their jurisdiction. Although this power weakened in some regions after local elections in 1994, executives continued to exercise considerable influence in the selection of local government personnel.[20] A more influential lever for regional governments is the tight grip they maintain over local budgets. After the center and the regional governments divide up revenues from the three main tax sources, each government receiving a fixed percentage of revenues, the regions then determine the amount of revenue to transfer to local governments. Local governments are consequently left with meager sources of autonomous revenue, and local budgets are dependent on the largesse of the region. Local revenue sources include a property tax, but until the legal status of property is more clearly defined, there are only limited revenues from this source. Other sources include "big moneymakers" such as parking fees, dog licenses, lotteries, and taxes on the resale of automobiles and computers. In stark contrast to their limited sources of revenue, local governments are expected to cover the costs of primary and secondary schools, health clinics and hospitals, sport and recreation facilities, local and urban roads, library services, local police, public utilities, day care centers, garbage collection, and other important services. In 1992, for example, local governments accounted for almost 100 percent of total expenditures on primary education, 85 percent of health, 80 percent of public utilities, and 60 percent of day care and housing.[21] As the center pushed responsibility for many issues to the regions, the regions in turn handed down numerous responsibilities to local governments. Yet the commensurate transfer of resources necessary to deal with these issues was not part of the package. The result was a fiscal squeeze that made local governments more dependent on regional resources.

One small escape from the budget woes of local government was extrabudgetary revenue, derived from fines on local enterprises, profits from joint ventures, and privatization revenue. This money was not included in local budgets and was immune to confiscation by regional governments. With this source of independent revenue, local governments could thus entertain a hope of autonomy from regional control. Yet there were limits to extrabudgetary sources. The privatization of local economic enterprises, for example, could not resolve the dilemma of inadequate revenue because profitable enterprises were routinely claimed by the regions and the unprofitable enterprises were left for the local governments.[22] Another downside of this source is that this money has also been misappropriated by local executives and elites and has served as slush funds for trips abroad and other boondoggles.[23]

In 1993, a new federal law attempted to address the predicament of local finance. The law affirmed the independence of local budgets yet paradoxically continued the established process of budget formation dominated by higher levels of government. Instead of a "unitary" budget, the law referred to a "consolidated budget" for the Russian Federation, which still meant that all local budgets had to be confirmed by regional governments. The law tried to offer local governments a guarantee that their revenues would not be less than 70 percent of their minimal requirements, and it granted them unspecified shares of personal and corporate taxes. This law had no viable enforcement mechanism, however, leaving local governments unable to demand the promises of this legislation.[24]

The power of regions over lower levels of government is not a feature exclusive to post-Soviet Russia. During the Soviet period, however, a greater degree of supervision over regional governments came from above. Now that regions are more autonomous from the center, their hands are not as tightly bound concerning their relationships with local governments. In other words, local governments have not been as successful in escaping the power of regional governments as the regions themselves have been in escaping central authority. This predicament has become more evident in developments since 1993. With the dissolution of local soviets and the commensurate rise of executive power after the October showdown between the president and parliament, the autonomy and power of local governments in many regions diminished further. What follows is an example of intergovernmental relations based on regional-municipal politics in the city of Omsk. Omsk is certainly not representative of all local governments in Russia. The great variety in political and economic development in regions and localities throughout Russia would make such a claim ludicrous. But Omsk does portray many of the general problems that confront all local governments in their relationships with regional power, particularly problems concerning budgets and personnel appointments.

OBLAST-MUNICIPAL RELATIONS IN OMSK

The city of Omsk is one of the larger cities in the Russian Federation. It has a population of roughly 1.2 million people, more than half of the oblast total. Since it is a large metropolis, one might expect the city government to have a reasonable degree of clout in regional politics. This, however, is not the case, as the following examples show.

One dimension of intergovernmental relations concerns control over the flow of information. Regions, of course, are vulnerable to the power of national television and press, but in local news, regions possess an abundance of control that strengthens power throughout their jurisdiction. In Omsk, the oblast head of administration, Governor Leonid Polezhaev, disliked the press coverage his administration received from both the local independent newspapers and the articles in the federal press. To resolve this matter, his administration reduced the availability of national newspapers (not readily available in Omsk) while simultaneously promoting the two oblast newspapers (which are heavily biased in favor of the oblast administration). This was achieved by slashing the subscription and single-copy rates of the oblast newspapers to less than half their previous cost while boosting oblast subsidies. In this manner, the oblast administration curbed the influence of alternative perspectives on local news, since the municipal and independent newspapers were forced to raise their prices to keep up with inflation. Significantly, the reduction in the prices for the oblast newspapers came during local election campaigns in the spring of 1994 and provided a subtle form of control over information. Not surprisingly, two-thirds of the deputies elected to the oblast assembly in 1994 supported Polezhaev. Such press subsidies allowed two regional newspapers with a subsidized advantage, newspapers known in Omsk as the "Governor's Tribunes," to dominate circulation throughout the city and the oblast.[25]

Another example of regional power concerns the governor's power of appointment. In February 1994, Polezhaev dismissed the mayor of Omsk, Yuri Shoikhet, who had served in that capacity for the previous two and a half years. Shoikhet's dismissal came in the form of a presidential decree, which was motivated largely by Polezhaev's lobbying efforts. The mayor received notification of this decision through the press. The explanation for dismissal was Polezhaev's allegation that the mayor was guilty of "destabilizing" the political and economic situation in Omsk. When supporters of the mayor defended him by pointing out that there had been no strikes or manifestations of disorder, no municipal crises in heating, and not even a single protest against municipal administration decisions, Polezhaev responded by pointing to the mayor's failed bid two months earlier to win election to the Council of the Federation. Shoikhet had run in the December 1993 elections under the banner of Yegor Gaidar's party, Russia's Choice, and had challenged Polezhaev's candidacy. Polezhaev decided to interpret Shoikhet's loss as a vote of nonconfidence in the mayor.[26]

The mayor's electoral loss was hardly a cause for dismissal, however. The real reason for the dismissal was that Shoikhet had been a thorn in the side of the oblast administration since taking office. He had consistently pushed for municipal power and greater autonomy at the expense of the oblast. Most important, he represented a consortium of small business interests that repeatedly came into conflict with large corporate interests connected to Polezhaev and the oblast administration.[27] Yet the dismissal was not unpopular with the majority of the local population and led to local elections for both the mayor and the city assembly (the city soviet had been dissolved the previous fall). The election, held in the spring of 1994, failed to give a majority to any of the mayoralty candidates and returned only eleven deputies to the seventeen-member city assembly. The city government was thus incapacitated until Polezhaev appointed one of his own assistants in the oblast administration to the mayor's office. Subsequent elections in the fall of 1994 eventually filled the remaining six vacancies in the city assembly. In the interim, municipal government relied exclusively on its executive, which was functionally subordinate to the oblast administration. In fact, it often became difficult to determine which level of government was formulating municipal policy, a situation that changed little during the first year of the new municipal administration's tenure.

The most telling example of regional control over local governments in Omsk concerns budget relations. Expenditure needs of the municipal government have increased dramatically over the past few years, as both the oblast and industrial enterprises dumped financial responsibilities on the city. Funding for day care centers, health clinics, and housing, much of which had formerly been provided by industrial enterprises and subsidized by the oblast, shrunk considerably. Between 1991 and 1994, the city more than doubled its previous share of all education costs (from 33 percent to 70 percent). All but 5 percent of medical clinics became dependent on the city budget, and 55 percent of residential services were also provided at municipal expense.[28] In contrast to rising expenditure needs, municipal revenues remained limited. The city depended on the oblast for the lion's share of the municipal budget, but its share of the oblast budget declined from 40 percent in 1990 to 35 percent in 1994.[29]

In 1994 the city government received only 60 percent of its budgeted revenue and was desperate to augment municipal funds. It set up local lotteries (awarding prizes of apartments, garden homes, and cash) and attempted to create a municipal commercial bank, which ran into conflict with the oblast administration and other existing financial institutions.[30] Yet each time the city found any new sources of revenue, the oblast decreased transfers to the city accordingly, justifying this action by pointing to the oblast's financial woes.[31] Ironically, Omsk oblast remained slightly above the national average in terms of oblast revenue, even as the city of Omsk crumbled. Municipal infrastructure required capital investment, housing shortages continued, and social services, in the words of the new mayor, Valery Roshchupkin, were in a state of crisis.[32]

While the city gained authority over a vast array of services, local self-government remained undeveloped in Omsk. This predicament left the municipality with little real power to address important matters on its own. As a result, the municipal administration failed to attract or keep qualified personnel; those with ability quickly moved on to the business world or to the oblast administration. In the latter instance, the oblast offered not only greater remuneration than the city but also more power to resolve local and regional matters. Perhaps the only sense of municipal power was found in the degree to which the city had influence over municipal wards and other levels of local government, which possess even less power than the city.[33]

GUBERNATORZATSIIA AND LOCAL SELF-GOVERNMENT

Post-Soviet Russia is a fledgling federal state without a legacy of divided power between Moscow and the regions. Political developments suggest that the regions are emerging from under Moscow's control. Yeltsin's early attempts to establish strong, unitary executive power throughout Russia have given way to an emerging federalism that demands negotiation and compromise among federal and regional executives. At the same time, however, regional leaders have relied on more traditional patterns of power in their push to consolidate executive power throughout their territory. Such integration ensures, at a minimum, that "things get done" and is particularly useful if there are worries over the delivery of supplies throughout the region. Regional governors and local executives are rarely unpopular with local populations because of their ability to make decisions and enforce the implementation of policy. Yet in spite of any advantages, the *gubernatorzatsiia,* or consolidation of power of regional executives, poses certain problems for the development of local self-government. Instead of local organs with sufficient autonomous power to resolve local issues, local politics are often only part of the broader domain of the regional government. In this regard, the prospects for local government seem to depend either on an unfair contest between increasingly powerful regions and comparatively weak local governments or on the largesse of the region itself.[34]

The benevolence of regional governments toward local self-government has definite limits, however. Though it is true that by the summer of 1995 some 21,000 constituencies throughout Russia had the opportunity to elect their own local executives, the overwhelming majority of these elections were for village elders *(starosty)*, who possess almost no power and serve more as plenipotentiaries than executives.[35] In municipal- and district-level elections, regional executives possess no small influence in manipulating results by virtue of their control over the local press, candidate selection, and the timing and location of elections. All of these factors can profoundly affect electoral outcomes.[36] Local elections in Vladimir oblast are a case in point. In 1995, Governor Yuri Vlasov responded to appeals from the oblast legislature for local elections to local councils and executives. But rather than hold simultaneous elections, Vlasov opted for legislative elections throughout the oblast while restricting elections for local executives to only three localities. He defended his decision with the claim that strong, integrated, executive power was still a necessity in Vladimir. Municipal and regional legislators in Vladimir were quite upset about this move, since in practical terms it meant the perpetuation of executive domination and of Vlasov's control of local government.[37]

Many regions pushed ahead of impending federal legislation and adopted their own charters or constitutions (depending on their status as oblasts/krais or republics), which, among other things, ought to provide the foundation for local governments in particular regions.[38] These charters allow regions to tailor local government to the needs of a local community, as opposed to a uniform system of local government for the whole of Russia. Yet such regional initiative also allows regions to continue their dominance over local affairs. Recent regional charters and republic constitutions, for example, often contain vague statutes and terminology, particularly regarding local elections and the accountability of executives, and occasionally violate the Russian constitution. Some regional charters even declare that representative organs cannot be created at the village level and that only general public assemblies can perform legislative functions. These measures are in direct contrast to the federal constitution, which states that this matter is for local communities to decide on their own.[39] Regional charters and constitutions generally praise the principle of local self-government but do little to ensure the development of local power. In this regard, regions suffer from the same challenges and complications in organizing power that are found at the center: they want to exercise authority and power throughout their jurisdiction but also need to divide power and transfer some of it to the subordinate levels of government. As with center-regional relations, there is also little clarity in the division of power between regional and local government. But in comparison with regional executives in federal relations, local executives in regional relations do not have much opportunity to strengthen their position through this lack of clarity. A primary concern for the future of local self-government in Russia is that regions may use their prerogative to continue to hand down responsibility to local governments while maintaining power, or the control of resources, for themselves.

ALTERNATIVE STRATEGIES

One way to counterbalance regional power at the local level would be for the federal government and central agencies to defend local authority and assert a stronger role for local governments. In cases of severe abuse of regional power, local governments have sought the support of federal agencies and the courts, and a number of cases of federal intervention have been successful. In the spring of 1992, for example, V. A. Barabanov, the oblast governor in Bryansk, grew tired of the municipal administration's complaints about alleged oblast sabotage of the delivery of foodstuffs to the city and of general political opposition from the city. He tried to resolve the matter with a directive *(rasporiazhenie)* that, among other things, dismissed the city mayor from his office and recommended the self-dissolution of the municipal soviet and administration.[40] The city tried to defend itself by appealing to the oblast court, which ruled in Barabanov's favor. Eventually, the Supreme Soviet Committee on Local Self-Government stepped in and made peace between the city and the oblast administration, affirmed the right of the mayor and the city soviet to function in their responsibilities, and challenged Barabanov to gain a more professional understanding of his responsibilities as governor.[41]

Another example of the benefit to local government of central involvement is a recent ruling by the Supreme Court of the Russian Federation. In February 1994, V. A. Chepelev, the mayor of Uglich, a small city in Yaroslavl oblast, was dismissed from his responsibilities by order of the oblast administration and was replaced by E. M. Sheremet'ev. This incensed the residents of Uglich, who complained that according to the existing law on local self-government, administrative organs should be formed directly by the local population without any interference from higher levels of government. In November, the oblast court supported the actions of the oblast administration and ruled that there were no anomalies concerning these events in Uglich. But when residents protested further, the case went to the Supreme Court of the Russian Federation, which ruled that the oblast involvement in Uglich contradicted both the constitution and presidential decrees. The court ruled that between November 1991 and October 1994, executive authority over appointments to lower executive offices was premised on Yeltsin's decree No. 239, which granted executives the right to appoint lower executives with the agreement of the corresponding soviet.[42] But since soviets could not participate in the decision after their dissolution in October 1993, the Supreme Court ruled that in this case, the selection of a new mayor was the sole purview of the city of Uglich.[43]

Without the support of the federal government and central agencies, organs of local self-government will remain under regional tutelage. There are at least two reasons to expect that such support will be forthcoming from Moscow. First, both the 1992 Federal Treaty and the 1993 Russian constitution declared that the creation of general principles for local self-government is an issue of joint jurisdiction between federal and regional governments.[44] In this regard, the new federal law on local self-government, passed during the summer of 1995, attempts to establish such general principles and guarantees for the autonomy of local organs.[45] Gone are the multidifferentiated tiers of local government and any mandated relationship between executive and legislative organs. Instead, principal attention is given to the primacy of the local assembly and to the definition of critical concepts such as municipal property. The law also allows for guaranteed budget revenue and obliges regional governments to transfer revenue sources to local governments should local revenue not satisfy minimal demands. Inasmuch as the federal government and the judiciary support these legal developments, the new law might be viewed as a great opportunity for the development of local self-government. Such optimism should be guarded, however, because joint jurisdiction over local government still allows important roles to be played by regional charters and constitutions, which may or may not promote local interests. In addition, the Council of the Federation, dominated by regional leaders, twice rejected the new law, before the Duma passed it to Yeltsin for approval. The council's opposition to the law was based on the difficulties that regional administrations would experience in controlling local affairs.[46] Nevertheless, there remain solid legal foundations for federal involvement in the development of local self-government.

The second reason why Moscow might become more active in promoting local government is that such a policy would be a sound political strategy. The new center-regional dynamic in Russia has led not only to strong regions but also to a relatively weaker center. One solution to Moscow's growing impotence in its relationships with the regions is to foster the development of local government autonomy, which may erode some of the power of the regions. In a figurative sense, stronger local governments would place regional governments between the proverbial hammer and anvil, would counter the political power of "regional barons," and would establish a foundation for a balance of power along the axes that extend outward from Moscow.[47] Even Deputy Premier Sergei Shakhrai, responsible for regional issues, regards local governments as critical components of a workable federal solution that recognizes both federal authority and the new role of the regions. Shakhrai has discussed local government as an example of the need for federal and regional cooperation.[48]

Post-Soviet Russian politics has been animated by a protracted struggle over power. This struggle has been over not only *who* would exercise political power but also, and more important, *where* power would be located. The first four years of the new Russia witnessed the ascendance of the regions as important players in Russian politics. The consequences of this development are being felt not only in Moscow but also in local governments and communities throughout the country. The further devolution of power from regions to local governments remains an important task in the arrangement and organization of power, the foundation of state-building.

NOTES

1. The word "regions" is used to refer to *respubliki, oblasty, krai,* and *okruga* collectively. As justification for the use of the term "region," it should be pointed out that, though highly probable, there is yet nothing set in stone concerning the perpetuation of different status among republics, krais, and oblasts. Some Russian politicians, at both local and federal levels, propose that asymmetrical federalism be replaced by an equitable distribution of powers among all *sub"ekty* of the federation. Recent research on Russian federalism includes Gail Lapidus and Edward W. Walker, "Nationalism, Regionalism, and Federalism: Center-Periphery Relations in Post-Communist Russia," in Gail Lapidus, ed., *The New Russia: Troubled Transformation* (Boulder, Colo.: Westview Press, 1995), pp. 79–113; Edward W. Walker, "Federalism—Russian Style: The Federation Provisions in Russia's New Constitution," *Problems of Post-Communism* 42, no. 4 (July-August 1995): 3–12; Christine I. Wallich, ed., *Russia and the Challenge of Fiscal Federalism* (Washington, D.C.: World Bank, 1994); James Voorhees, "Russian Federalism and Reform: The Declining Effectiveness of the Russian Central State," *Demokratizatsiya* 2, no. 4 (fall 1994): 549–65.
2. The analogy of a multilayered chess game can be found in the conclusion of Guillermo O'Donnell, Philippe Schmitter, and Laurence Whitehead, eds., *Transitions from Authoritarian Rule: Tentative Conclusions about Uncertain Democracies* (Baltimore: Johns Hopkins University Press, 1986), p. 66.
3. R. A. W. Rhodes, *Control and Power in Central-Local Government Relations* (Farnborough, Eng.: Gower Publications, 1981), pp. 1–32.
4. There are exceptions to such rights among republics. Karachaevo-Cherkessia,

for example, delegated to the Russian president its right to appoint its executive leader.
5. See, for example, the decree of the Supreme Soviet: "O razgranichenii gosudarstvennoi sobstvennosti v rossiiskoi federatsii na federal'nuiu sobstvennost', gosudarstvennuiu sobstvennost' respublik v sostave rossiiskoi federatsii, kraev, oblastei, avtonomnoi oblasti, avtonomnykh okrugov, gorodov Moskvy i Sankt-Peterburga, i munitsipal'nuiu sobstvennost'," *Ekonomika i zhizn'*, no. 3 (January 1992); and "O kraevom, oblastnom sovete narodnykh deputatov, i kraevoi, oblastnoi administratsii," *Vedomosti s"ezda narodnykh deputatov RSFSR i Verkhovnogo Soveta RSFSR*, no. 10 (March 5, 1992). The latter piece of legislation was never signed by President Yeltsin because of his objections to what he perceived as excessive legislative control over the regional executive, especially concerning the power of appointment.
6. See Yuri Khrenov, "Kak ni trudno razdelit' vlast', a pora uzhe eto sdelat'," *Rossiiskaya federatsiya* 11 (1995): 10–22. For a concise analysis of the treaty and the constitution as they relate to the consequences for Russian federalism, see Walker, "Federalism—Russian Style." There is some concern among both Russian and Western scholars as to whether or not the provisions of the Federal Treaty are fully included in the new constitution. See, for example, the comments by A. Kotenkov, deputy minister for nationality issues and regional politics, in Khrenov, "Kak ni trudno," p. 13, and Voorhees, "Russian Federalism and Reform," p. 559.
7. See Konstantin Titov, "Kak obustroit' nash obshchii dom," *Rossiiskaya federatsiya* 10 (1995): 16–19. Titov is the governor of Samara oblast.
8. Voorhees, "Russian Federalism and Reform"; Jennie I. Litvack, "Regional Demands and Fiscal Federalism," in Wallich, *Russia and the Challenge*, pp. 218–40.
9. Yeltsin's relationship with Vitaly Mukha, governor of Novosibirsk, is a case in point. Mukha's opposition to reforms and his leadership of "Siberian Agreement" put him at odds with Moscow. But his removal was no easy task: Yeltsin had to back down from an initial attempt to oust Mukha in March 1993 because the political costs were too high. Mukha was dismissed after the president's Pyrrhic victory over parliament in October. Mukha's fate is discussed in detail in James Hughes, "Regionalism in Russia: The Rise and Fall of Siberian Agreement," *Europe-Asia Studies* 46, no. 7 (1994): 1133–61. Another example was the response to Yeltsin's decision to sack the governor of Stavropol krai in July 1995, a response that included public demonstrations and demands to either revoke the dismissal or allow for gubernatorial elections. The best example, however, is that of Eduard Rossel, the governor of Sverdlovsk oblast. Dismissed from his position as governor by Yeltsin in late 1993, he resurfaced a few months later in regional elections and served a stint as chairman of the oblast legislature. In gubernatorial elections in August 1995, Rossel upset the candidate endorsed by the central government. See Laurence Peter, "Urals Leader Seeks Power Pact," *Moscow Tribune*, August 26, 1995, pp. 1–2.
10. Ukaz Presidenta Rossiiskoi Federatsii, "O merakh po ukrepleniiu edinoi

sistemy ispolnitel'noi vlasti v Rossiiskoi Federatsii," *Sobranie zakonodatel'stva Rossiiskoi Federatsii,* no. 24 (October 10, 1994), pp. 3531–37. This claim, however, was temporary: its primary purpose was to prolong presidential perogative until after the presidential elections in 1996. See also Igor Belikov, "Regional Governors in Russia," *Analytica Moscow: Politica Weekly Press Summary* (October 29–November 4, 1994). At the end of 1991, Yeltsin had also appointed "presidential representatives" to function as his "eyes and ears" in oblasts and krais and to ensure the implementation of presidential decrees and government policy in these regions. Although these representatives were relevant to regional politics in the aftermath of the collapse of the government of the Soviet Union, they appear to have been a transitional measure and, with few exceptions, were of declining significance. By 1993 the role of governor was much more important—in both regional and federal politics—than that of presidential representative.

11. See *Current Digest of the Post Soviet Press* 47, no. 2 (1995): 22–23.
12. See World Bank, *Russian Federation: Toward Medium-Term Viability* (Washington, D.C.: World Bank, 1996), p. 45.
13. *Nezavisimaya gazeta,* September 1, 1993, as cited in Voorhees, "Russian Federalism and Reform," p. 553. According to one governor, the high rates of inflation make such recalcitrance necessary. Transfers to Moscow and then back to the region are often in fixed amounts, and inflation rates mean a net loss for the region: see Titov, "Kak obustroit'," p. 19.
14. Moscow and St. Petersburg are exceptions to the rule. They both possess status akin to that of regional governments.
15. There is some confusion over the concept of local government. During the Soviet period, with the existence of fifteen republics as the "secondary tier" of government, what we now refer to as *regions* were also included as organs of local government. Since the collapse of the Soviet Union, however, this regional tier has been bumped up a notch and is no longer part of local government. It is, however, not uncommon to find the term "local" used in the Russian press with reference to regional government.
16. The demarcation of power, which extends beyond the federal or center-regional dimension, is a fundamental component of the modern democratic state. A recent article by Jonathon Fox points out the role of local governments in transitions away from authoritarianism: "Latin America's Emerging Local Politics," *Journal of Democracy* 5, no. 2 (April 1994): 105–16. See also Joanna Regulska, "Self-Governance or Central Control? Rewriting Constitutions in Central and Eastern Europe," in A. E. Dick Howard, ed., *Constitution Making in Eastern Europe* (Washington, D.C.: Woodrow Wilson Center Press, 1993), pp. 133–61.
17. Regardless of the various arguments about *how much* power local governments in Russia should possess, there is general agreement that they require more than presently exists. See Ol'ga Belikova, "Narodovlastie otkladyvaetsia," *Rossiiskaya federatsiya* 10 (1995): 33–34.
18. Zakon RSFSR, "O mestnom samoupravlenii v RSFSR," *Sovetskaya Rossiya,* July 20, 1991.

19. See, for example, the complaints of Yuri Shoikhet, the mayor of Omsk, about oblast sabotage of municipal reforms, in *Omskii vestnik*, February 4, 1992, and *Vecherny Omsk,* January 31, 1992. Compare these allegations with the more general picture described in M. Steven Fish, *Democracy from Scratch: Opposition and Regime in the New Russian Revolution* (Princeton, N.J.: Princeton University Press, 1995), p. 193. While working with the oblast administration in Omsk during the summer of 1992, I queried the deputy governor on how implementation of oblast policy was enforced at the municipal level. He responded by slamming his fist down on his desk and exclaiming, "*Vot tak!* (That's how!)"
20. For examples of how governors manipulated the electoral process during the December 1995 campaign, see Andrei Zhukov, "Regional Governors: The Election's Wild Cards," *Prism* 2 (November 17, 1995): 1–6. The opportunities for manipulation and influence are greater during local elections.
21. Christine I. Wallich, *Fiscal Decentralization: Intergovernmental Relations in Russia*, Studies of Economies in Transformation, paper no. 6 (Washington, D.C.: World Bank, 1992), pp. 39–40.
22. For an example of the conflict over property between city and oblast, see *Vecherny Omsk,* February 5, 18, 1992. See also John F. Young, "Institutions, Elites, and Local Politics in Russia: The Case of Omsk," in Theodore H. Friedgut and Jeffrey W. Hahn, eds., *Local Power and Post-Soviet Politics* (Armonk, N.Y.: M. E. Sharpe, 1994), pp. 150–53.
23. This insight comes fom my own experience working with the Omsk oblast administration during the summer of 1992. Although such insights are unsubstantiated except by rumor, the ubiquity of rumors concerning misappropriation in both oblast and municipal administrations, as well as similar rumors in other areas (Yakutsk, Moscow), suggests that this is not a rare phenomenon.
24. Zakon Rossiiskoi Federatsii, "Ob osnovakh biudzhetnykh prav i prav po formirovaniiu i ispol'zovaniiu vnebiudzhetnykh fondov predstavitel'nykh i ispolnitel'nykh organov gosudarstvennoi vlasti respublik v sostave Rossiiskoi Federatsii, avtonomnoi oblasti, avtonomnykh okrugov, kraev, oblastei, gorodov Moskvy i Sankt-Peterburga, organov mestnogo samoupravleniia," *Rossiiskaya gazeta*, April 30, 1993.
25. Sergei Suslikov, "Kak v Omske priruchili pressu," *Izvestiya,* June 22, 1994, p. 4. Before his dismissal, Shoikhet tried to defend against this oblast control of the press and subsidized the municipal paper. These subsidies were no match for oblast support, and the subsidy war was won by Polezhaev. My own impression of the municipal paper since 1994 is that it has adopted a very supportive stance toward the oblast administration. Some of this favorable press may be accounted for by the fact that Polezhaev's administration includes a full-time committee devoted to ensuring positive press coverage.
26. Shoikhet ran far behind Polezhaev in the election, garnering about 20 percent of the vote compared with Polezhaev's 65 percent. For more on the circumstances behind the mayor's dismissal, see Sergei Suslikov, "Otstavka mera Omska—rezul'tat mnogokhodovoi politicheskoi intrigi," *Izvestiya,* February 2, 1994, p. 3.

27. Young, "Institutions, Elites, and Local Politics," pp. 141–49.
28. "God proshel pod znakom skudnogo biudzheta," *Vecherny Omsk,* January 5, 1995, pp. 1–2. Other large shares of these expenditures are carried by municipal raions and other forms of local government.
29. Ibid. The 1993 share was 33 percent, so there was marginal improvement in 1994. The city, however, demands a 50 percent share, to compensate for greater expenditure needs.
30. "V poiske variantov," *Vecherny Omsk,* August 25, 1994, p. 2.
31. "God proshel," *Vecherny Omsk,* January 5, 1995.
32. "Administratsiia dolzhna reshat' prakticheskie zadachi," *Vecherny Omsk,* March 31, 1994, pp. 1–2.
33. It is important to note, however, that neither Polezhaev nor Roshchupkin are unpopular leaders in Omsk. Indeed, the governor and his protégé are both praised as capable and effective administrators. The relative harmony between oblast and city is in stark contrast to the political battles and squabbles that dominated Omsk politics before 1994. These good relations led some of my acquaintances in Omsk to suggest that local self-government is not a necessary condition for political, social, and economic development. Yet this observation misses the primary point: the conflict between oblast and city in Omsk was not a consequence of self-government but of its absence. Conflict between oblast and city before 1994 was based on the city's struggle to exercise authority and strengthen its power in an environment in which it possessed little of either.
34. The role of regional legislative organs in regional politics has been excluded here. The results of Yeltsin's dissolution of regional soviets in October 1993 curbed the relevancy of representative organs at the regional and local levels. With recent legislative initiatives and recent elections, regional legislatures may now become more relevant and provide a balance to executive domination. But at present, executive power remains beyond legislative control. See, for example, the comments made by the numerous chairs of regional legislative bodies to the Russian Duma during its discussion of a draft law concerning the separation of powers between executive and legislative bodies among the *sub"ekty* of the Russian Federation: *Parlamentskie slushaniia po proektu federal'nogo zakona "Ob obshchikh printsipakh organizatsii sistemy organov gosudarstvennoi vlasti sub"ektov Rossiiskoi Federatsii,* Stenograficheskii otchet, December 27, 1994.
35. *Rossiiskaya gazeta,* March 2, 1995; Ivan Nikul'shin, "Sel'skii starosta: Bez bulavy i kalacha," *Rossiiskaya federatsiya* 10 (1995): 24–25.
36. Zhukov, "Regional Governors."
37. Iurii Shatalov, "Prokuroru gubernator ne ukaz," *Rossiiskaya gazeta,* March 2, 1995, p. 2.
38. By the early summer of 1995, at least sixteen of the eighty-nine regions had adopted their own charters or constitutions.
39. Vsevolod Vasil'ev, "Chei monastyr', togo i ustav," *Rossiiskaya federatsiya* 11 (1995): 32–35. Statute 131 is the relevant part of the constitution of the Russian Federation.

40. The mayor was also one of Barabanov's assistants in the oblast administration. See "Rasporiazhenie No. 396 'O zamestitele glavy administratsii oblasti'" (March 30, 1992), in "Materialy po rezul'tatam proverki v Brianskoi oblasti," documents from the Komitet Verkhovnogo Soveta RSFSR po voprosam raboty sovetov narodnykh deputatov i razvitiiu samoupravleniia.
41. The oblast soviet, which was also at odds with Barabanov, was left to mediate between oblast and city.
42. Ukaz Presidenta Rossiiskoi Federatsii No. 239, "O poriadke naznacheniia glav administratsii," *Vedomosti RSFSR* 48 (November 28, 1991).
43. A mitigating circumstance may have made this ruling easier, since the Uglich appointment was made not by the governor but by his assistant. Igor' Murav'ev, "Glava administratsii—dolzhnost' vybornaia," *Rossiiskaya federatsiya* 10 (1995): 36–37; *Rossiiskaya gazeta*, April 12, 1995, p. 13.
44. See statute 72 of the Russian constitution and the second statute in each of the agreements in the Federal Treaty. *Konstitutsiia Rossiiskoi Federatsii* (Moscow: Iuridicheskaia Literatura, 1993), pp. 29, 66, 76, 89.
45. The new law, "Ob obshchikh printsipakh organizatsii mestnogo samoupravleniia v Rossiiskoi Federatsii," is published in *Rossiiskaya gazeta*, September 1, 1995, pp. 4–6. The contents of the law are discussed in John F. Young, "Local Self-Government and the Russian State," (paper presented at the 27th National Convention of the American Association for the Advancement of Slavic Studies, Washington, D.C., October 28, 1995).
46. L. F. Boltenkova, "Pochemu Sovet Federatsii otklonil zakon 'Ob obshchikh printsipakh organizatsii mestnogo samoupravleniia v Rossiiskoi Federatsii'?" *Regionologiia* 3 (1995): 19–30; Leonid Gil'chenko, "Pochemu ne khotiat gosudarevy liudi' podelit'sia vlast'iu s narodom," *Rossiiskaya federatsiya* 17 (1995): 41–44.
47. This is one solution proposed by Vladimir Kuznechevskii, "Komu ne po dushe edinaia rossiia," *Rossiiskaya gazeta*, April 6, 1995, pp. 1–2.
48. Sergei Shakhrai, "Federalizm i novaia regional'naia politika," *Rossiiskaya gazeta*, February 4, 1995, pp. 1, 4.

III

ECONOMIC REFORM AND SOCIAL CHANGE

5
Regional Aspects of Privatization in Russia

Darrell Slider

Privatization is the most important structural reform in post-Soviet Russia, a program intended to break decisively with the command economy and to transform state-run enterprises into new, relatively autonomous actors essential to a market economy. Russian reformers expected that privatization would lead to changes in enterprise structure and management, replacing the Communist-era *nomenklatura* with managers capable of operating in a market economy. If effective, according to the reformers, privatization would also break the dependence of enterprises on subsidies from the state budget. The reformers further expected that restructured enterprises would attract significant private investment, both foreign and domestic, that would allow the enterprises to modernize and compete under the new conditions.

At first glance, Russia's privatization program has been an overwhelming success. By early 1995, 112,625 enterprises—approximately 46 percent of all economic units in Russia—had been privatized.[1] This was the result of a process that had actually been under way since the late Gorbachev period. There was no single process under which state enterprises changed their form of ownership but rather a complex and sometimes ad hoc set of procedures that varied over time. Among the methods of privatization used were the direct purchase or auction of enterprises, the creation of joint-stock companies with mixed or wholly private ownership, the splitting of enterprises into several units (sometimes with different forms of ownership), the free transfer of property to workers and management, the sale—to current users on preferential terms—of property that had been leased, and the conditional sale of property based on promises of future investment or other terms.[2] Further complicating the situation were the different levels of state property: federal, provincial (referring to republic or oblast), and municipal. The various claimants to enterprises included the branch ministries, managers, employees, and national, regional, and municipal governments.

In negotiating terms of privatization, regional leaders and their representatives in central legislative institutions were able to force the center to make a number of concessions that undermined the initial goals of privatization. Instead of attracting new owners and outside investment (meaning both from Moscow or other regions and from foreign areas), privatization most often transferred effective ownership to local "insiders" such as enterprise managers and local officials.[3] The inability of reformers within the Russian government to enact a privatization program that would conform to their initial goals reflected the weakness of Boris Yeltsin's presidency and the Russian government.[4] Yegor Gaidar, the acting prime minister at the time the privatization program was worked out and introduced, admitted that compromises in the privatization program were part of a deal designed to "buy off" the *nomenklatura* by allowing it to take over property in exchange for giving up political power. Instead, as Gaidar has argued, the *nomenklatura* made every effort to keep both property and power.[5]

The *nomenklatura* in the regions represented the largest part of the Soviet-era elite, and the reformist version of privatization was particularly threatening to this group.[6] Under the Soviet system, regional officials were able to use their influence and ties with local enterprise managers to exercise extensive discretionary power over a wide range of local issues.[7] Local enterprises, even those not administratively subordinate to the region, provided funds, material, labor, social-cultural institutions, housing, and other resources to the region. Managers of these enterprises, as a result of their interaction with local party and administrative officials, were effectively brought into the local elite irrespective of their administrative subordination. Privatization threatened to disrupt local elite networks by bringing in outsiders or by creating a new elite of entrepreneurs unbound by past conventions. As this chapter will show, however, the ability of local elites to shape the practice of privatization limited this threat.

The success of regional and municipal elites was aided by the institutional weakness and conflicts between executive and legislative authority at the center. Ineffective supervision of the implementation of privatization led to substantial regional differences both in the rates of privatization and in the methods used.[8] The most explicit devolution of power came about through ad hoc negotiations between Yeltsin and selected regional leaders. This approach was applied most often to "republics within the federation"—most of which were formerly autonomous republics under the Soviet administrative framework. Agreements emerged in the form of bilateral treaties between the center and individual republics. The first of these agreements were with Tatarstan (February 1994) and Bashkortostan (August 1994), followed by agreements between Moscow and Kabardino-Balkaria, Sakha (Yakutia), Komi, Buryatia, and Udmurtia, respectively.[9] The first oblast to negotiate an agreement was Yeltsin's home province of Sverdlovsk.

These treaties, which as a rule were not published, did not represent a new phase in Kremlin policy. They had been preceded by a number of ad hoc deals—negotiated by Yeltsin and the Russian government—that included major concessions on privatization. These concessions often expanded the rights of regional governments to dispose of state property. Moscow allowed Tatarstan, one of the most demanding of the republics, to write its own program for privatizing major enterprises, one that varied considerably from the national program.[10] Republic officials were able to establish their own republic-wide system of privatization checks that were distributed to each resident and that could be used only for the purchase of shares in the republic's major enterprises. The republic government retained, on average, 41 percent of the shares of the Tatarstan enterprises.[11]

When treaties were signed beginning in 1994, this pattern of concessions by Moscow to regional elites was formalized. As part of the Bashkortostan agreement, for example, specific enterprises were assigned to federal, republic, or joint ownership. The most profitable enterprises were given republic or joint status, whereas military enterprises that needed large subsidies were left to federal authorities.[12] Other regions also sought to use separate deals with the center to enhance their control over the privatization process.

In the earliest stage of privatization, the principal method applied to large state enterprises was the creation of shareholder-owned companies, or AOs (*aktsionernye obshchestva,* or stock societies). A portion of state property was distributed free to the population in the form of privatization checks, or vouchers, which could be sold or traded for shares in newly privatized enterprises. Regional officials were extremely inventive in preventing voucher privatization or in adapting it for their own purposes. In Moscow, the voucher stage of privatization of large enterprises was effectively sabotaged by the mayor, Yuri Luzhkov, who engaged in a sustained battle with the head of the State Committee on Property (*Goskomimushchestvo,* or GKI), Anatoly Chubais, over this and other privatization issues. The Moscow city government in May 1994 made itself the chief arbiter on matters concerning the privatization of federal property in Moscow. In mid-1994, after appeals by both parties to the president, Yeltsin instructed Chubais to "stay out" of Moscow's affairs. As a result, very few federal enterprises underwent stock privatization in the capital.[13] Luzhkov also championed turning over municipal property to labor collectives in ways that conflicted with the national program. City enterprises were transferred at very low prices, but with the Moscow city government retaining the right of ultimate ownership and using its powers to levy a wide assortment of fees and taxes.

Even where the creation of joint-stock societies and the system of voucher privatization were carried out for large enterprises, a potential controlling portion (30 to 40 percent was sometimes sufficient) of shares in privatized enterprises remained in the hands of the federal and provincial governments. Check privatization encountered substantial opposition from both branch ministries and regional elites, which found ways to preserve some measure of control over privatized enterprises. Through the creation of holding companies, ministries in many cases were able to obtain a controlling interest in enterprises that had previously been under their control.[14]

Regional officials used a wide range of strategies to retain control over joint-stock companies in their territory. In many regions, local officials sponsored the creation of check investment funds. Local residents would be encouraged to turn over their privatization checks to the funds, which would then invest them in enterprises in the region. In this way, control over a significant share of enterprise stock could remain in the hands of local elites.[15] In any event, the most common result of the creation of AOs was that effective ownership rights were taken by the current enterprise managers. This was a result that regional and local officials for the most part approved and encouraged.

At the expiration of the validity of privatization checks in mid-1994, the Russian government worked out a new program for the next stage of privatization. When the parliament refused to enact the new program as law, Yeltsin implemented the program by decree.[16] The principal element of the "post-voucher" stage of privatization was the sale of shares for cash, a stage that did not begin in earnest until April 1995. The delay resulted from several personnel changes at the top of GKI. Chubais left as "privatization minister" when he was promoted to first vice-premier, with overall control of economic policy. From November 1994 to January 1995, the chairman of GKI was Vladimir Polevanov. At the time of his appointment, Polevanov was a provincial official—the governor of Amur oblast. The appointment came as a shock to many at GKI and to Chubais. Not only was the Amur region not particularly distinguished in the area of privatization, but Polevanov was under attack from virtually all political movements in Amur. Opposition leaders accused Polevanov of steering contracts to past and current business partners (Polevanov had previously been a gold-mining geologist), of maintaining links to a pyramid investment scheme, and of illegally diverting funds designated for social programs. The opposition also argued that Polevanov allowed a corporation in which he was a partner to manage the state share of ownership in privatized enterprises in the oblast.[17]

As GKI chairman, Polevanov repeatedly battled with Chubais over the results of the first stage of privatization. Polevanov sought the renationalization of a number of enterprises in strategically important sectors (such as mineral resource processing, transportation, and military-related industry), and he tried to shift the subordination of GKI from Chubais to the more conservative first deputy prime minister, Oleg Soskovets.[18] Yeltsin finally removed Polevanov in January 1995, and GKI set up a commission to reverse or annul decisions that had been made when Polevanov had been in charge.[19] In February 1995, Sergei Belyaev, Chubais's first choice as his successor, became the head of GKI.

Under Belyaev's tutelage, the second stage of privatization began to be implemented. Government-owned shares of federal enterprises were to be sold at auction over a period of one year. In April, a list of 7,186 enterprises for which shares were to be sold at open auctions began to appear in *Rossiiskaya gazeta*. The list did not include enterprises from the sensitive fuel sector or from the military-industrial complex.[20] The second stage of privatization would, like the first stage, have implications for provincial control over local enterprises. A struggle between regional authorities and the center over who should have the right to manage (or sell) government shares *(gosudarstvennyie pakety)* in privatized enterprises was inevitable. The federal government struck first when, in a measure recommended by GKI, it adopted a decision in November 1994 to place representatives of the government in stock companies in which the federal government owned a share, thereby establishing greater control over AOs in which it had stockholdings.[21]

Regional governments opposed federal control for obvious reasons: to retain some measure of influence over the activities of "privatized" enterprises and/or to achieve a greater financial benefit from the sale of these shares. The most valuable enterprises in a region were almost always federal property. In some cases, the state-owned shares represented a controlling interest and allowed the government to select enterprise management. In other enterprises, the federal government's share was enough to guarantee a seat on the board of directors of an enterprise. Provincial leaders were intent on retaining a controlling interest in those privatized enterprises that had been designated provincial property. In Kabardino-Balkaria, for example, the republic government kept a controlling share of 72 percent of the AOs created in 1994.[22] A special agreement between GKI and the government of Bashkortostan allowed it to create "state AOs" and to have a decisive voice in other "privatized" enterprises.[23]

The process by which Moscow authorities declare federal enterprises in the regions bankrupt and then name new management has also been resisted by regional elites. The lack of an effective bankruptcy procedure (though a law on bankruptcy was approved in the early stages of Russia's reforms) was one of Russia's major deviations from a true "shock therapy"; instead, loss-making federal enterprises were allowed to continue to operate, thanks to state subsidies. In September 1993 the Federal Bankruptcy Agency was established under GKI.[24] However, procedures for selling debtor enterprises were not issued by a Yeltsin decree until June 1994.[25] One of the earliest cases of a Moscow-imposed reorganization of a major bankrupt enterprise was that of Rybinsk Motor Works in Yaroslavl oblast; Rybinsk was declared bankrupt in April 1995. Rather than allow a new manager to be appointed by the Federal Bankruptcy Agency, oblast authorities supported the current director and ordered local police to prevent federal officials from entering the premises.[26] Later, when the Russian government announced it would sell its share in the company, the director of Rybinsk Motor Works declared the sale "illegal."[27]

Another type of threat to local control over key industries was the plan put forward by several of Russia's major private banks (all based in Moscow) to take over the state's share in major industrial and fuel-sector enterprises (not scheduled for privatization until sometime in 1996–97) as collateral for a loan to the central government.[28] This program, which Yeltsin approved in September 1995, began to be implemented in late 1995, and it threatened to undermine regional efforts to gain control of large federal enterprises in their jurisdiction.[29]

There were genuine grounds for regional elites to be concerned about the uneven distribution of financial resources. In 1995 over 70 percent of Russia's finance capital was estimated to be concentrated in Moscow banks. As a defense against the anticipated onslaught of takeovers (which are invariably viewed as "hostile" by regional elites) by these financial powers, several regions and cities took steps to create their own banks, which would give local elites more leverage in defending their regional interests. The attempts by Moscow banks to set up affiliates in other regions were rarely successful unless someone with local ties was named to head the branch.[30] Even city leaders in Moscow were wary of the power of Moscow-based private banks, and city authorities created, in early 1995, a municipal bank that would give them greater control over the city's budgetary funds for investment and other purposes.[31] Where local governments have served as a source for capital, they have used this role to increase their hold on regional enterprises. In Astrakhan, the oblast legislature adopted regulations mandating that loans made by the oblast to local enterprises would be repaid in stock. This in turn would increase the share of state ownership in newly privatized enterprises.[32]

Some regions also sought to achieve direct control over the terms for attracting foreign investment to local enterprises. Foreign companies attempting to obtain a share of Russian enterprises have often been met with additional conditions imposed by local and regional governments—demands for investment in infrastructure, for example. Regions have also sought to bypass the Ministry of Foreign Economic Relations, to achieve greater control over foreign operations. Most aggressive in this area—and reflecting the special conditions it succeeded in wresting from Moscow—was the republic of Tatarstan, which announced the creation of its own Investment-Financial Corporation in February 1995 to bring all foreign investment activity under the control of the republic leadership. The institution was created to insure foreign investments and provide investors with guarantees in the form of assets and shares contributed by member banks and enterprises. The corporation announced it was opening an office in London or Brussels.[33]

Regionally based concentrations of capital and large enterprises in the form of financial-industrial groups (*finansovo-promyshlennye gruppy*, or FPGs) represented another institutional innovation that would allow retention of regional control over privatized enterprises. FPGs can be constructed on a sectoral rather than territorial basis, in a structure reminiscent of the Moscow-based ministries—and indeed, FPGs are sometimes the creations of these ministries. The debate over how FPGs would be organized became the chief battleground for local elites and the branch ministries in Moscow. Nonregionally based FPGs could just as easily threaten the control of local elites. As one account put it, many regional elites viewed FPGs as "the latest plot against the regions, an act of war which [was] being conducted against them by the center, the ministries, branches, banks, foreigners, the mafia, the tax service, and others who [were] attempting to extract local resources."[34]

In December 1993, a group named Urals Factories became the first officially registered FPG. A creature of republic industrial and banking elites in Udmurtia, it comprised eleven factories, a research institute, banks, insurance companies, and the republic privatization check investment fund. The FPG pooled resources within the republic for producing a wide range of goods, including telecommunications, medical equipment, and defense technology.[35] By providing a regionally integrated conglomerate with local management and financing independent of the center or Moscow-based banks, the Urals Factories FPG sought to insulate a significant part of the republic's economy from outside control. Part of the reason that the group was formed in Udmurtia was that this republic had the largest concentration of defense plants of all Russian regions. Republic leaders had frequently complained about a lack of support from federal authorities for the conversion of local military industry.[36] Similar large, regionally based FPGs were formed in 1994 and early 1995 in Kemerovo, Murmansk, Samara, Saratov, and Vladimir oblasts.[37]

In January 1995, the Russian government approved a program for the formation of FPGs, and a law was adopted by the parliament and signed by Yeltsin in November 1995. The law provided for a number of tax breaks as well as exemptions from antimonopoly legislation. It was also clear that the framers of the legislation anticipated continued subsidies for the enterprises in officially registered FPGs.[38] From the standpoint of local elites, this represents the best of all worlds—a mechanism that might permit local control, federal budgetary largesse, and monopoly power. The Moscow city government has been enamored of FPGs as a way to retain an economic stake as a founding partner. For some in the Moscow administration, this represents an efficient alternative to privatization.[39]

Landownership rights became another issue that had major implications for regional control over privatized enterprises. Enterprises as a rule did not have clear title to the land that they occupied, and often they had no documentation allowing for the use of the land under their de facto control. In the center of St. Petersburg, for example, around 70 percent of the land-users had no documentation.[40] The lack of clear title and full property rights not only decreased the options available to enterprises (such as selling unused land to raise capital or using it as collateral for a loan) but also tended to scare off outside investors and, particularly, foreign investors.

In June 1992 Yeltsin signed a decree authorizing the sale of land to enterprises during the privatization process, and a July 1994 decree by Yeltsin on the federal privatization program reaffirmed the principle that privatized enterprises could purchase their land.[41] In practice, however, local authorities prevented such purchases while awaiting a more general land code.[42] In Sverdlovsk oblast, regional officials rejected outright the land-sale provisions of the federal program for postvoucher privatization. They argued that land sales conducted in this way would not yield a high enough price.[43]

In fact, prices set for the sale of land to enterprises were most often seen as too high by potential purchasers. In the absence of a true real estate market, the value of any particular piece of land was not known. As a result, the formula was often established arbitrarily: for example, the price might typically be set at two hundred times the assessed property tax—a cost prohibitive for most enterprises. By contrast, the deputy head of GKI recommended in April 1995 that the land price be set at ten times the property tax.[44]

A pioneer in this, as in so many other areas of privatization, was Nizhni Novgorod oblast, led by Boris Nemtsov, one of the few committed reformers in charge of a province. In November 1994, for the first time, an auction was held for several small, empty lots on the outskirts of the city. One of the purposes of the auction was to determine the real market value of the land, though it turned out that no one submitted bids higher than the initial offered prices, and three of ten lots went unsold. Also, this was land designated for residential housing rather than commercial property.[45] In early 1995, auctions for the purpose of selling land were also held in Astrakhan and Vladimir.[46]

St. Petersburg was another region in the forefront of efforts to encourage the sale of land to enterprises. Mayor Anatoly Sobchak signed a decree allowing land purchases in November 1994,[47] and city officials, desperate to raise needed city finances, tried to sell to enterprises the land they were using. However, the price set—adjusted for location—was prohibitively expensive for most enterprises, especially those located near the city center. According to one calculation, the price for a typical industrial enterprise was equivalent to 100–140 years of lease payments at current rates. City officials responded to the lack of interest by sharply increasing leasing fees.[48]

The preference of most local officials was for some form of leasing agreement between the enterprise and the city, with ultimate ownership rights retained by the city. This gave city officials both control and a source of income for local budgets. Even long-term leases, however, could often be obtained only after lengthy bureaucratic delays (and the attendant bribes). The mayor of Moscow, Yuri Luzhkov, was perhaps the regional official most adamantly opposed to land sales. All land remained under the control of the Moscow city government, which allowed auctions or bidding only for long-term leases. The leases included conditions on how the land was to be used. The right of enterprises to negotiate a forty-nine-year lease was part of Yeltsin's decree on Moscow privatization.[49] Half of the rental revenues went to the Moscow city government.[50] Other regions adopted similar measures without authorization. The republic of Chuvashia, for example, adopted a privatization program that allowed privatized enterprises to arrange only long-term leases, not purchases, of land.[51]

Regional elites have fought to retain or achieve control over supposedly privatized enterprises, and they appear to be winning the battle. In the privatization process, the central government was forced by its own weakness to make considerable concessions to the regions. In this way, the reformist goals of privatization were compromised. This conclusion applies to the first stage of privatization and, most likely, also to the "second stage" of privatization, which is more specifically focused on the problem of attracting investment.

The result of retaining government control (whether through shares, representatives on boards of directors, FPGs, or landownership) will be to prolong or delay genuine privatization—with the effect of extending conflicts that are often at the heart of other disputes. In areas with significant ethnic conflict, the decisions of state enterprises can disrupt political stability. One of the regions where this has already manifested itself is Dagestan, the republic with the most volatile mix of ethnic groups. As the head of the Dagestan committee on property put it, "real" privatization "could smooth over many of the conflicts in the North Caucasus."[52] In other words, privatization of state property could remove a substantial amount of economic decision-making from the political arena, thus reducing the potential grounds for ethnic conflict.

The first stage of privatization and the prevailing legal and regulatory climate in the second stage would be enough to dissuade most outside investors. De facto insider or management control over enterprises gave outsiders few levers to oversee the object of their investments. The lack of regulations governing the issuance and registration of shares also left investors open to potential surprises that would lessen the value of their shares. In the much-publicized case of the Krasnoyarsk Aluminum Plant, a British company lost a $300 million investment when, after a dispute with the Russian directors, the record of their shares was erased from the plant registry.[53] Another implication of retaining control at the regional level through a packet of state-owned shares is that there might be no other source for investment other than the local budget. Needless to say, most regions are incapable of providing the investment funds needed for upgrading the industrial base.

Rather than adhering to the national privatization program—which is what the logic of a developing federalism would imply—Russia's regions have continued aggressively to seek legal sanction for exceptions and deviations from the national program. An outspoken advocate of this approach is Sergei Burkov, head of the State Duma Committee on Property, Privatization, and Economic Activity and a leader of the large deputy faction "New Regional Policy." His committee had overall responsibility for preparing a new draft program on privatization; if adopted by the parliament, his program would have superseded the one that Yeltsin had signed into force in mid-1994 and would have given much greater discretionary power to regional elites and labor collectives.[54] Many of the compromises in government policy on privatization can be attributed to the effective lobbying of regional interests in the Duma and the Council of the Federation.

With very few exceptions—such as Boris Nemtsov's Nizhni Novgorod—the privatization policies implemented by regional elites are motivated by their perceived self-interests. These have little in common with genuine privatization and the development of a market economy. Whereas Moscow's concessions reflected the existing distribution of power between the regions and the center, the resulting "privatization" was most likely to further entrench regional elites in the local economy, where they will be in a position to establish new obstacles to demonopolization and marketization of the economy. Much will depend on future developments in Russian federal relations; if the emerging relationship between the center and Tatarstan is the model, Russia could evolve into a loose confederation of provinces with widely varying economic systems, few of them oriented toward private property and markets.

NOTES

1. *Rossiiskie vesti,* March 31, 1995.
2. For a review of the methods of privatization, see Morris Bornstein, "Russia's Mass Privatisation Programme," *Communist Economies and Economic Transformation* 6, no. 4 (1994): 419–57.
3. For an overview of the early record of privatization in the context of economic reform, see Peter Rutland, "Privatisation in Russia: One Step Forward, Two Steps Back?" *Europe-Asia Studies* 46, no. 7 (1994): 1109–32.
4. This argument has also been made by Michael McFaul, "State Power, Institutional Change, and the Politics of Privatization in Russia," *World Politics* 47, no. 2 (January 1995): 210–43.
5. See Ygor Gaidar, *Gosudarstvo i evoliutsiia* (Moscow: Izdatel'stvo "Evrasiia," 1995), pp. 143–65.
6. At a meeting of regional officials organized by Yeltsin to discuss local self-management, the assembled provincial governors reportedly applauded Alexander Solzhenitsyn when he proposed that privatization be halted for five to six years in order to "give it some thought." *Segodnya,* February 21, 1995.
7. For a recent and detailed examination of the role of local elites in the Soviet economy, see Peter Rutland, *The Politics of Economic Stagnation in the Soviet Union: The Role of Local Party Organs in Economic Management* (Cambridge: Cambridge University Press, 1993).
8. See Darrell Slider, "Privatization in Russia's Regions," *Post-Soviet Affairs* 10, no. 4 (October-December 1994): 367–96.
9. At the time of writing, treaties with several other regions were in the final stages of negotiation.

10. For an early report on the Tatarstan privatization approach, see *Kommersant*, September 23, 1993.
11. *Segodnya*, April 27, 1995.
12. Ibid., April 19, 1995.
13. Ibid., May 13, 1994.
14. See the remarks by the newly appointed chief of GKI, Sergei Belyaev, at a conference on privatization, in ibid., February 21, 1995.
15. For details, see Slider, "Privatization in Russia's Regions."
16. *Izvestiya*, July 15, 1994; *Rossiiskaya gazeta*, July 26, 1994.
17. A lengthy list of charges against Polevanov was published by the chairman of the Amur branch of Gaidar's party, Russia's Choice, in *Rossiiskie vesti*, November 1, 1994.
18. *Kommersant*, no. 3 (January 31, 1995), pp. 10–11.
19. *Segodnya*, February 1, 1995.
20. Ibid., April 14, 1995.
21. *Nezavisimaya gazeta*, November 25,1994.
22. *Kabardino-Balkarskaia pravda* (Nal'chik), February 8, 1995, in *Russian Regional Press Bulletin* (*RRPB*), March 13, 1995.
23. See the report by Irgiz Temirkhanov, "Respublika Bashkortostan: Tendentsii politicheskogo razvitiia," *Politicheskii monitoring* (April 1995), pt. 1, p. 8.
24. The resolution, signed by Viktor Chernomyrdin, was published in *Kommersant*, September 26–October 3, 1993.
25. The regulations appeared in *Rossiiskie vesti*, June 8, 1994.
26. This case was reported by Chrystia Freeland in *Financial Times*, September 15, 1995. For an account critical of the federal agency, see *Rossiiskaya gazeta*, October 5, 1995.
27. *Financial Times*, December 5, 1995.
28. The proposal was outlined in ibid., April 26, 1995.
29. Ibid., September 5, 1995.
30. *Kommersant-Daily*, April 29, 1995.
31. Ibid., March 16, 1995.
32. *Astrakhanskie izvestiya*, February 23, 1995 (*RRPB*, March 17, 1995).
33. *Kommersant-Daily*, February 9, 1995.
34. *Izvestiya*, November 24, 1994.
35. *Nezavisimaya gazeta*, December 7, 1993; *Rossiiskie vesti*, December 16, 1993.
36. *Ekonomika i zhizn'*, no. 13 (April 1995), p. 28.
37. *Segodnya*, February 12, 1994, March 17, 30, and 31, 1994, February 21, 1995; *Izvestiya*, January 19, 1995.
38. *Rossiiskaya gazeta*, February 2, 1995; *Rossiiskie vesti*, November 4, 1995.
39. *Segodnya*, May 17, 1994; *Rossiiskaya gazeta*, July 20, 1994.
40. *Kommersant-Daily*, March 23, 1995.
41. *Kommersant*, no. 28 (August 2, 1994), p. 54.
42. *Kommersant-Daily*, February 11, 1995.
43. *Oblastnaya gazeta* (Yekaterinburg), January 21, 1995.
44. Albert Kokh, cited in *Segodnya*, April 26, 1995.
45. *Segodnya*, November 15, 1994.

46. *Kommersant-Daily,* February 11, 1995.
47. *Rossiiskaya gazeta,* November 10, 1994.
48. *Kommersant-Daily,* February 18, 28, 1995.
49. *Ekonomika i zhizn',* no. 7 (February 1995); *Kommersant-Daily,* February 11, 1995.
50. See the report on the property market in Moscow in *Financial Times,* September 22, 1995.
51. *Segodnya,* January 11, 1995.
52. State Duma hearings on state ownership were reported in ibid., April 19, 1995.
53. On the risks of share investing, see *Financial Times,* October 4, 1995.
54. See the interview with Burkov in *Rossiiskaya gazeta,* November 30, 1994, and the article in *Segodnya,* January 20, 1995. Burkov, from Kemerovo, has close ties to Aman Tuleev, who has frequently clashed with Yeltsin over economic issues.

6
Labor Institutions in Post-Communist Russia: The Rise of Regionalism

Carol Clark

INTRODUCTION

The transition to a market economy in Russia has been characterized by uncertainty. A number of old institutions have crumbled while new ones remain terribly weak or have yet to take shape. An example of the last case is the absence thus far of a stable system of labor relations based on the development of representative, independent labor institutions. At the macroeconomic level of labor relations, one is struck by the lack not only of any agreement on what form labor relations should take but also of any governmental strategy to move toward a stable system. The government's attempt to create a mechanism for cooperation among workers, employers, and itself—in the form of the Tripartite Commission—has yielded few results, none carrying practical weight.[1] The old, official trade union federation, Federatsiya Nezavisimaya Profsoyuzov Rossii (FNPR), has maintained a dominant position on the labor side in the formal negotiations and, in fact, has even increased its role on the commission since early 1993. At the same time, FNPR has been slow to change its orientation from that of the administration's partner to that of an independent federation representing and defending labor's interests. Alongside the failed official attempts, efforts to create a new, independent trade union federation (composed of trade unions formed since 1989) have likewise yielded no positive results.[2] Furthermore, government policy on social and labor issues has lacked a consistent strategy and has vacillated with personnel changes in the Ministry of Labor.[3] The original policy of reregistering trade union members, lending credibility to the phrase "representative trade union" by allowing workers to choose their preferred trade union, was abandoned by early 1993.

At the microeconomic level of labor relations, FNPR has lost power in its internal relations with its regional and branch-level trade union associations,[4] and at the enterprise level, the official FNPR union has weakened vis-à-vis enterprise management.[5] Simultaneously, alternative trade unions have arisen, beginning with the formation of the Independent Trade Union of Miners (NPG) after the 1989 strikes. In terms of their combined political and economic orientation, the new trade unions cover a wide spectrum: they range from trade unions that support the current political changes and, to varying degrees, the economic reforms introduced since 1992, to trade unions that espouse strongly nationalistic agendas and advocate a return to a more state-managed economy.[6] Although their appearance undoubtedly signals change, what one does not see is a strong movement toward the establishment of an institutionalized system of negotiation, mediation, and implementation of collective bargaining agreements. Moreover, many observers do not expect such a system, in which unions defend labor's interests, to arise in the near future.[7] This lack of significant change suggests that the redesigning of labor institutions in Russia is (and will continue to be) a particularly difficult task. The difficulty is further appreciated once one acknowledges that by the end of the Soviet period, the official trade unions were thoroughly discredited institutions whose alienated membership perceived the trade union not so much as a representative body as a social services agency.[8]

Explanations for the weak state of Russian trade unions vary. One group of scholars offers the interpretation of a "social contract": an agreement between the workers and the state, leading to acquiescence and a relatively passive labor force. Another group emphasizes that paternalism and the associated mutual dependence between manager and worker underlie the lack of change.[9] A worker's enterprise provides not only a place of work and the ability to earn income but also a wide range of goods, services, and in general, in-kind benefits that make up the basic necessities on which workers come to depend. As one author describes this relationship, the enterprise is in the business of "reproducing the labor force" insofar as it has become the provider of workers' "basic life needs."[10] This argument raises an interesting question: what factors help to maintain paternalism and dependence at the enterprise level during the transitional period? Two factors are arguably important: one is the economic policies introduced under *perestroika*,[11] and the other is the continuation, during the transitional period, of a long-standing socialist policy of distributing social services at the place of production. Together, these factors strengthened management's position as enterprises increased their autonomy during the late 1980s, allowing management to maintain (if not strengthen) a paternalistic system of labor relations during the early stages of the transition. Moreover, these factors help to explain the defeat of new trade unions, fighting against the old FNPR trade unions while exerting no control over social services themselves, and the difficulty of any union to be truly independent of the administration, since the administration over the past five years has gained greater control and leverage over the distribution of those services.

A third factor, related to the previous factor, is that neopaternalism in the post-Communist period fits nicely into the short-term survival strategy adopted by many industrial enterprises after the initial market reforms were introduced in January 1992. As one group of experts explains, the "restoration of authoritarian paternalism and consolidation of monopoly position" must be seen as "ways to secure enterprise prosperity," especially during a relatively chaotic and uncertain period.[12] Mutual dependence, then, survives at the enterprise level as workers, whose real living standards have declined dramatically since 1990, rely heavily on their respective enterprises for the payment of wages plus the distribution of many important social services and goods (which cannot be purchased on the open market with their declining real wages) and, likewise, as enterprise managers desire to retain workers, especially highly skilled and experienced workers, in the presence of production disruptions, financial constraints, and the relative shortage of skilled labor. This distribution of an in-house benefits package helps to regulate the internal labor market at large industrial enterprises and provides a means by which managers can continue their "rhetoric of conscience and care" toward the work collective.[13]

The maintenance of paternalism, furthermore, helps to explain the emergence of certain tendencies in the response of labor institutions to the post-Communist transition. In particular, it may help to reinforce branch unionism in Russia, because enterprise-level paternalism and mutual dependence are strikingly different across branches of industry. That is, the package of benefits offered to workers at the enterprise level depends on the industry to which the enterprise belongs. This differentiating feature would help to separate workers' interests and prevent cooperation, or collective action, across sectors or industries.[14] In this way, the differing pattern of paternalism and mutual dependence at the enterprise level can influence how labor defines its interests, suggesting a model in which labor organizes along sectoral lines and strives for sectoral independence, in contrast to the old FNPR structure, in which sectoral interests had to compete with other interests. This trend toward sectoral independence and, sometimes, occupational independence within a given sector is seen in the development of the independent trade unions since 1989. Not only the miners' union but also the other strong, militant, grassroots unions, including those of pilots, air traffic controllers, railroad workers, and seafarers, have striven for sectoral independence. One of the more recent examples is the Mining and Metallurgy Trade Union of Russia (GMPR). GMPR represents the largest branch-level trade union to have broken away from FNPR in an effort to secure its sectoral demands and to gain sectoral independence over the distribution of the social security funds controlled by the official trade union federation.[15] It saw an internal contradiction in the structure of the old federation and believed that branch unionism was essential in building a new, more democratically based trade union that would engage in "real" trade union work more actively than the official trade unions had traditionally done.[16]

Although the above factors help to highlight some of the important issues, and hence the lingering difficulties, associated with efforts to establish and build independent trade unions, other factors—often neglected, or at least not fully developed, in the trade union and labor relations literature—have significantly influenced labor's response to the post-Communist transition. Without addressing these issues, one cannot fully understand why it has been so difficult to create a stable system of labor representation that will be capable of effectively articulating labor's distinct interests. These factors can be grouped under the rubric of "regionalism," and together they identify the difficulties in defining labor's interests: to which organizations should labor appeal, and on what basis should cooperation be built? Furthermore, it is possible that these factors will compete with those that support branch unionism, the result being different, and potentially conflicting, bodies from which to form representative labor institutions. Moreover, their significance may grow as economic policies begin to place limits on the institution of neopaternalism.

One can see the importance of regional factors, first by reexamining the reforms of the *perestroika* period; those reforms helped to redefine Russia's economic space, to initiate both the growth of political power away from the center and a greater sense of regional identity.[17] That is, the economic changes that began in the late 1980s occurred against a backdrop of growing regionalism. This trend has been expressed in a number of different ways and continues in the post-Communist period. It is apparent, for example, in the role that regional political and managerial elites play in privatization. The center has failed to impose one model on the various regions, although it appears, at least on the surface, to wield control over policy design and implementation. The implementation and control over enterprise privatization exists de facto within regional and local bodies.[18]

Other forms of regionalization include campaigns for regional autonomy and greater control over regional resources, along with efforts to lobby the center as a "regional body." A more subtle form of regionalization arises from the fact that individual industries will undergo certain adjustments during the transitional period, carrying with them particularly strong regional effects and thereby introducing a regional focus to cooperation and institution-building. Specifically, one can argue that regional disparities and structural adjustments will be significant in Russia in the medium to long run and that local-regional conditions will influence the form that labor institutions will take. The first point stems from the fact that industrial activity and employment structures in the former USSR were both relatively highly concentrated and relatively specialized at the regional level. The post-Communist Russian economy, moreover, will undergo significant shifts in the sectoral composition of its GDP over the longer term, if the experience of the more advanced, OECD countries is anything by which to judge. In particular, one would expect some sectors of the economy to expand relative to others, the service sector being perhaps the most obvious example, because the USSR had an underdeveloped tertiary sector, an overdeveloped heavy industry sector, and as one author put it, a superagrarian economy for the better part of the twentieth century.[19] For these reasons, one would expect relatively strong growth of light industry (manufactured consumer goods and some intermediate products) and of services in large metropolitan areas.[20] As a consequence of the combined effects of the anticipated sectoral shifts and the highly specialized regional production of the Soviet period, the potential for economic growth should differ significantly across regions. This regional differentiation should make efforts at cooperation across regional lines difficult (e.g., in the case of a national trade union organized along branch lines).

Together, the above tendencies form a regional focus for organizing interests and institutions. In the case of industrial activity highly concentrated in certain geographic areas, a different organizing principle may emerge, so that one finds the expression of a regional focus in the development of labor institutions. The regional pull, moreover, can come into direct conflict with, or at least present a challenge to, interests as defined by the national, branch-level approach to unionism. If this is true, one can better understand the fluidity in labor structures and the absence to date of strong, coherent institutional development.

It is this potential tension between broad-based regional institutions and national, branch-level institutions that is explored in this chapter. First, the role played by enterprise paternalism in historically defining interests along branch lines is examined in greater detail, including a discussion of the reasons underlying paternalism. Second, the forces of regionalism are examined, both in terms of a regionalization of policy and a growing sense of regional identity. This section is followed by a discussion of the likely regional adjustments to be experienced in post-Communist Russia and of how those adjustments will reinforce the trends toward regionalization. The analysis finally turns to a specific case study, that of the newly independent GMPR. This case study illustrates how regionalism fits into the equation for the institutional development of labor organizations during the post-Communist transition and, in doing so, highlights the difficulty of accomplishing such a task.

NEOPATERNALISM AND CRISIS IN THE TRADE UNION MOVEMENT

The lack of independence of labor institutions and the presence of neopaternalism can be seen as an outgrowth of the drive toward greater enterprise autonomy during the late 1980s. Beginning with *perestroika*, enterprises slowly gained greater decision-making powers, expanding tl:eir production and financial autonomy by transferring assets away from ministerial control.[21] Expansion of enterprise decision-making power occurred in three phases. First, in 1987, the Law on the State Enterprise gave firms greater rights over the use of their assets and introduced a weak form of worker management, and then in 1988, cooperative activity allowed enterprises to take advantage of the price irrationalities and supply shortages characteristic of the administrative-command system.[22] The second phase included the "destatization" of state property, in which firms were allowed to choose from a number of options to transfer assets to new organizational entities and thereby further escape ministerial control. The leasing of enterprise shops or departments (with an option to buy) by the labor collective and the setting up of independent cooperatives within the state enterprise are just two examples.[23] By 1990 the choices had expanded with the establishment of small enterprises (within the parent state enterprise) and the transformation of state enterprises into joint-stock companies. These options essentially continued the transferal of assets and eventually led to the third phase, the privatization of state property.[24] During all three phases, the overriding goals of enterprise management were freedom from the administrative system and minimization of outside interference (in both the operations of the enterprise and, eventually, the ownership structure).[25] This continued desire to limit outside interference and preserve enterprise autonomy explains why industrial enterprises overwhelmingly chose variant #2 when drawing up their privatization plans.[26] That variant allowed for the controlling interest in an enterprise to be held by the employees; it specified that workers and management, that is, the labor collective, could buy up to 51 percent of their enterprise's shares at 1.7 times the historical price and thereby effectively limit outside interference.[27]

In return for increased autonomy, the privatized enterprise assumed some of the previous responsibilities of the state and, in the process, strengthened the paternalistic institutions that were already present in the Soviet enterprise. The enterprise managers were willing to provide more goods and services and even job security in exchange for internal support, as part of their short-term survival strategy.[28] For example, "large industrial enterprises even purchased collective farms, construction companies, and food-processing, clothing and footwear companies in order to guarantee such supplies [to their workforce]."[29] As a consequence, by the beginning of the post-Communist transition, the traditional FNPR trade union found itself relatively weak, and the norm continued to be a basically passive labor force with no effective, independent representative body (the same as in the Soviet period). How, then, did this balance of power at the enterprise level come about? First of all, under the old system the trade union always functioned as one part of the party-administration-trade-union troika. In this role, it ideally was to perform a dual function, that of representing the working class as a whole and that of serving as a transmission belt, communicating the goals of the party-state to the workers.[30] In practice, however, the union worked to implement party policy and maintain control over the labor force.[31] It essentially represented an "integral part of the management structure of the enterprise, and was universally seen as such,"[32] with its main administrative duty being the distribution of social and welfare services. In the transitional period, FNPR has continued to assume this traditional role, choosing not to fight for change, and has remained an arm of the administration, representing management's and the industrial *nomenklatura*'s interests to the state. This response follows from the traditional source of FNPR's power: not only its control over but its ownership of all assets and property associated with the provision of social services (day care centers, sanatoria, vacation centers, pioneer camps, etc.), along with its control over membership dues automatically taken out of members' wages by the enterprise administration.

Herein lies the two-pronged problem for the traditional trade union during the post-Communist period. First, workers in Russia have long been alienated from and distrustful of the official trade union, and therefore a large percentage of workers remain in the union purely to take advantage of its distribution network.[33] And second, the trade union's monopoly position over the distribution of services and goods has been successfully challenged by both the enterprise administration and the government of Boris Yeltsin during the transition. Since 1992, the administration of the enterprise has increasingly taken control of the trade union's distribution functions,[34] and in the fall of 1992 the Yeltsin government announced that the responsibility for the distribution of social security was to be assumed by a state committee.[35] This problem suggests that the traditional trade union has lost its legitimacy, triggering an "identity crisis" within the old trade union federation. In summary, workers still view the trade union not so much as defender of their rights vis-à-vis the administration as a distributor of social benefits, and they therefore see this type of organization as unnecessary in a market economy setting. This attitude of the workforce, combined with an old union structure under crisis, has changed the balance of power dramatically in favor of management and against the unions: management has gained control over enterprises while, simultaneously, the traditional trade union has significantly lost any base of power it might have had.[36] Even strikes organized by the traditional trade unions are arranged with the permission of the enterprise director.[37]

More to the point, however, the continuation (albeit in a different form) of paternalistic relations at the enterprise level suggests a possible explanation for the few independent trade unions that have arisen since 1989 and for the weakening of FNPR as branch-level trade unions fight for their rights within the federation (refusing, for example, to pay dues to the federation's central soviet) or, as in the case of GMPR, officially declare their independence. A study completed in 1992 points to the reasons why.[38] It examines the reaction of the steelworkers to the miners' strikes and the emergence of NPG. Clearly, the two groups of workers failed to build an intersectoral alliance in 1990; they built neither a coherent regional strategy nor a meaningful solidarity. The reason for this separation of interests included the prevalence of paternalism and mutual dependence at the workplace. This institution prevented intersectoral (or interoccupational) cooperation because the nature and strength of the steelworkers' dependence on a paternalistic employer differed greatly from that of the miners. In other words, the levels of dependence differed across branches of industry and thereby helped to define a worker's interests as tied to his or her branch of industry. In this case study, the steelworkers saw the costs of striking as significantly higher than did the miners; at stake were many more paternalistic benefits. One may therefore expect that as the system of paternalism breaks down under increasing pressure from the transition and as FNPR continues to fail to meet the needs of its member trade unions, the historical experience of the Soviet system will naturally lead to unions based on sectoral independence.[39] The ways in which union leaders perceive their interests and formulate their goals are, in part, influenced by the very system under which they have lived for so many years. GMPR, for example, followed such an approach in its struggle to break away from FNPR. One of its main points of disagreement with the FNPR leadership concerned branch-level control of the social services fund.[40] Advocates of branch unionism, however, must confront another factor—the growing trend toward regionalization—as they attempt to redesign labor institutions and to organize workers. This factor is outlined in the following two sections.

LEGACIES OF THE *PERESTROIKA* PERIOD: THE RISE OF REGIONALISM

The desire to limit outside control found expression not only at the level of the enterprise but also at the level of the region. Beginning in the *perestroika* period, as political power began to shift from the center to the regions, the regions began to more actively participate in the formulation and implementation of economic policy. This was most evident during the first stage of privatization.[41] Regional control over the implementation of the government's plan ensured that regional elites would be actively involved in economic decisions at the enterprise level.[42] This control thereby provided the means by which local authorities could minimize the risks associated with the privatization program—the risks of loss of control over local resources, of high local unemployment, and of outsiders gaining control over regional property.

In particular, authorities in the regions influenced the outcome of the first stage of privatization in two ways. First, the balance of power between the Committees on State Property (which existed at the central, regional-provincial, and local levels and which were organized in a strictly "vertical" hierarchical structure) and the regional-local Property Funds (which reported to the appropriate soviet and which consisted mostly of regional elites) clearly shifted in favor of the Property Funds.[43] The Property Funds gained real control over the property and resources being privatized in their respective areas; they effectively established a presence in enterprise management by maintaining 20 percent of the enterprise's voting shares and by using those shares to influence, if not outright choose, members for the board of directors of local enterprises.[44] Second, voucher auctions were by and large a regional affair: absent were both national auctions and an effective mechanism for the exchange of information across regions. In addition, the amount of enterprise capital that was actually auctioned remained less than 25 percent, and "open" auctions were easily transformed into "closed" ones when local authorities disallowed bidding by the public and/or individuals from outside the region.[45]

Regional authorities have used other measures as well to influence economic outcomes and to enforce a more regional approach to resolving economic problems. In essence, their efforts amount to a "restructuring of economic space" and to growing "regional protectionism."[46] The more formal measures include regional associations, the most prominent being the Siberian Agreement, and the formation of regionally based financial-industrial groups.[47] The Siberian Agreement, signed by six Siberian oblasts, initiated a formal approach to economic bargaining on behalf of a group of regions: Siberian cooperation was seen as a vehicle through which collective Siberian interests could be defended vis-à-vis the center.[48] At the base of such cooperation is a strong sense of regional, communal identity combined with a feeling of being exploited by Moscow. A good example of this combination is the Siberian oblast of Kemerovo, in which NPG maintains a strong following and in which the miners fought for regional self-management of resources and control over export revenues from regionally based economic activity during the first wave of strikes in 1989–90. Well-organized and strong regional structures in Kemerovo, moreover, make such a policy sustainable.[49] Other, less formal and more ad hoc measures have included the refusal to surrender federal taxes to the center, as a way to secure greater control over resources. Both types of measures, along with the active role played by regional authorities in privatization, suggest that the level at which decisions are made, policy is implemented, and more generally, a group's interests are represented, has clearly shifted.

INDUSTRIAL ADJUSTMENTS IN THE POST-COMMUNIST PERIOD: STRENGTHENING REGIONALISM

In addition to the efforts of regional authorities, the post-Communist industrial restructuring may indirectly reinforce the trend toward regionalization. Restructuring will have a differential impact on the various regions in part because of the industrial strategy used during the Soviet period. In this way, it may lead to a strengthening of regionalism. To understand this effect, first consider the industrial structure inherited from the Soviets: the secondary sector had played a dominant role (as measured by employment shares) until the 1980s, and within that sector heavy industry was emphasized, leading to what one author described as a "pronounced development of the military-industrial complex."[50] This pattern of industrial activity differed from that observed in most industrialized countries during the same time period. First, the tertiary sector became dominant rather late in the Soviet case, and second, when it did overtake the employment share of the secondary sector, its dominance was relatively slight.[51] Therefore, one would expect the transition to a market economy in Russia to include a significant change in the sectoral composition of GDP, namely a shift away from heavy industry and toward light industry and an increase in services relative to the industrial sector. Examining data from the early transitional period, one indeed finds industrial decline in Russia outpacing the GDP decline, the hardest-hit industries being fuels, metallurgy, and chemicals. Metallurgy's decline in the first years of the transition was three times greater than the all-industry decline in Russia.[52]

Furthermore, not only the sectoral composition of Soviet GDP but also the geographic concentration of production and regional specialization differed from that observed in industrialized market economies. The Soviet model of development and industrialization yielded "monopolism": the policy of production specialization in large enterprises. As a result, the output profile of many industrial enterprises was quite narrow in comparison with that of firms in similar industries in market economies.[53] For example, more than 50 percent of the output registered in 209 out of the 344 major commodity groups was produced by one enterprise; in 109 of the cases, one enterprise produced 90 percent of the output.[54] This specialization was apparent in the regional data: locational patterns in Russia indicate a very uneven distribution of output, with some oblasts both highly industrialized and highly specialized, relying on only a few production lines for a significant proportion of their output.[55] In addition to this regional specialization, some sectors tend to be spatially concentrated; 10 oblasts produce 74.4 percent of ferrous metallurgy, for example. Nonferrous metallurgy is the second-most-concentrated sector, followed by fuels, which has 57 percent of its output produced in just 10 oblasts.[56] Taking all three factors into account—the decline in heavy industry in the early transitional period, the spatial concentration of this industry, and the high levels of regional specialization—we see that regions in which metallurgy is an important component of output will be especially hard hit during the transition. More generally, the anticipated sectoral shifts discussed above should yield strong regional effects.[57] In this way, the center of gravity may shift toward the regions in terms of defining goals and approaches toward economic policy. Will a similar shift in focus, then, take place in the development and reorientation of labor institutions and/or interests?

TRADE UNION REVITALIZATION? THE MINING AND METALLURGY TRADE UNION OF RUSSIA

GMPR decided to break away from FNPR in November 1992. Its motivation for the split derived from its desire to conduct policy based on its own branch-level interests and, more specifically, to have greater control over the distribution of the social services fund for its branch industry. Moreover, the leadership's goals for the longer run included actively conducting real trade union work and creating a more democratically structured trade union. The main result of such work, in the view of the leadership, would be the establishment of collective agreements at the enterprise level and of branch-level tariff agreements, which would ensure minimum branch guarantees for wages and working conditions. Eventually, the leadership would also seek a more Western-styled social security system in which the state would provide guarantees and services; provision of benefits would not be linked to a worker's place of employment (at least not directly).[58]

GMPR is an important case study. First, with over two million members, it is the largest branch-level trade union to have split with FNPR. It represents, therefore, the possibility of a traditional trade union establishing its independence and breaking away from the protection of the old, conservative trade union federation. The importance of this type of reformation has been debated in the literature. Some experts argue quite persuasively that maintaining new, independent, representative labor institutions has been equally as difficult as reforming the old, official trade unions. They therefore conclude it is unlikely that an independent labor organization will arise and successfully challenge enterprise administration and, hence, challenge the paternalistic relations at the enterprise level.[59] Others argue that although reform within the old trade union federation may be difficult, it is necessary if an independent trade union movement and representative labor organizations are going to develop in Russia.[60] A new system of labor relations oriented toward real trade union work and establishing a framework for negotiation and mediation between labor and management cannot exclude the old trade unions. Proponents of this viewpoint argue that the large number of members in the old trade unions cannot be ignored and that a continuing decline in the standard of living works in favor of the maintenance by the old trade unions of some degree of influence.[61] For this reason, GMPR might serve as a model for reforming other traditional trade unions.

Second, GMPR represents a sector whose output declined significantly in the first two years of transition and a sector that suffered from "overdevelopment" during the Soviet period. Therefore, its transformation during the transitional period will indicate whether Russia can successfully restructure its economy. More to the point, however, GMPR can be seen as a trade union organization subject to regional tensions and, therefore, to potentially competing interests from member unions in different areas of the country. It is trying to define its interests along a sectoral line, but it is doing so in a sector that is highly spatially concentrated. As the analysis in this chapter suggests, strong regional association would result in areas where there is a high degree of specialization. This association can derive both from the fact that enterprises, in their efforts to restructure and adjust their production profiles, will respond to the particular local conditions that exist and from a strong desire for regional autonomy, often carrying with it some notion of regional self-sufficiency. If this is so, then highly specialized regions may move in diverging directions, their interests no longer so closely tied to a single sector, and as a consequence, the importance of maintaining close ties to a national trade union body may slowly diminish in those regions.

Information gathered from three union sites, each from a different region, lends support to this hypothesis.[62] The variations in regional industrial structures, in levels of regional autonomy, and in development of regional bodies appear to play a role in how the local trade unions respond to the transition, that is, how they perceive union identity and, in part, how they determine with whom to cooperate.

To illustrate this relationship, we first consider the Staleprokatny Factory in St. Petersburg. The factory is a rolling mill producing a number of items, including steel tapes, nails, screws, and wires, with one division producing consumer goods. This last division employs only one hundred individuals out of a total workforce of more than two thousand people; therefore, metallurgy remains the factory's principal concern. The production profile of the enterprise and the general process of restructuring are influenced by the regional setting. The factory is situated in a large, metropolitan area that possesses a highly diversified industrial structure. Staleprokatny has not risked significantly changing its output mix, instead relying on known technology and, to a good degree, on old business partners. In this way, it has not sought to undertake competition with other industries in the same metropolitan area—industries that have inherited an established business network from the previous Soviet period. Although it has been able to pay its workforce regularly without experiencing periods of nonpayment of wages, it remains in a relatively weak financial position, and three hundred workers who are formally on the payrolls are, in practice, on "part-time" payrolls and receive few if any wages.[63] Part-time workers in turn use informal employment in the service sector as a way to supplement their income. This safety valve—the possibility of informal employment in a large metropolitan area—affects the enterprise's response to employment issues during its restructuring and influences the relationship between trade union and management.[64] Given this regional and local setting, then, one would expect that the local trade union would maintain close ties to the national branch-level trade union organization. Its identity and agenda would remain firmly within the sectoral-branch concept of trade unionism, since the factory is situated in a highly diversified industrial region without either a strong sense of regional identity or the development of regional bodies to challenge the center.

The general picture emerging from the union site confirms this approach to trade union activity at the enterprise level. In fact, the relationship between the grassroots, local trade union, and the Moscow leadership seems to be closer than before the split with FNPR.[65] There also is interest in remaining strongly tied to the national branch union. First of all, the local union committee clearly identifies with the national leadership in Moscow and has often sought and received help from it. As the local trade union leader, Eduard Zatitsky, explained, members of the local union committee were very relieved that their national trade union organization was saved and that, through their efforts and those of the new leadership at the regional and national levels (such as Yuri Strelkov, leader of the Leningrad regional trade union committee of GMPR), they were able to reorient their union toward real trade union work and to separate its interests from those of management. This separation does not suggest, however, that the trade union has been able to establish a good working relationship with management or that it is seen as a strong partner with whom to negotiate and compromise. The administration is very powerful, and it has maintained a neopaternalistic system of labor relations. The trade union is no longer under the administration's wings, yet it remains terribly weak. The local leaders thus have received help from the central soviet on matters concerning collective agreements; for example, when they were locked in a long-drawn-out battle with the administration over whether, by law, a collective agreement had to be signed, and when they were fighting for better working conditions and for the right to continue to collect trade union dues centrally, the central council sent representatives to work with the local activists.[66]

In addition to working with the GMPR leadership in Moscow, the local leaders have looked to regional bodies to resolve issues of a specifically local or regional nature. The enterprise trade union committee has discussed the idea of forming a citywide council of trade unions and has had informal talks with other steelworks in St. Petersburg (regardless of whether the trade unions at those sites are GMPR members) to address municipal problems such as the acute housing shortage and the communal housing arrangements for workers. On balance, though, the local and regional cooperation that the factory trade union leaders have sought—including participation in the regional intertrade-union association, which includes FNPR unions—is best described as complementary to their sectoral allegiance. The local ties do not represent an alternative to working with the national GMPR leadership, nor do they function as alternative forums within which to discuss real trade union work (in the narrow, Western sense of the phrase). Rather, they serve as a place for discussion of social and more community-based issues such as housing. Allegiance to the national metallurgical trade union remains strong, since output is firmly based in this sector—thereby uniting production interests—and since the local trade union resists a purely company-based model (i.e., company unionism in which the trade union works exclusively with the enterprise administration).

In contrast to the Staleprokatny Factory, the Tulachermet Concern in Tula has a regional setting less diversified in terms of industrial and employment structures. Tula, a city of over 500,000 inhabitants, is located approximately two hundred kilometers south of Moscow, and it relies more heavily on a few important factories, including the Tulachermet Concern. The concern comprises several joint-stock companies employing eleven thousand workers, with approximately fifteen thousand employees in total. In comparison with Staleprokatny, Tulachermet responded early to the challenges of market transition: it had already converted into a joint-stock company by 1991, and it began to alter its production mix and search for new business partners, on both the supply and the purchasing sides. Furthermore, it sought to establish a regionally based financial-industrial group to assist the enterprise in its restructuring.[67] This group includes a pension fund, a medical facility, a regional industrial bank, and a machine-building factory, thereby connecting productive units to financial resources and factories that are linked to one another in the production cycle. In response to changes during the late *perestroika* and early post-Communist periods, then, the enterprise diversified its output, not only introducing new products but also moving into new areas of production. Now a significant portion of its output is exported, and 50 percent of its output is composed of consumer goods, such as gas water-heaters, vacuum cleaners, shoes, TV and VCR assembly, and intermediate goods such as cinder blocks and finished slates of marble and granite.

The regional setting helps to explain the change in output profile and the response to employment issues. First of all, enterprise restructuring has occurred in a region without a highly diversified output profile: it was possible to fill regional niches and find export markets without confronting long-established firms. This was necessary, moreover, since the region was more vulnerable in terms of unemployment and loss in income from the decline suffered by metallurgy and related industries during the first two years of post-Communist reforms. Second, the region does not have a large metropolitan area within which informal service employment can coexist with part-time, reserve work at the principal factory—at least not on a scale comparable to that offered in a city such as St. Petersburg. Lastly, labor-management relations are affected by the fact that the individual enterprise is an important local employer and that the region lacks a tradition of strong independent trade unionism. Following the analysis in this chapter, one would expect the local trade union to adopt an approach to union activity reflecting these regionally specific features. Over time, the importance of maintaining close ties to the national trade union body may then slowly diminish in this region.

There are clear signs of this approach. Tulachermet has followed a different survival and restructuring strategy, and its local trade union leaders seem to have adjusted to this change. There are indications that the local labor leaders are reorienting their attention and redefining their identity so as to diverge increasingly from the notions of identity and interests espoused by the Moscow leadership of GMPR. It was clear, for example, that among the leaders of the trade union committees at the concern, including the leader of the regional trade union committee, the GMPR split with FNPR was not important.[68] What was more important was working with the administration of the concern and working with others in the region to maintain profitability and to tackle the big problems at the local level, including maintenance of employment levels and providing summer passes to children's camps.[69] In other words, the relative importance of GMPR as a partner in comparison with the administration has decreased.

In terms of union identity, there also are indications of change. With the reorientation of production, the export of mainly nonmetallurgy products, and the growing regional business ties, metallurgy has become less important to the concern's survival. Second, union membership at Tulachermet has remained open to managers, a principle that differs from the one adopted by the GMPR leadership. In fact, one of the main goals of the central council is to remove management from union ranks.[70] Third, it is evident that Tulachermet union leaders identify with management. For example, many trade union activists described the company as a "family" in which members of individual families move between labor and management over generations and sometimes within a given generation. The aspirations of the local trade union leader, furthermore, support this interpretation. His eventual goal is to secure a position within the administration, and he continues to see trade union work as a means to that end. (These aspirations and this approach to trade union work are very different from those espoused by either Zatitsky or Strelkov.) In essence, as management responds and redirects output and as trade union leaders seek a working partnership with management, both parties are focused on other economic sectors, whose concerns, interests, and economic cycles may be very different from those of the metallurgical sector. Moreover, as documented in the literature on trade union structures in advanced market economies, these lower-level partnerships can call into question the role and function (and power) of the more centralized union structures. Company partnerships (or productivity coalitions, in the case of some market economies) become the forums within which problems are resolved, and consequently they challenge the model of branch trade unionism. Although the system of labor relations has yet to take a permanent form, elements of this model are clearly emerging at Tulachermet.

The third site, Zapsib (Western Siberian) Metallurgical Combinat in Novokuznetsk, Kemerovo oblast, represents the site with the strongest regional elements: well-organized regional structures, as discussed above in the Siberian Agreement, and a clear sense of regional identity and the role it should play. Kemerovo oblast is also a highly industrialized and specialized region. For this reason, during the early post-Communist period it faced similar opportunities to diversify production as did Tulachermet, but also similar vulnerabilities in terms of income and employment loss. Furthermore, it is an area that possesses both a strong desire for greater autonomy and control over regional resources and a strong independent trade union tradition, with NPG being prominent in the region since 1989. Thus, it is not surprising that Zapsib's response to the transition reveals a strong regional focus with growing diversification of production. As a very important employer in Novokuznetsk (over thirty thousand people are employed in the factory), Zapsib has responded to the post-Communist production decline as would a factory running a "company town." It has taken over the former responsibilities of the state, suggesting a scenario not too different from the neopaternalism described above. This is most obvious in its attempt to maintain employment levels. It has built a number of additional plants to provide alternative employment opportunities and to diversify output: a mechanical bakery, a brewery, and a clothing factory that specializes in leather shoes. One therefore would expect the local trade union to adjust its strategy; its identity and agenda would no longer necessarily remain firmly within the sectoral-branch concept of trade unionism, at least not without a strong commitment to regional decision-making.

The evidence suggests that such an adjustment has occurred in the local trade union's approach to union activity and in its commitment to the national GMPR leadership. First of all, the local trade union committee has illustrated its ability to do battle with the administration and to come away from such battles with a greater sense of its role as defender of labor's rights. Moreover, the battles that it has won at the enterprise level have been fought without significant help and assistance from Moscow, and thus it exhibits more independence than most other GMPR local trade union committees.[71] In comparison with the other two case studies, Zapsib, unlike Tulachermet, has not adopted a "cooperative" model to labor relations at the enterprise level, and it has more effectively defended its interests than has the local trade union committee at Staleprokatny. In addition, Zapsib has adjusted its approach to trade union relations. It has adopted a much more decentralized approach in which its relationship to the center is less important than its relationships at the regional level. Although it has a strained relationship with the GMPR leadership in Moscow,[72] the local trade union committee has built and continues to maintain good regional relations with the official (FNPR) oil, coal, and chemical trade unions, irrespective of GMPR's split from FNPR in late 1992. The local trade union committee continues to exhibit cooperation in their regional, intertrade-union association.[73] In summary, it appears that the local trade union's ties and allegiance to the national GMPR organization are relatively weak and continue to weaken.[74]

CONCLUSION

The absence of a stable system of labor relations, including the creation of a set of institutions capable of independently representing labor's interests, has been widely documented. Scholars have offered a number of reasons for this failure, and in evaluating labor's response to the challenges of the transitional period, they have focused their attention on the opportunities for labor to achieve sectoral independence in its institutions (e.g., NPG). They have noted that the more successful independent trade unions are the ones that represent workers in a single branch or occupation, the pilots' union being a prime example. This case study, however, illustrates that against the backdrop of growing regionalism in Russia and the force it exerts, sustaining a coherent, effective institution based on the principle of branch unionism can be difficult. That is, the trend toward regionalization must be acknowledged if one is to understand better the lack of strong, independent labor organizations in Russia. The branch union approach as exemplified by GMPR can give rise to a number of tensions. In the case of GMPR, the leadership is attempting to build an independent, branch-level trade union within a branch of industry that is highly geographically concentrated. As the regions try to tackle local economic problems, the policies pursued suggest a growing internal contradiction for GMPR. Furthermore, the communal interests of enterprise directors, as seen in the mutual support of an "essential few" in new business dealings,[75] underpin a regional solution to economic problems, as evidenced by the regionally based financial-industrial groups.

Moreover, such tensions are visible not only in GMPR but also in other independent trade unions, including the pilots', air traffic controllers', and NPG unions. Essentially, tensions arise as Russia restructures its economic space; consequently, a gap opens up between the national leadership and the regional organizations of different trade unions. NPG is a good example of this phenomenon. As one expert explains, NPG lost touch with its members at the regional level in a matter of only a couple of years. In recognition of this failure, NPG has adopted a new strategy: the national leadership will spend a year traveling around the country to reacquaint the center with the specific concerns of the various regions in which NPG has membership organizations.[76] The transport and maritime workers (pilots, air traffic controllers, railroad drivers, seafarers, dockers) likewise must meet the same challenge. They helped to form a new Confederation of Labor in April 1995.[77] From the outset, however, tensions between the national leadership of these unions and some of their regional organizations have been present.[78] Members in regions outside the major metropolitan areas feel as though they are on their own and their interests are not represented; in response, they sometimes look to local structures to solve their problems. Therefore, founding members of the Confederation of Labor must resolve this problem of diverging interests if the confederation is going to be an organization in practice and not just on paper and if it wants to have any claim to representing member associations.

Finally, this chapter, in acknowledging the importance of regionalism, supports the conclusions reached in previous studies: many uncertainties remain as to whether Russia will establish, in the long run, a stable set of institutions for labor representation, for resolution of conflicts in the workplace, and in general, for the negotiation, implementation, and monitoring of some system of collective bargaining agreements. This chapter highlights just one of the uncertainties: labor's response to the trend toward regionalization. Will labor leaders successfully find ways to incorporate distinct regional concerns? In an effort to create a more active membership, will they rethink the principles around which labor organizes? Whereas these tensions can be seen as a normal part of the pluralization of public life, they present a difficult challenge for fledgling independent trade unions. In Western market economies, which already possess effective institutions for conflict resolution and have a history of relatively well-functioning trade union and labor relations systems, tensions have arisen and demands for changing trade union bargaining structures and trade union identity (including interests and agenda) have been made. In some cases, these tensions have led (or are leading) to resolution involving the decentralization of decision-making, including the bargaining and negotiation of important work conditions at a lower level. In the process of making these changes, the role of branch-level trade unionism remains uncertain in a number of countries. In the case of Russia, trade unions face a more difficult task for two reasons: first, they face not only the pressures of enterprise restructuring in terms of work organization and output profile, and the challenges those represent for trade union power and identity, but also the other "regionalization" pressures outlined in this chapter; and second, they must acknowledge the fact that enterprise restructuring alone has relatively strong regional effects in a country characterized by a high level of regional specialization and production concentration. Thus, the ability of trade unions to respond effectively to regional interests is one factor, among many, that will help determine whether, in the long run, a stable system of labor relations will emerge in Russia.

NOTES

Research for this paper was supported by a grant from the International Research and Exchanges Board, with funds provided by the U.S. Department of State (Title VIII) and the National Endowment for the Humanities. None of these organizations are responsible for the views expressed. The author would like to thank Lisa Baglione for her work on this joint project and Nana Tsikhelashvili and the members of the Free Trade Union Institute in Moscow for their assistance.

1. See Linda J. Cook, "Russia's Labor Relations: Consolidation or Disintegration?" in Douglas W. Blum, ed., *Russia's Future: Consolidation or Disintegration?* (Boulder, Colo.: Westview Press, 1994); Linda J. Cook, "Workers in the Russian Federation: Responses to the Post-Communist Transition, 1989–1993," *Communist and Post-Communist Studies* 28 (1995): 13–42; Leonid A. Gordon, "Russia on the Road to New Industrial Relations: From Unipartite Commands to Tripartite Partnership via Bipartite Conflicts and Bargaining," in Bertram Silverman et al., eds., *Double Shift: Transforming Work in Post-Industrialist Societies* (Armonk, N.Y.: M. E. Sharpe, 1993).

2. An attempt to form such a confederation occurred in the wake of the miners' strikes in the city of Novokuznetsk in 1990. For a discussion of this attempt and the failed outcome, see Peter Rutland, "Labor Unrest and Movements in 1989 and 1990," *Soviet Economy* 6 (1990): 345–84. A new Confederation of Labor was founded on April 12, 1995. It is too early to determine whether this confederation will achieve greater success, but the early signs are not positive. In fact, within the first year of operation, this confederation split into two competing confederations. Interview with Scott Reynolds, director of the Free Trade Union Institute, Moscow, June 29, 1996.

3. Interview with Yakov Berger, head of the Russian-American Foundation for the Research and Training of Free Trade Unions, Moscow, June 1994.
4. See a number of articles in *Delo*. This is a relatively new Russian newspaper that began operations in October 1992. It is devoted to various labor and social issues, and it describes itself as a newspaper reporting on the social partnership among representatives of government, employers, and workers. In terms of the shift of power within FNPR, the branch-level organizations at the regional level appear to have gained at the expense of the central soviet. Interview with Reynolds, June 29, 1996.
5. See Galina A. Monusova, "Profsoyuzy na Promyshlennykh Predpriyatiyakh: Realii Perekhodnova Perioda," unpublished manuscript, 1993.
6. See Yuri Milovidov, "Profsoyuznyi Dvizhenie v Rossii: Istoriya, Sovremenost' i Perspectivy Razvitiya," *Ekonomika i Stroitel'stva* (August 1993), pp. 5–11.
7. Rutland, "Labor Unrest and Movements," commented on this possibility in the wake of the coal miners' strikes in 1989 and 1990. He concluded that the possibilities were remote, due to the political and economic chaos present at that time. Vadim Borisov, Peter Fairbrother, and Simon Clarke, "Is There Room for an Independent Trade Unionism in Russia? Trade Unionism in the Russian Aviation Industry," *British Journal of Industrial Relations* 32 (1994): 359–78, suggest once again that this possibility is highly unlikely. In their case study of the independent airline pilots' and the air traffic controllers' unions, they point to the desire on the part of the pilots, one of the strongest independent trade unions besides NPG, to maintain their "labor aristocracy," and they point also to the defeat of the air traffic controllers at the combined hands of the administration and the pilots' union. In other cases, different factors explain defeat, factors including the weakness—and therefore openness to victimization by the administration—of new, independent trade unions.
8. See Simon Clarke, Peter Fairbrother, Michael Burawoy, and Pavel Krotov, *What about the Workers? Workers and the Transition to Capitalism in Russia* (New York: Verso, 1993); Borisov, Fairbrother, and Clarke, "Is There Room?"; Mark Kramer, "Blue-Collar Workers and the Post-Communist Transitions in Poland, Russia, and Ukraine," *Communist and Post-Communist Studies* 28 (1995): 3–11; and interview with Thomas Bradley, former head of the Free Trade Union Institute, Moscow, July 1993.
9. See Kramer, "Blue-Collar Workers," pp. 8–9, for a discussion of the two views.
10. See Stephen Crowley, "Barriers to Collective Action: Steelworkers and Mutual Dependence in the Former Soviet Union," *World Politics* 46 (1994): 594. Simon Clarke and Peter Fairbrother, "Post-Communism and the Emergence of Industrial Relations in the Workplace," in Richard Hyman and Anthony Ferner, eds., *New Frontiers in European Industrial Relations* (Oxford: Blackwell, 1994), p. 373, characterize workplace paternalism as a system in which enterprises "provide workers with a range of social and welfare benefits and scarce consumption goods."
11. See Clarke and Fairbrother, "Post-Communism and the Emergence of Industrial Relations."

12. See Simon Clarke, Peter Fairbrother, Vadim Borisov, and Petr Bizyukov, "The Privatization of Industrial Enterprises in Russia: Four Case-studies," *Europe-Asia Studies* 46 (1994): 179–214.
13. See Oleg Kharkhordin and Theodore P. Gerber, "Russian Directors' Business Ethic: A Study of Industrial Enterprises in St. Petersburg, 1993," *Europe-Asia Studies* 46 (1994): 1075–107.
14. For an exposition of the argument that paternalism and mutual dependence vary across industries, see Crowley, "Barriers to Collective Action." As the author explains: "The distribution of these goods and services is also highly uneven between industries. . . . In some industries and enterprises workers have been better provided for, while in others, such as coal mining, workers have had less to lose" (p. 596).
15. The chairman of the trade union's central council, Boris Misnik, led the fight to leave FNPR. The union first threatened to leave FNPR in June 1992, and finally, in November 1992 at a plenum session of FNPR, the union decided to leave the official trade union federation.
16. Interview with Boris Misnik, Moscow, June 1994.
17. For a discussion of those and related issues, see James Hughes, "Regionalism in Russia: The Rise and Fall of Siberian Agreement," *Europe-Asia Studies* 46 (1994): 1133–61, and Peter Kirkow, "Regional Politics and Market Reform in Russia: The Case of the Altai," *Europe-Asia Studies* 46 (1994): 1163–87.
18. Darrell Slider, "Privatization in Russia's Regions," *Post-Soviet Affairs* 10 (October-December 1994).
19. See Andrei I. Treyvish, Kavita K. Pandit, and Andrew R. Bond, "Macrostructural Employment Shifts and Urbanization in the Former USSR: An International Perspective," *Post-Soviet Geography* 34 (1993): 157–71.
20. The service sector may grow rapidly because the vast majority of operating joint ventures in Russia have been in services. With a relatively capital-scarce Russian economy, this development should influence the development of this sector.
21. Scott Thomas and Heidi Kroll, "The Political Economy of Privatization in Russia," *Communist Economies and Economic Transformation* 5 (1993), and Clarke et al., *What about the Workers?* Both of these works explain the expansion of enterprise power during the *perestroika* period and the consequences of it for the transitional period (e.g., how it helped to shape enterprise behavior and how its legacy influenced the dynamics of transition). See also Alexander S. Bim, Derek C. Jones, and Thomas E. Weisskopf, "Hybrid Forms of Enterprise Organization in the former USSR and the Russian Federation," *Comparative Economic Studies* 35 (spring 1993).
22. See Clarke et al., *What about the Workers?*
23. Michael Burawoy and Kathryn Hendley, "Between Perestroika and Privatization: Divided Strategies and Political Crisis in a Soviet Enterprise," *Soviet Studies* 44 (1992), provide an excellent case study of this process. They follow the events in four different shops of a Moscow state enterprise: the choice of organizational setup, the operations in each of the four, and the often conflicting interests that arise within one state enterprise.

24. Peter Rutland, "Privatization in Russia: One Step Forward, Two Steps Back?" *Europe-Asia Studies* 46 (1994): 1109–31, for example, argues that privatization was not "revolutionary"; rather, it evolved from the policy changes first introduced in the late 1980s.
25. Pekka Sutela, "Insider Privatization in Russia: Speculations on Systemic Change," *Europe-Asia Studies* 46 (1994), discusses management behavior during this period.
26. Over 70 percent of enterprises participating in privatization auctions had chosen variant #2 by February 1993. See Thomas and Kroll, "Privatization in Russia." More recent estimates indicate that 75 percent of participating enterprises chose variant #2.
27. The remaining shares were both (1) distributed between federal and local authorities and (2) sold for vouchers (and sometimes cash), with insiders (i.e., enterprise employees) purchasing additional shares at the time of open auction. See Thomas and Kroll, "Privatization in Russia," and *PlanEcon Report* 9 (December 19, 1993).
28. See Clarke and Fairbrother, "Post-Communism and the Emergence of Industrial Relations," p. 375.
29. Ibid., p. 376.
30. For a description of the "dual functions" of the official trade unions, see Blair Ruble, *Soviet Trade Unions* (Oxford: Oxford University Press, 1981).
31. See Clarke et al., *What about the Workers?* and Borisov, Fairbrother, and Clarke, "Is There Room?" The desire of the old trade unions to subordinate the workers to both management and the party was achieved in two ways. First, the enterprise boss was typically the union leader at the workplace, and second, the union organizations were a "cemetery for Party cadres." (This characterization is taken from Clarke et al., *What about the Workers?* pp. 97–98, and is made by Vladimir Kuzmenok, former deputy chairman of the General Confederation of Trade Unions, of which FNPR was a member until the confederation's demise in late 1991.) Also, interview with Bradley, July 1993, for a description of how the old trade unions remained a bastion of the party apparatus.
32. This identification with management went deeper, though. As one author argues, the worker's position was one of "general helplessness and defenselessness . . . before the administrative apparatus," and hence "non-economic coercion of labor was widespread under Soviet-type socialism." Andrei Kuznetsov, "Economic Reforms in Russia: Enterprise Behavior as an Impediment to Change," *Europe-Asia Studies* 46 (1994). D. A. Semenov further explains that the salaries of trade union leaders were always expressed as a percentage of the enterprise director's salary. Interview with D. A. Semenov, deputy chairman of Sotsprof, Moscow, June 1994.
33. See Milovidov, "Profsoyuznyi Dvizhenie v Rossii."
34. See Clarke and Fairbrother, "Post-Communism and the Emergence of Industrial Relations," p. 378. As one expert explains: "It is worth it for the administration . . . to take away from trade union committees the distribution functions, as the bankruptcy of the majority of trade union organiza-

tions in the literal and figurative sense will follow shortly thereafter. Therefore, it is not surprising that in the case of the appearance of collective labor conflicts, trade union committees frequently stand on the side of the administration." See Milovidov, "Profsoyuznyi Dvizhenie v Rossii," and "'Starye i Novye' Profsoyuzy: Kto voidet v rynok?" *Rossiiskii Stroitel'* (1994): 6.

35. Cook, "Workers in the Russian Federation," and interview with Scott Reynolds, director of the Free Trade Union Institute, Moscow, June 1994. It is questionable, however, whether this change in government policy has had any concrete effects on the way distribution of social services is carried out in practice.
36. See Clarke et al., *What about the Workers?*; Clarke and Fairbrother, "Post-Communism and the Emergence of Industrial Relations"; and Kuznetsov, "Economic Reforms in Russia."
37. See various issues of *Delo*.
38. Crowley, "Barriers to Collective Action."
39. Tensions during the transition have strained the paternalistic system of labor relations. From the workers' side, tensions develop between cadre workers (core production, highly skilled workers), who are in relatively strong demand and therefore can demand higher wages, and other workers, who have fewer options and would like to preserve the collective distribution of goods and services through nonmarket channels at the place of production. From the other side, financial pressures will force management to seek another model of relations. Therefore, the "rhetoric of conscience and care" may be something that management will increasingly abandon. See Clarke and Fairbrother, "Post-Communism and the Emergence of Industrial Relations."
40. As the leader of GMPR, Boris Misnik, explained, an important reason for leaving FNPR was its desire to defend and lobby for its branch-level interests. Interview with Misnik, June 1994.
41. See Slider, "Privatization in Russia's Regions." The discussion in the following paragraph is based largely on his study.
42. In terms of regional versus central power, some authors have argued that the balance of power has tilted more recently in favor of the center, especially after October 1993. For an example of this argument, see Jeffrey Hahn, "Latest Developments in Russian Local Government," mimeograph, March 1995.
43. Slider, "Privatization in Russia's Regions."
44. By October 1993 a majority of Property Funds engaged in such activity. Ibid., p. 387.
45. Ibid., pp. 374–75. The 25 percent figure was as of August 1993.
46. See Hughes, "Regionalism in Russia."
47. For a discussion of financial-industrial groups, see Irina Starodubrovskaya, "Financial-industrial Groups: Illusions and Reality," *Communist Economies and Economic Transformation* 7 (1995): 5–19, and Larisa Gorbatova, "Formation of Connections between Finance and Industry in Russia: Basic Stages and Forms," *Communist Economies and Economic Transformation* 7 (1995): 21–34.

48. Hughes, "Regionalism in Russia," pp. 1134–35. The six oblasts were Kemerovo, Novosibirsk, Tomsk, Tyumen, Altai, and Krasnoyarsk. The agreement was signed in November 1990.
49. Rutland, "Labor Unrest and Movements."
50. See Treyvish, Pandit, and Bond, "Macrostructural Employment Shifts," p. 167.
51. Ibid., pp. 158–60. There is a difference among the market economies, though, in terms of level, duration, and time period of secondary-sector dominance. For example, the experiences of the United States and Japan are much different from that of Western Europe.
52. See Matthew Sagers, "Regional Industrial Structures and Economic Prospects," *Post-Soviet Geography* 33 (1992): 492. After the first two years, the textile and other "feminine" industries have experienced the greatest percentage decline in output.
53. See Irina Starodubrovskaya, "The Nature of Monopoly and Barriers to Entry in Russia," *Communist Economies and Economic Transformation* 6 (1994): 3–18.
54. See Matthew Sagers, Tim Heleniak, and John Dunlop, "High Concentration of Production of Certain Product Lines at Particular Plants," *Soviet Geography* (1991), p. 190.
55. See Sagers, "Regional Industrial Structures," p. 498.
56. Ibid., pp. 510–11.
57. As one study explains, "What is also clear is that given the low diversification of most areas in terms of industrial structures (high degree of dependence on a single sector or economic activity) that economic polarization between distressed and prosperous areas is going to be high." See ibid., p. 512.
58. Misnik talked about changing to a new system of social security over the next five years. New legislation governing the social security system was to be considered in 1996. Interview with Misnik, Moscow, July 1995. A discussion of the leadership's goals and the reasons underlying the union's split with FNPR are given in interviews with Misnik in Moscow, June 1994, and in New York City, September 1994.
59. See Clarke and Fairbrother, "Post-Communism and the Emergence of Industrial Relations," p. 389.
60. See, for example, Milovidov, "Profsoyuznyi Dvizhenie v Rossii."
61. Interview with Yuri Milovidov, Moscow, June 1994, and also interview with Thomas Bradley, New Castle, Delaware, September 1994.
62. Two sites, Staleprokatny Factory in St. Petersburg and Tulachermet Concern in Tula, were visited in June and July 1995, and the information collected on the third site, Zapsib Metallurgical Combinat in Novokuznetsk, was gathered in the summer of 1994 through two sets of interviews (one in Moscow and the second in New York City) with the trade union leadership.
63. For all intents and purposes, they are on unpaid leave. Interview with Yuri Strelkov, leader of the Leningrad regional trade union committee, St. Petersburg, June 1995.
64. Interview with Eduard Zatitsky, trade union leader at Staleprokatny Factory, St. Petersburg, June 1995.
65. One must be careful, however, not to overstate the closeness of this rela-

tionship or the level of satisfaction felt by the local activists. Rather, what is important for the present analysis is the direction of change in center-local relations and not the absolute level of cooperation between them.
66. Interview with Zatitsky, June 1995.
67. The marketing director of the concern explained to the author how the concern would not have survived without the business ties provided by the financial-industrial group. Interview with Mark Tseitlin, Tula, July 1995.
68. One of the shop trade union leaders did mention, however, that they received more information from the central soviet in Moscow after the split and that he believed the split was good. Interview with Anatoly Sadomov, Tula, July 1995.
69. Interview with Viktor Sadomov, leader of both the Tulachermet trade union council and the Tula regional trade union committee. Also, interviews with a number of trade union leaders of various shops at Tulachermet, Tula, July 1995.
70. Interview with Misnik, July 1995.
71. Ibid.
72. It is unclear whether this relationship is more strained now than it was three years ago. Crowley, "Barriers to Collective Action," mentions that the local trade unions believed that what happened in Moscow (e.g., the GMPR split with FNPR in 1992) was really of very little concern to them and was not terribly important in terms of how they conducted business.
73. Interview with Misnik, June 1994 and September 1994.
74. The relationship between the local GMPR leader in Lipetsk and the Moscow leadership suggests another case in which both regional concerns and the factory response to the transitional period are coming into conflict with branch unionism. The local trade union leader argues that there is very little coordination or help from Moscow; the working relationship is quite distant at best. Furthermore, the Lipetsk factory, in which forty thousand people work, has followed a route similar to that of Tulachermet and Zapsib. It has remained "profitable" as it has diversified output; the factory now runs a brewery, zoo, vacation camps, and resorts, along with its metallurgical production. So, as in the other cases, the importance of metallurgy to the survival of the firm is diminishing, and the firm is taking on the social functions of the state and establishing a type of company town. Interview with Christine Mulligan, Education Director, Russian-American Foundation for Trade Union Research and Education, and Elena Sheveleva, Assistant Education Director, Russian-American Foundation for Trade Union Research and Education, Moscow, July 1995.
75. See Kharkhordin and Gerber, "Russian Directors' Business Ethic," for a discussion of the concept of the "essential few."
76. Interview with Mulligan and Sheveleva, July 1995. They noted that this distance between the leadership and the rank and file helps to explain (although it is just one of many factors) why workers have become more pessimistic and more withdrawn and fearful over the last year.
77. The independent trade unions of pilots, railroad drivers, air traffic controllers, seafarers, and dockers and NPG formed the Confederation of Labor

on April 12, 1995. It took eight months to organize, one of the key problems being the tension between the national leadership of the unions, who believe the "vertically" organized unions should make all the important decisions, and the regional structures of some of the unions, who favor more "horizontal" forms of cooperation and decision-making. Interview with Scott Reynolds, director of the Free Trade Union Institute, Moscow, July 1995. Reynolds commented on this tension and explained that he feels that the center of gravity in the confederation should be at the regional level. He believes that the more broad-based regional structures of the free trade unions, including some of the Sotsprof regional associations, will become more important in the future as they are able to respond better to the specific concerns of the individual trade unions in their respective areas.

78. Interview with Reynolds, July 1995. These regional tensions may also be an important factor underlying the split of the new confederation into two competing bodies (see note 2, above).

7

The Regionalization of Russia's Economy and Its Impact on the Environment and Natural Resources

D. J. Peterson

Western observers have extensively documented the Russian Federation's environmental problems that were wrought by seven decades of Soviet central planning and development.[1] But since the nation embarked on reforms in 1991, market liberalization, "destatification" of the economy, and political decentralization have created new forces affecting the state of Russia's natural landscape. One of the most striking outcomes of these processes has been the economic, social, political, and—I would add—environmental regionalization of Russia. In order to understand the forces shaping regional environment and natural resources outcomes, we need to explore the patterns of economic change in the post-Soviet reform era.[2]

Despite political and economic uncertainty and institutional impediments, economic reform is moving ahead, forcing a radical restructuring of the Russian economy—whether intended by politicians or not. Several factors are driving the restructuring process: (1) a decline in state orders for industrial production, most importantly for defense needs; (2) a reduction in state-backed capital investment; (3) a reduction and reorientation of government subsidies; and (4) an integration of the Russian economy into the global economy.

In addition to the impact on macroeconomic conditions—the focus of most economists' attention—these changes have exerted a substantial impact on the health of individual sectors of the economy. Most important, the Russian economy is undergoing a transition toward a postindustrial model, characterized by a reduced emphasis on industrial production and the rise of services and mass consumerism, a trend that has special significance for cities. Second, over the short to medium term, the fate of Russia's economy at the regional level can be placed on a continuum: those regions characterized by uniform primary goods (e.g., materials) production will fare best overall, whereas those regions dominated by firms producing finished goods will perform most poorly.

Since Russia's industries tend to be spatially concentrated, the strong sectoral orientation of many regions means economic reform is playing out differently across the federation.[3] Variation in structural adjustment at the regional level is further influenced by the Russian Federation's large size. The closer a region is to the geographic periphery (i.e., to export markets), the greater is its ability to sell its produce on international markets, especially those regions purveying lower-value bulk commodities. Finally, economic development and population growth within Russia should be shifting southward, to regions with a more favorable climate.

Given these conditions, this chapter will examine the nexus between sectoral adjustment to structural economic change and regional environmental and natural resources issues.[4] Because of the immensity of the Russian Federation and the diversity of its regions, the present study does not attempt to describe the situation in each and every part of the country. Rather, its basic arguments are illustrated with respect to the following regions currently of major importance in Russia's economic transition: (1) the Far East and eastern Siberia, characterized by raw materials production and a trade orientation toward Pacific Rim markets; (2) central and northern European Russia, where the economy features a blend of light manufacturing, forest products, and agriculture as well as the diversified metropolitan economies of Moscow and St. Petersburg; (3) the traditional heavy industry heartland of the Ural Mountains and southern Siberia; and (4) southern European Russia, a region noted for its agriculture and mild climate. The discussion begins with a general overview of some important economic, environmental, and demographic trends to provide a framework for the regional coverage that follows.

OVERVIEW OF ECONOMIC TRENDS

According to official statistics, industrial output in Russia declined by almost 50 percent from 1989 to 1994. A breakdown of output data by sector is presented in table 7.1. These figures probably overstate the actual decline, but the important issue is the relative declines registered by individual sectors.[5]

By 1995, a pattern of restructuring had become evident. Although the economic downturn had affected all sectors, energy and agriculture had

Table 7.1
DECLINE IN LEVEL OF PHYSICAL OUTPUT OF SELECTED SECTORS IN 1994 AS PERCENT OF 1990 OUTPUT

Sector	1994/1990 (Percent)
Light industry	21.2
Machinery	31.5
Timber and forestry products	35.1
Construction materials	43.9
Chemicals and petroleum processing	44.9
Food processing	51.6
Ferrous metals	52.5
Nonferrous metals	54.2
Fuel and energy	70.7
Agriculture	76.4

Source: *Kommersant,* no.1 (1995), p. 21; Russian Federation State Committee for Statistics, *Sotsial'no-ekonomicheskoe polozhenie Rossii 1994 g.* (Moscow, 1995), pp. 223–30.

fared relatively better. The hardest-hit performers were light industry (e.g., consumer goods) and machinery—the decline in the former resulting from the increased availability of cheap imports and the drop in the latter caused by a sharp reduction in capital investment. Conversely, the retail and service sector has recovered in recent years: in 1995, retail sales exceeded their 1989 level in real terms.[6]

In addition, a large share of Russia's primary products output has been diverted from domestic to global markets, a trend that strengthened in 1994 and braked the decline in output of many sectors.[7] In 1994, for example, the performance of nonferrous and ferrous metals producers improved in relation to the rest of the industrial economy as a result of sharp increases in exports. Exports of timber, pulp, paper, and chemicals also accelerated (see table 7.2). In sum, a realignment of the Russian economy away from manufacturing and toward the increasing dominance of the service sector, agriculture, and natural resources development has been occurring, facilitated by greater integration into the world economy.

Despite the sharp downturn in domestic output, the consequent environmental impact has been mixed. Air pollution emissions from stationary sources declined by 27 percent between 1990 and 1993, a decline that was significantly less than the fall in industrial output reported during this period. From 1991 to 1993 the volume of suspended solids discharged in wastewater decreased by a similar amount. The total amount of discharged wastewater that did not comply with water pollution

Table 7.2
INCREASE IN SELECTED EXPORTS BY VOLUME, 1992–1994

Product	Percent
Newsprint	403
Copper	280
Plywood	231
Cellulose pulp	228
Aluminum	220
Electricity	199
Hewn timber	193
Pig iron	176
Ammonia	158
Frozen fish	154
Crude oil	134
Natural gas	124

Source: Russian Federation State Committee for Statistics, *Sotsial'no-ekonomicheskoe polozhenie Rossii 1994 g.* (Moscow, 1995), p. 303.

regulations, however, remained unchanged over this period. In short, although the gross impact on the environment has decreased significantly, the Russian economy has become *more* pollution intensive.[8]

There are several reasons why the decrease in emissions has not kept pace with the decline in production. First, and most important, enterprises, many fighting for their economic survival, have cut spending on their pollution-control efforts. Second, production lines have been working below design capacity, thereby reducing efficiency. Frequent disruptions of continuous processes (such as refining and smelting) have increased emissions. Third, pollution derived from personal consumption, such as automobile emissions and generation of solid waste, is rapidly increasing as a result of the increasing consumer orientation of the Russian economy and is offsetting the environmental gains from the decline in industrial output. Fourth, increases in specific types of pollution reflect the reduction of public funding and/or the growth in obsolescence of infrastructure. The lack of an improvement in wastewater discharges, for example, reflects the poor state of municipal sewage-treatment systems. During the Soviet era, municipal sanitation services frequently were funded by the central government and were provided by local enterprises free of charge. With economic and political decentralization, federal funding no longer exists, and enterprises have been eager to shed the costly responsibilities. Municipalities have been left with little money to invest in infrastructure maintenance or even to purchase essential treatment agents. Thus, whereas municipal wastewater treatment loads have fallen by about one-quarter, overall compliance with discharge regulations and, by default, the state of Russia's rivers and lakes have not improved.

Finally, a trend that also will have a significant impact on the environment is the long-delayed suburbanization of Russia. Central planning favored the development of large but spatially compact cities, with their ubiquitous multistory apartment blocks. This policy, which left Russia with relatively few small towns, has been abandoned.[9] Large Soviet enterprises that once drew people to the cities are now shedding labor, and some are closing their doors. Cities are no longer the commercial meccas they once were. As the retail economy has developed rapidly, consumer goods and services are increasingly available in smaller towns and rural areas. A residential building boom also is under way in the countryside as the new upper and middle classes invest their money in real estate and elbow room.[10] In the early 1990s, the share of Russia's population residing in cities fell for the first time, and this is likely to continue in the coming years. Birthrates in urban areas also have fallen.[11]

Once Russia's general economy revives, a similar "suburbanization" trend can be visualized for commercial and industrial development. Industrialized urban centers are likely to remain blighted by "brownfields"—giant aging industrial plants noted for their outdated technology and infrastructure, vertically integrated works, and pervasive environmental hazards—which few investors will find attractive. Russia's future investors will want to seek rural "greenfield" sites to build new, less-centralized production facilities, much like the postindustrial development patterns witnessed in the United States.

What these trends portend is a redistribution of pollution loads from a relatively small number of large, concentrated industrial point sources to a much larger number of diffuse yet cumulatively significant sources. Expansion of suburban development, for example, entails increased water pollution from sewage and storm-water runoff, wildlife habitat loss, and wetlands destruction. These trends, though universal around the world, assume particular importance in the case of Russia. As noted above, Soviet urban planning and economic development patterns promoted the relatively compact development of Russia's cities. This has allowed the survival of vast open spaces (and their indigenous flora and fauna) between urban centers.[12] Indeed, Russia today possesses a significant share of the world's remaining large tracts of undisturbed landscapes where natural processes, such as great fires and wildlife fluctuations, have been allowed to proceed according to regular rhythms.[13]

To sum up, the Russian economy has been undergoing a far-reaching and irreversible restructuring since the government initiated reform in

1992. Overall, the relative role of natural resources development in the economy has *increased* while the efficiency of many sectors has *decreased*, and the pollution intensity (emissions per unit of output) of the economy also has worsened. The following sections examine how these trends are affecting Russia's regions.

THE FAR EAST AND EASTERN SIBERIA

The natural environment in the Far East[14] and eastern Siberia has remained the least developed and the most pristine region of Russia, for several reasons. First, the region hosts a small, highly urbanized population: in 1991, the Far East counted about eight million residents, three-quarters of whom lived in provincial centers. Second, a harsh climate and inaccessible terrain has thwarted development. Commercial transport throughout the area is largely limited to river and coastal navigation and to the Trans-Siberian Railway, which skirts the Chinese border. Finally, national security interests have limited development along the Amur River on the Chinese border and along the Pacific Coast.

All this is changing quickly, however. The Far East and eastern Siberia area appears to be the region of the Russian Federation most directly affected by integration into the global economy, largely due to its geographic position. Since Russia's independence in 1992, Russia's international trade has shown a significant shift away from the former Soviet bloc and Western Europe in favor of dynamic economies of Asia—namely China, South Korea, and Taiwan—a trend that represents a return to prerevolutionary trade patterns.[15] Because of the region's small population and relatively pristine character, the environmental impacts of new development in the Far East have greater significance for nature conservation than for human health concerns.

The greatest immediate environmental impact in the Far East comes from logging. Southeast Asia—most importantly Japan and North and South Korea—traditionally has been a large market for wood products from the Russian Far East. Public pressure to limit logging in the western United States and Canada also has increased demand for timber from Russia.

Logging operations in the Far East had been confined largely to the areas adjacent to the Trans-Siberian and Baikal-Amur Railways, but recent investment from abroad has expanded logging in coastal areas, such as along the coast of Primorsky krai.[16] Unfortunately, most logging operations have entailed clearcutting of trees with insufficient efforts at regeneration, a trend that has intensified with economic reforms as logging firms have sought to cut costs and speed operations.[17] The result has been widespread erosion that has degraded landscapes, polluted local streams and rivers, and disturbed the region's rich fish resources. Clearcutting in northern regions of the Far East is particularly pernicious given the very slow growth rates, thus ensuring that the effects will be long-term. Historically, logging operations have been rather inefficient, but as international companies become more involved, they will bring more modern technology, such as harvesters and forwarders, which will dramatically increase the speed of cutting operations.

The international cause célèbre concerning the Far East environment is the demise of two charismatic animal species: the Siberian or Amur tiger and the Amur or Far East leopard. The survival of these two species has been impaired by long- and short-term forces. Over the past several decades, logging has destroyed valuable habitat—an important issue given the great range each animal requires.[18] The second and more immediate factor is commercial poaching, which has increased dramatically in recent years as trade opportunities with the outside world have opened up. A tiger pelt may command up to thirty thousand dollars in Japan or the United States, and in China and Taiwan, tiger bones and whiskers are valued for their medicinal properties. Such commercial demand has attracted professional hunters whose activities thus far have been constrained only marginally by local game wardens, who lack technical, institutional, and local political support.[19] Russian officials believe that about fifty tigers were killed yearly in the early 1990s, and the number of leopards dropped almost as precipitously. Most recent estimates suggest that the number of tigers in the wild had fallen to two hundred to three hundred by 1995. The number of remaining leopards was pegged at just thirty.

The Russian Far East is strikingly unpopulated; as noted above, the region counted only eight million inhabitants in the mid-1990s. Sakha, a republic roughly the size of India, had a population of 1.1 million, four-fifths of which resided in Yakutsk. Furthermore, the population of the Far East dropped by a quarter million inhabitants between 1989 and 1992, largely as a result of economic uncertainty and the reduction of military forces posted in the region.[20] This trend may not continue, however, if the region attracts additional residents as its economy recovers and integrates into Pacific markets. With the relaxation of relations between the Russian Federation and the People's Republic of China, cross-border trade has exploded, and a significant number of Chinese have emigrated north. If investments in sanitation systems in provincial centers such as Khabarovsk and Blagoveshchensk are not made, local economic and population growth could exacerbate already existing water pollution and could decimate the remaining fisheries along the

Amur River.[21] Similarly, environmentalists are concerned about efforts, led by the United Nations Development Program, to create a major shipping and manufacturing center on the Tumen River, which separates the Russian Federation, China, and North Korea.

The southern reaches of Khabarovsk and Primorsky krais are noted for their mild climate, beautiful rugged terrain, wild rivers, and temperate rain forests. In these aspects, the region can be seen as analogous to Washington State or British Columbia. It would not be surprising to see the rise of domestic and international tourism in this area in the coming years. Like its analogue in North America, the Far East may see the rise of environmental and leisure lobbies that challenge the prerogatives of extractive industries.

CENTRAL AND NORTHERN EUROPEAN RUSSIA

A substantial share of Russia's manufacturing and light industries are located in the northwestern region of the federation. In the first few years of restructuring, this region has suffered with the sharp downturn in the economy. Ivanovo (Russia's textile center), Pskov, and Yaroslavl oblasts and Mordovia and Chuvashia republics have been particularly hard-hit. In the future, the north is likely to be dominated by the oil, forest products, trade, and service sectors. As restructuring moves the economy toward a postindustrial model, the wealthy cities of north and central Russia—St. Petersburg, Kaliningrad, Nizhni Novgorod, and most importantly, Moscow—will decline as defense-industrial centers to emerge as major commercial and trading hubs, much as Pittsburgh moved beyond its "steeltown" profile in the 1970s. Given the rich history of the region, areas such as the Golden Ring and the upper Volga watershed may revive somewhat as tourist centers, to become the New England of Russia.

For the north, the fate of the forest products sector plays a large role in the region's overall economic health. Historically, two-thirds of the Russian timber harvest has come from forests in this section of the country, most importantly from Arkhangelsk oblast and Komi republic.[22] Yet the logging industry in the north has been severely depressed in the 1990s as a result of the economic downturn. In Komi republic, for example, cutting in 1994 had fallen to less than one-third the levels of the late Soviet era. The recession has eased the development pressure on the remaining old-growth stands located in Komi, in southern Arkhangelsk oblast, and on the Kola Peninsula. Presently, most exports from this region are shipped as raw logs to Finland, where they are processed into intermediate and final products for reexport.

Paper and pulp producers are concentrated in the north (Arkhangelsk oblast, Karelia and Komi republics). The major environmental problems associated with pulp and paper production in Russia are waterborne sulfates, chlorides, phenols, formaldehyde, and airborne particulates, sulfur dioxide, and carbon monoxide. Two mills in Arkhangelsk oblast—Arkhangelsk and Kotlas—account for 23 percent of the total wastewater discharges of the entire pulp and paper sector. Cities with the worst environmental impact are Kaliningrad, Perm, and Arkhangelsk. This sector has been hard-hit by the recession. Moreover, the sharp increase in transport tariffs has raised costs, especially for supplies coming from Siberia and the Far East. Nevertheless, many producers are now marketing their output abroad. Given that paper production in Russia averages just 24 kilograms per person (compared with 142 kilograms in the United States), one can expect that output, especially of higher-quality paper, will surge to meet the demand of the emerging commercial and service sectors. Not surprisingly, numerous Western firms have invested in (or expressed an interest to invest in) pulp and paper operations in Russia's northwest.

Land use patterns are changing quickly in the northwest. Strict security measures sharply limited logging on the Soviet side of the Finnish border, and a fifteen- to twenty-mile-wide strip of old-growth forest, the "green belt of Karelia," has survived from the Kola Peninsula down through Karelia to Lake Ladoga. This stand represents the last unfragmented boreal forests in the area and an important biogeographical bridge between Scandinavia and the Russian landmass.[23] Environmentalists and biodiversity specialists are concerned about the fate of this and other remaining virgin stands. In 1995, for example, the government of Viktor Chernomyrdin issued a decree ordering a clearcut and sale of the woods to facilitate patrolling the Finnish border.[24]

A countervailing trend to the continued logging of virgin forests is the restructuring of the farming sector and the concomitant reduction in the area of tilled land, especially in marginal agricultural areas. Growth rates have outpaced logging—a long-term trend that is likely to accelerate and that is similar to a phenomenon observed in the eastern United States since the beginning of the twentieth century.[25] Thirty-seven percent of Arkhangelsk oblast, for example, was forested in 1983, up from 33 percent in 1956.[26] The region also will see less of an environmental impact from livestock operations set up in the 1960s and 1970s to supply the big cities. In a free-market environment, the high cost of shipping in grain from the south has made many of these large complexes extremely unprofitable.

In urban areas, the load on the environment is shifting from manufacturing-oriented pollutants emitted from concentrated point sources to more diffuse and varied loads. A simple case in point is air pollution.

During the 1970s and early 1980s, the Soviet government invested in a large-scale program to convert electric power and urban heating plants to natural gas. This resulted in a significant improvement in air quality in the urban centers of central and northern Russia. Over the past decade, that progress has been eroded as a proliferation of cars, mostly imported, has begun to choke roads and highways and boost levels of urban smog. Despite the economic recession, the number of vehicles in Moscow, for instance, increases by an estimated 30,000–50,000 annually. In 1993, transport accounted for over three-fourths of the capital's air pollution.[27] Thus, we can expect a decrease in airborne heavy metals and highly toxic micropollutants and a rise in nitrogen oxides and carbon monoxide.

Another problem facing municipalities in the coming years will be to manage the explosion of solid-waste generation created by the rise of the service industries and a mass consumer society. Before the advent of reform, the average Soviet citizen generated less than one-third the solid waste generated by the average American.[28] Solid-waste disposal was not a major concern of municipal governments. Another challenge of municipal governments will be the provision of safe drinking water, of sewerage, and of wastewater-treatment services to growing suburbs. To meet all of these needs, municipal governments are being forced to come up with unpopular tax and service charge schemes.

THE URALS REGION AND SOUTHERN SIBERIA

Soviet central planning favored the industrial development of Siberia, a policy that began with Stalin's first Five-Year Plan in 1928 and was epitomized by the rise of Magnitogorsk and Komsomolsk-on-Amur. This policy accelerated dramatically during World War II, when many industries were relocated beyond the Urals in the face of advancing German troops. In subsequent years, the region's defense-oriented economy continued to grow as new industries, such as oil and gas, developed. In the 1990s, however, the downgrading of national security concerns and the rise of Russia as a trading state are forcing major changes in the Rust Belt economy of the Ural Mountains and Siberia. Demand has plummeted for steel, machinery, and armaments, and a sharp drop in state-sponsored investment has depressed the region's economy, especially the construction sector. Being situated at the heart of the Eurasian landmass puts local industries at a disadvantage when it comes to trading on domestic and world markets. The harsh climate boosts operating costs, and since 1992, Russia's state railroad monopoly has dramatically boosted freight tariffs to compensate for falling subsidies and to underwrite passenger services. This has priced many of the region's bulk commodities—such as coal, steel, and timber—above world market prices. Therefore, the region should see a shift away from such sectors and toward higher value added industries, unless the government intervenes in the coming years to reorder transportation costs.[29]

Oil and gas production is central to the economic well-being of Russia, both as a fundamental element of the domestic economy and as the most important source of export revenue. The country's most important oil- and gas-producing region lies in western Siberia: Tyumen oblast alone accounts for two-thirds of Russian oil production. As a result, conditions in this region represent the continued and intensifying pressures on the environment as a result of economic change.

Oil and gas production in western Siberia has been sliding and is likely to continue to fall throughout the rest of the 1990s due to decaying capital stock, the drop-off in investment, material supply problems, and the decreasing quality and increasing complexity of remaining deposits.[30] Despite the decrease in production, the oil and gas sector's impact on the environment remains severe. According to one Russian forestry expert, the oil and gas development has affected 30–50 percent of the taiga in western Siberia.[31] The number of accidents at well sites and along oil and gas pipelines has been increasing in recent years as a result of the overall aging of the capital infrastructure and a decrease in maintenance and safety practices. In 1994, the accident rate on main pipelines increased by almost 20 percent.[32] Total losses have been pegged at ten million tons annually.[33] In 1992–93, twenty major oil spills occurred in Tyumen oblast alone.[34] This has seriously contaminated many rivers in western Siberia, including the Tobol, Irtysh, Ob, and Tom—a problem that has worsened in recent years with the deteriorating state of the region's oil transport infrastructure.

As oil fields have been depleted, development has extended north toward the Yamal-Nenets autonomous okrug of Tyumen oblast, where the balance of energy reserves shifts to gas. One environmental implication of this trend is that the risk of long-term devastation caused by the oil spills that have been so prevalent to the south is less prominent in the north. The downside of the northward migration of production is that the use of heavy equipment and indiscriminate traffic patterns have devastated the tundra. Areas not in production have been seriously degraded by geological prospectors. A decline in reindeer population has been attributed to the region's expanding pipeline network, which has interrupted their migration patterns. This is of particular concern to the small remaining population of indigenous farmers.[35]

The fate of the coal and steel sectors epitomizes the effect of reform on heavy industry and the potentially positive environmental impact of restructuring. The Russian coal industry is clustered in several regions of the Urals and Siberia: most importantly, in the Urals basin in Chelyabinsk oblast, the Kuznetsk (Kuzbass) basin in Kemerovo oblast, and the Kansk-Achinsk basin west of Krasnoyarsk krai. The Urals and Siberian coal industry has experienced a precipitous decline in output in recent years due to a drop in state investment, a collapse in industrial consumption, and rising transportation costs. According to a 1993 World Bank survey, economic criteria dictate that a large share of the region's coal producers (mostly deep mines) should be closed. This would leave a smaller number of more modern, largely open-face pits operating in the Kuzbass and Kansk-Achinsk regions.[36]

Regardless, coal companies in Chelyabinsk and the Kuzbass continue to work many problem mines by dint of massive subsidies from the federal government, which fears the social and political repercussions of massive unemployment. Most of these operations are underground mines characterized by thin, complex, or deep seams. As a result, the proportion of overburden to salable coal extracted is excessive. Mine operators do not backfill exhausted works but discard waste rock in huge cone tips. Acid drainage has polluted local surface-water resources while mine-water pumping has lowered the water table in many locales. Subsidence has imperiled some cities and towns, most notably those in the Prokopyevsk area of the Kuzbass. Deep mines in and around Novokuznetsk are rather gassy, and in some cases the estimated energy value of the methane presently vented into the atmosphere exceeds that of the coal mined. Although coal-bed methane utilization could mitigate both environmental and public safety hazards, no coal companies have identified this as a promising new avenue for development. In short, if the government were to shut down unprofitable coal mines in the Urals and Kuzbass regions, the environmental benefit, in terms of pollution avoided, would be significant.

Forty-three percent of Russia's steel production is located in the Urals. The second iron and steel center is Novokuznetsk in Kemerovo oblast. The Russian iron and steel sector overall has been depressed by the drop in domestic industrial demand, cuts in state investment for construction, and a disruption of traditional trade networks after the collapse of the USSR. Ural smelters have been hard-hit as the cost of coking coal from the Kuzbass has been rendered prohibitive by skyrocketing freight costs. In the steel center of Magnitogorsk, air emissions declined by almost 50 percent in the early 1980s after several steel and coke furnaces were decommissioned.[37]

Russia's nonferrous metals production, the largest share of which is located in northern and eastern Siberia, has fared better than coal and steel. The outlier in terms of environmental impact is the Norilsk nickel plant, which produces nickel, copper, cobalt, platinum, and other rare metals. In 1993 its smelters discharged 2.3 million tons of pollutants (mostly sulfur dioxide), down by 333,000 tons from the previous year. Nevertheless, Norilsk accounted for over 10 percent of all industrial emissions in Russia (26 percent of sulfur dioxide emissions), making the complex the single largest point source in the world.[38] Eastern Siberia is home to Russia's five largest aluminum smelters—Bratsk, Krasnoyarsk, Sayansk, Irkutsk, and Novokuznetsk—which account for 80 percent of the country's smelting capacity. All except Novokuznetsk are situated near large hydroelectric facilities. With secure access to this cheap source of electricity (which is a major input in aluminum production), these facilities are very competitive on the world market. As a result they have been able to export up to two-thirds of their output and thus maintain relatively stable production levels in spite of domestic industrial upheaval, namely the cutback in military procurement. Siberia's aluminum smelters have shifted so much output into international markets that they have depressed prices.[39] Although wages in aluminum-producing cities have remained high, the impact on the environment and public health is grim. The city of Bratsk, for example, continues to suffer some of the worst air pollution in Russia.

Soviet development policy promoted the rapid population and urbanization of the Urals and Siberia, which account for almost one-third of Russia's population.[40] This trend has now reversed, and Siberia has experienced a net emigration in recent years. Between 1989 and 1992, the population of western Siberia (not including the Urals) dropped by 36,000 while the population of eastern Siberia declined by 114,000.[41]

In remote areas, planners created entire cities to support local enterprises. Norilsk, located two hundred miles north of the Arctic Circle, boasts a metropolitan population of a quarter million inhabitants. In western Siberia, nine auxiliary personnel support each oil worker.[42] With privatization and cutbacks in state support for the north's industrial workforce, industries no longer have the resources to maintain large payrolls, the cities they built, and the broad range of ancillary operations they once provided (e.g., heat and power supply, dairy and livestock operations, recreation facilities). In the future, enterprises in remote areas will rely more on contract labor brought in for short terms without the provision of extensive amenities. This is increasing the pressure for more emigration in the future from remote areas of the north and east. Given the fact that such urban settlements have had a heavy impact on the region's natural resources, depopulation represents a positive environmental trend.[43]

SOUTHERN EUROPEAN RUSSIA

Just as the Sun Belt has witnessed rapid growth in the postindustrial-era United States, southern Russia is poised to experience a period of economic and population growth; its relatively mild climate and access to world markets through Black Sea ports enhance the region's attractiveness. Already, the federal government has drafted plans to channel Siberian and Caspian oil exports through the port of Novorossiisk, and this could stimulate ancillary development. For the near future, two of the most important influences on the environment as a result of economic transition will be population and agriculture.

In contrast to Siberia, large areas of Russia's southern margins are experiencing a significant increase in population. One source of this trend is the continued positive rates of natural increase among titular nationalities of the non-Russian republics (e.g., Ingushetia, Dagestan, Kalmykia). Already, the region has received a large share of immigrants from other republics of the former Soviet Union (notably Ukraine and Kazakhstan) and from the north and Siberia. The military conflict in Chechnya has only worsened the situation by generating streams of refugees. In the future, coastal resort communities on the Black Sea—Anapa, Sochi, Adler—are likely to grow as Russia's new wealthy classes invest their resources in leisure activities.

The major environmental challenge in many areas of the south, therefore, will be the provision of essential communal services such as sewerage and safe drinking water to meet the growing population's needs. In the poorest regions, we are seeing the emergence of many environmental and public health problems characteristic of developing countries. In 1993–94, for example, the Russian media reported several outbreaks of typhoid and cholera.[44] The Russian public health service has reported that the quality of drinking water is worst in Kalmykia, Dagestan, and Karachaevo-Cherkessia.[45] Along the Black Sea littoral, the expansion of sewerage systems did not keep pace with tourist development during the Soviet years, and this problem is likely to worsen with increased tourist traffic. The probable result will be increased water pollution and beach closings in urban areas.

The Black Earth area, which covers much of Russia's south-central region, serves as the country's breadbasket, accounting for one-half of tilled farmland and four-fifths of production.[46] Structural adjustment is beginning to reshape the Russian agricultural sector, and the Black Earth and North Caucasus areas could be centers of a revitalizing farming sector in the coming years as higher food prices and land privatization create incentives for increased production and investment in the countryside. Historically, the region's favorable climate has made it a major producer of grains, corn, sunflower oil, and rice. The southern provinces are well situated geographically to supply international markets, and if rural reform is successful, Russia could eventually regain its prerevolutionary status as a major food-exporting nation.

To date, the impact of economic reform on environmental quality in farming regions has been mixed. The decrease in public investment has curtailed soil-conservation programs, leading to faster depletion of soil fertility across all of southern and central Russia. The intensive grazing of arid grasslands in Kalmykia and in Astrakhan oblast also has led to desertification. On the other hand, the draining of wetlands has also been reduced (see table 7.3). Furthermore, the rapidly increasing cost of agrochemicals has forced farmers to cut their consumption of fertilizer by over one-half in the early 1990s. Although experts have warned of deteriorating soil fertility as a result of reduced chemical inputs, food production has declined by less than one-quarter over the same period. The reduction in the often improper and excessive application of fertilizers and pesticides is likely to reduce pesticide contamination of foods, soil, and water resources, especially in the North Caucasus.[47] Yet despite the 60 percent drop in pesticide use, the Russian environment ministry noted in 1994 that "extremely high levels of pollution" of the Kuban and Don Rivers persisted as a result of pesticide runoff in Rostov oblast and Krasnodar krai.[48]

REGIONAL RESPONSES TO ECONOMIC AND ENVIRONMENTAL CHANGE

This chapter has illustrated how economic reform is playing out differently across sectors and regions in Russia and how the variation is largely determined by territories' natural resource and industrial endowments. In industrial (capital-rich) areas, such as Chelyabinsk and Kemerovo oblasts, restructuring is having a positive effect on short-term environmental problems such as air pollution. Nevertheless, long-term problems such as accumulated hazardous waste dumps and groundwater contamination will not be mitigated by restructuring. On the other hand, resource-rich regions that have been able to divert their output to international markets, regions such as Tyumen oblast, continue to pursue materials development (albeit at overall lower rates), resulting in the continuation of preexisting problems.

The ability of regions to respond to their different environmental challenges also varies. The Russian Federation is marked by a great variation in socioeconomic development across its regions. Soviet development policy, though oriented toward sustaining national security interests, also

Table 7.3
THE IMPACT OF RESTRUCTURING ON AGRICULTURE, 1986–1993[a]

Activity	Percent
Organic fertilizer use (tonnage)	48
Pesticide use[b]	41
Land drained	19
New/repaired irrigation systems	8
Tree-planting for erosion control	8

[a]Figures expressed as 1993 as a percent of the annual average for 1986–90 in area.
[b]Figure is 1993/1990 (percent).
Source: Ministry of Environmental Protection and Natural Resources, *Gosudarstvennyi doklad: O sostoyanii okruzhayushchei prirodnoi sredy Rossiiskoi Federatsii v 1993 godu* (Moscow, 1993), p. 133.

was guided by a strong redistributive ethic aimed at reducing this disparity. Every region shared in the "pork" doled out by Moscow. The demise of central planning ended this leveling policy, and we are beginning to see a notable increase in income disparity among regions—largely along the Rust Belt and natural resources cleavage. Given the reduced role of the federal government, efforts to manage Russia's complex and expensive environmental problems will have to be funded largely with local resources. At the same time, the ability of different regions to pay for conservation and remediation programs also is diverging. The challenge for Rust Belt regions is to devise and implement strategies to manage industrial decline with modest or dwindling resources. The question for natural resource regions is whether to use their continuing income to manage current threats or to prevent future degradation.

One question that Rust Belt regions need to address is whether the decision to shut an enterprise should be made solely on economic criteria or should include environmental factors. Operations may exist that are relatively sound financially but that have a markedly negative and costly environmental impact, which is not registered on a traditional balance sheet. In addition, Rust Belt resources must be directed to maintaining existing, cost-effective environmental-protection investments in, say, wastewater-treatment systems. Rust Belt regions also must decide how to allocate scarce and dwindling resources to manage persistent (and often expensive) environmental threats. In other words, should money be spent on long-term stabilization and eventual cleanup, or should brownfields be written off as "sacrifice zones"? Finally, these regions face the challenges of managing the environmental impact of new growth, such as extending sewerage systems to expanding suburbs. These are questions of the more immediate issues of public health and finance and resource allocation.

The environmental policy challenges confronting resource-rich regions are more abstract. Most immediately, the issue of property rights must be resolved. Uncertainty over ownership of natural resources (an issue that has been kept separate from debates over land privatization) has promoted a short-term, exploitative, "Klondike" mentality.[49] To the extent that Russia's sizable wealth in natural resources remains in the hands of the state (which appears likely for the immediate future), the state must assert its rights and adopt strong and enforceable measures to regulate the best use of the resources. The finite nature of the resource wealth dictates that regions must decide how best to manage the long-term development of natural resources. Should the Far East, for example, use its income to promote sustainable forestry practices or to diversify into finished goods production? This leads to the broader issue of the future of materials—and implicitly, of the region—in the national economy. What is the value, for instance, of old-growth forest in the Far East, and who should benefit from it? Questions such as these have significance far beyond an individual region's boundaries. The answers to these questions promise to shape the economic and environmental policy emerging in twenty-first-century Russia.

NOTES

An earlier version of this paper appeared in *Post-Soviet Geography* 33 (May 1995): 291–309, and is republished with the permission of V. H. Winston and Son, Inc.

1. See, for example, D. J. Peterson, *Troubled Lands: The Legacy of Soviet Environmental Destruction* (Boulder, Colo.: Westview Press, 1993); Joan DeBardeleben and John Hannigan, eds., *Environmental Security and Quality after Communism* (Boulder, Colo.: Westview Press, 1995); Murray Feshbach and Alfred Friendly Jr., *Ecocide in the USSR* (New York: Basic Books, 1992); and Philip R. Pryde, *Environmental Management in the Soviet Union* (New York: Cambridge University Press, 1991).
2. Federal and regional governments have adopted numerous new laws and regulations governing environmental protection and natural resources management. Efforts to implement these measures by regional authorities vary across Russia—another important factor shaping outcomes. For more on this subject, see D. J. Peterson, "Building Bureaucratic Capacity in Russia: Federal and Regional Responses to the Post-Soviet Environmental Challenge" in DeBardeleben and Hannigan, *Environmental Security*. Ultimately, the economy and its institutions must stabilize before these legal instruments can prove effective.
3. On the regional distribution of sectoral development in Russia, see Matthew

Sagers, "Regional Industrial Structures and Economic Prospects in the Former USSR," *Post-Soviet Geography* 33 (1992): 487–515.
4. My arguments are not intended to be encyclopedic and to cover all sectors but to highlight what I see as important phenomena and trends regarding the physical environment. I intentionally downplay the human impacts and address them only indirectly through issues such as migration and consumption. The long-term fate of economic reform in Russia remains undetermined, as evidenced by the heat of political struggles over its direction. Nevertheless, some trends, such as reforestation and the increasing dispersion of pollution, appear inevitable regardless of the political superstructure.
5. The command economy created incentives for managers to overstate production, whereas in the present era, managers understate production to avoid taxation. One Western analyst has estimated that Russian GDP fell by about 35 percent between 1989 and 1994. See Vincent Koen, "How Large Was the Output Collapse in Russia? Alternative Estimates and Welfare Implications," *IMF Staff Paper*, November 1994.
6. "Russia's Emerging Market," *Economist*, April 8, 1995, p. 13.
7. In the first ten months of 1995, for example, Russian exports had increased by one-fifth over the same period in 1994 (*Interfax*, November 22, 1995).
8. This is most clearly manifested in the rate of energy use: while industrial production decreased by 50 percent from 1990 to 1994 (according to official government statistics), electricity consumption fell by only 20 percent. For more on this, see V. Vasiliev et al., "Strategiya ispol'zovaniya energoresursov," *Ekonomist*, no. 12 (1994), pp. 6–14. The increase in pollution intensity was one of the findings of the autumn 1992 "White Book" report on the status of the Russian environment. See *Post-Soviet Geography* 34 (1993): 74–78.
9. G. M. Lappo, "Urban Policy in Russia: A Geographic Perspective," *Post-Soviet Geography* 33 (1992): 516–32.
10. To illustrate the extent of urban development in Russia, take the cases of St. Petersburg and Moscow. In 1992, the population of the city of St. Petersburg surpassed 5 million. The population of the surrounding oblast numbered just 1.7 million. Compare this with Boston or Chicago, where the central city accounted for less than one-third and one-half of the greater metropolitan population, respectively. In 1992, the population density of Moscow was over 9,000 people per square kilometer, about the same as New York City (9,140) and more than twice as high as another major European capital, Berlin (3,900).
11. The federal government estimated that Russia's overall population dipped slightly in 1992–94 and that the birthrate dropped below replacement. Russian commentators tend to view this trend as decidedly negative in terms of ethnic and social well-being, yet this trend has long-term positive implications for the environment.
12. Lappo, "Urban Policy in Russia."
13. Laura Williams et al., "An Emergency Strategy to Rescue Russia's Biological Diversity," *Conservation Biology* 8 (1994): 934–42.
14. For the purposes of this discussion, this region includes Amur, Magadan, and Sakhalin oblasts, the republic of Sakha, and Khabarovsk and Primorsky krais.

15. Andrei Illarionov, "Vneshnaya torgovlya Rossii v 1992–93 godakh," *Ekonomist,* no. 6 (1994), pp. 74–91.
16. Alexei Grigoriev, "Mapping the Shrinking Taiga," *Taiga News,* no. 9 (1994), p. 8.
17. Inadequate regeneration efforts in the region were typical during the late Soviet period as well. See Brenton M. Barr and Kathleen E. Braden, *The Disappearing Russian Forest: A Dilemma in Soviet Natural Resource Management* (Totowa, N.J.: Rowman and Littlefield, 1988).
18. Both species inhabit remote regions of Khabarovsk and Primorsky krais.
19. B. J. Chisholm, "Cooperation in the Taiga: The Key to Saving the Amur Tiger," *Surviving Together* (spring 1994), pp. 36–39.
20. Allen Bloom and S. V. Zakharov, "Vzaimosvyaz natsional'nogo i regional'nogo aspektov issledovaniya prostranstva SNG," *Problemy prognozirovaniya,* no. 6 (1994), pp. 86–107.
21. In August 1994, the fisheries conservation service of the Jewish autonomous oblast canceled the fall salmon fishing season to protect salmon populations along the Amur (*Rossiiskaya gazeta,* August 31, 1994, p. 8).
22. Grigoriev, "Mapping the Shrinking Taiga."
23. Jarmo Pyykkö, "The Green Belt of Karelia at Risk," *Taiga News,* no. 10 (1994), pp. 6–7.
24. *Rossiiskie vesti,* May 25, 1995.
25. According to data reported by Minpriroda, annual increase in the stock of timber across Russia averages 830 million cubic meters. In 1993, a total of 556 million cubic meters of wood was taken. Ministry of Environmental Protection and Natural Resources, *Gosudarstvennyi doklad: O sostoyanii okruzhayushchei prirodnoi sredy Rossiiskoi Federatsii v 1993 godu* (Moscow, 1993).
26. *Zelenyi mir,* no. 8 (1994), p. 6.
27. *Nezavisimaya gazeta,* August 12, 1993, p. 1.
28. U.S. and Soviet annual solid-waste generation in 1989 totaled 655 and 195 kilograms per capita, respectively (Peterson, *Troubled Lands,* p. 130).
29. For more on transportation issues, see Jane Holt, *Transport Strategies for the Russian Federation* (Washington, D.C.: World Bank, 1994).
30. Leslie Dienes, "Prospects for Russian Oil in the 1990s: Reserves and Costs," *Post-Soviet Geography* 34 (1993): 79–110.
31. Grigoriev, "Mapping the Shrinking Taiga."
32. *Segodnya,* January 11, 1995, p. 7.
33. Alexei Yablokov, member of the Russian Federation Security Council, cited in *Kommersant-Daily,* February 3, 1995, p. 3.
34. Ministry of Environmental Protection and Natural Resources, *Gosudarstvennyi doklad,* p. 139. For more on the pipeline issue, see D. J. Peterson, "Bleeding Arteries: Pipelines in the Soviet Union," *Report on the USSR* (June 15, 1990), pp. 1–3.
35. V. Pakhamov and V. Loginov, "Khozyisvennoe osvoenie Tyumenskogo severa i problemy korennykh narodnostei," *Voprosy ekonomiki,* no. 5 (1994), pp. 125–32.
36. Another important Russian coal-mining center, Vorkuta in Komi republic, is also noted for its inefficient and worked-out deep mines and is facing

severe cutbacks in production as a result of economic pressures.
37. *Chelyabinskii rabochii,* March 22, 1994, p. 2.
38. Ministry of Environmental Protection and Natural Resources, *Gosudarstvennyi doklad,* pp. 97, 119. For more on this interesting case, see D. J. Peterson, "Norilsk in the Nineties," *RFE/RL Research Report* (January 29, 1993), pp. 24–28.
39. By 1993, the nominal price for aluminum had fallen by 56 percent from its peak in 1988. Similarly, prices for nickel and platinum dropped by 61 and 30 percent, respectively. As an aside, other aluminum producers, especially those in the United States, have complained that they have had to cut back production at their more modern and cleaner operations in the face of the onslaught from the Siberian "mega-polluters" (*Financial Times,* October 28, 1992, pp. 29–32).
40. Despite their common image as forbidding and barren territories, Siberia and the Urals are very urbanized. Seven cities boast a population of almost one million inhabitants or more: Yekaterinburg, Chelyabinsk, Omsk, Ufa, Perm, Novosibirsk, and Krasnoyarsk. In the 1990s, 86 percent of the forty-five million people living in the Urals and Siberia resided in urban areas.
41. Bloom and Zakharov, "Vzaimosvyaz natsional'nogo i regional'nogo aspektov issledovaniya prostranstva SNG." One could surmise that emigrants would favor destinations in the western and southern regions of the country. Of the large number of Ukrainians who went to work in Siberia and the Arctic, many now are leaving Russia for their native country.
42. A. Pozdniakov and V. Kurnyshev, "Sotsial'no-ekonomicheskoe polozhenie Rossiiskogo severa i mery po ego stabilizatsii," *Voprosy ekonomiki,* no. 5 (1994), pp. 119–24.
43. For background on the severe social and economic problems of the Russian north under the transition to a market economy, see the special coverage of the subject in *Post-Soviet Geography* 36 (1995): 195–245.
44. See, for example, *Izvestiya,* August 31, 1993, p. 2.
45. *Pravda,* July 13, 1993, p. 1.
46. Ministry of Environmental Protection and Natural Resources, *State Report on the Environment in 1992,* translated in JPRS-TEN-94-05 (February 25, 1994).
47. In 1992, the southern agricultural region accounted for over two-thirds of pesticide use in Russia (ibid.).
48. Ministry of Environmental Protection and Natural Resources, *Gosudarstvennyi doklad.*
49. Many Communist and nationalist commentators have decried the exploitation, by international capital, of Russia's new global status as a "raw materials colony." They have argued that Russia should withdraw from the global economy to protect its environment as well as its natural resource wealth. Although their concerns about the character of the global economy and the exploitation of nature are valid, the performance of the Soviet regime (which was dominated by Russians) suggests that returning to Soviet-style socialism or autarky would not solve the problem.

8

Health in Russia: The Regional and National Dimensions

Mark G. Field

Russia's decreasing population is one measure of the dimensions of the country's health crisis.[1] A decreasing population is not necessarily a cause for alarm, particularly if it is temporary, but the causal components of this phenomenon in contemporary Russia and the long-term trends and implications are ominous. According to projections by the Russian Health Ministry, the population will continue to decline until 2005.[2] This population decrease is but one of the many symptoms of the deep social crisis and systemic breakdown that is affecting all aspects of Russian life, to varying degrees. This chapter will examine this crisis and the state of the health care system, taking into account both the regional and the national dimensions.

BACKGROUND

The Soviet Union was the first country in the world to pledge universal health care to its citizens, and that provision was enshrined in its various constitutions. People from around the world traveled to the Soviet Union to admire its system of medical care, hailed by many (including the state propaganda apparatus) as the way to the future, as an example for the world to emulate.[3]

The realities of Soviet medical care were, however, a bit at odds with the rosy picture painted by official proclamations. An idea of the true nature of the situation emerged in the late 1960s when statistics began to show, to everyone's surprise, a reversal in the downward trend of an infant mortality rate that had fallen to about one-tenth of what it had been before the Revolution of 1917.[4] That drop had been attributed to the salutary effects of Soviet socialized medicine and of the Soviet system. Infant mortality (defined as the death of an infant who was born alive and who died within its first year or on its first birthday, and usually reported as such deaths per 1,000 newborns) is generally considered a proxy measure not only of the state of medical care but also of the well-being of a population—an indicator, for example, of income, education, cultural level, housing, nutrition, and other components of the standard of living.[5] After the Soviet statistical handbooks had shown, over a period of three to four years, an embarrassing 20 percent rise in infant mortality, an embargo was placed, for a number of years, on the further publication of these data as well as on the publication of several other equally dismaying vital statistics. It was only in the period of *glasnost'* that more complete data were eventually released, permitting analysts and demographers not only to get a better grip on the health and the demographic situation of the former Soviet Union but also to work their way back in time to see what had actually happened.[6] It is noteworthy that several observers of the Soviet demographic scene stated that the data were unprecedented for a society in "peace time." Thus in 1983, Roland Pressat, a French analyst examining the mortality increase in the USSR, remarked, "One has never seen, in time of peace, a regression of health conditions on such a scale."[7] Later on, in the spring of 1994, Lee Hockstader observed, "Russia is facing . . . troubling trends that add up to demographic and public health crises virtually unprecedented in peacetime."[8] And even more recently, Nicholas Eberstadt, an American demographer examining the falling birthrates in Eastern Europe and in Russia (where a 35 percent decrease had occurred), wrote, "In the past such abrupt shocks were observed in industrial societies only in war time."[9]

It may be suggested that the situation in the Soviet Union beginning in the mid-1960s (and even earlier) was a time not of peace but of war. The cold war was not a conventional conflict where most of the casualties were military. But it was a confrontation nonetheless and most of the casualties were civilian. What we are witnessing today in the former Soviet Union is the aftermath of that lost conflict.[10] The Soviet Union lost that round because of its insistence on matching the West in military outlays, with a gross national product (GNP) several times smaller than its main adversary (the United States) and with an inefficient and corrupt economy. The proportion of the GNP that went to health (*zdravookhranenie*) declined from about 6 percent in the 1960s (a respectable figure then in line with Western industrial societies) to about one-third that amount by the time of the collapse of the Soviet Union, the only major industrial country where a decrease in this figure took place.[11]

THE HEALTH SITUATION IN TODAY'S RUSSIA

Although history never repeats itself, observers of the Russian contemporary scene have sometimes been tempted to compare it with the Weimar Republic. Some of the ingredients are there: a lost "war" after a protracted and costly conflict; a bitterness about national humiliation; the loss of an empire and of a position as a "Great Power"; a demoralizing level of inflation (though not hyperinflation); a polarization of society between a small group of profiteers and growing, increasingly impoverished and bitter middle and lower classes; crime in the streets and in high places; the unpredictability of daily life; and a nostalgia about a past when life was difficult but predictable. The purpose in describing the general situation of the Russian Federation is to suggest a link between a deteriorating national and regional situation and the state of the health of the population.

At the same time, a cautionary note should be sounded about assuming a direct relationship between health care and the health of a population. Granted, the activities of physicians, nurses, and other health personnel and the availability of facilities, pharmaceuticals, equipment, and budgetary allocations affect health, but the impact is smaller than usually assumed. Health is the end product of a multiplicity of factors, not simply of medical care. The World Health Organization estimates that living conditions and lifestyles account for about 50 percent of the variance, the environment about 20 percent, and genetics another 20 percent. This leaves only 10 percent attributed to medical care.[12] Living conditions (the state of the economy, housing, the food supply, individual income, and education) and lifestyles (smoking, alcohol consumption, sedentariness, and poor diet) are critical, and physicians can do very little about them. In addition, political events, ethnic conflicts, forced mass migrations, and of course, conventional wars have devastating effects on a population. The cold war had its victims and its impact on health and demographic indicators. But this impact was modulated, in some respects, by varying economic conditions in the different regions of what is today the Russian Federation. The result was significant regional variations in health levels and in the supply of health resources, reflecting differences in economic development, degree of urbanization, population density, pollution levels, and other related variables.

Of the variety of indicators, for comparative purposes, of the state of the health of a population, the most important are morbidity and mortality. *Morbidity* is the index of the incidence and prevalence of sickness, trauma, and disability. It is often a slippery measure because definitions and diagnoses of morbidity are affected by cultural factors, definition problems, reporting, and aggregation. *Mortality* is a more accurate and simpler index. Here the critical point, for the individual or society, is longevity, or life expectancy. This expectancy is thus a leading health indicator and is often cited in international and cross-regional comparisons. The life expectancy in Russia has dramatically decreased, particularly for men.

If the Soviet regime was parsimonious in the provision of health (and other) data, the government of Boris Yeltsin has been far more generous. A most important benchmark, in this regard, was the commissioning and the release, in October 1992, of two official reports, one on the state of the health of the population in the Russian Federation[13] and the other on the state of the environment.[14] Both provide aggregated national and regional data for 1991, and many signs indicate that the situation has not materially improved since publication.[15] For example, the suicide rate has dramatically increased, as has the rate of mortality from homicide and alcoholism.

Perhaps the most telling part of the report on health is that, since the collapse of the Soviet regime, the population not only has stopped growing but has begun to decline. As of 1994, this decline was on the order of .66 percent per year, and the effects are compounded over time. In a population of 150 million, this is a yearly decline of about a million persons. The natural decrease in population varies from region to region, but in 1995 such a decrease was reported for all the regions of the Russian Federation (excluding effects of migration to particular regions). This situation is the result of two phenomena: an increase in mortality, particularly adult male mortality at the ages forty to fifty-nine, and a drastic reduction in births, as well as an increase in abortions.[16] Officially there are three or more times as many abortions as live births, though the figure is presumably considerably higher, since many terminations are done privately. (By contrast, in the United States in 1992, there were three times as many live births as abortions.)[17] In the years between 1985 and 1993, the birthrate declined from 16.7/1,000 to 9.6/1,000, that is, by 43 percent.[18] The mortality rate rose from 11.3/1,000 to 14.1/1,000, that is, by 25 percent, in the first seven months of 1993. For each birth in 1993 there were almost one and a half deaths. In Moscow and St. Petersburg, two to three times as many died as were being born. In 1994, in Moscow, there were 2.3 deaths for each birth.[19]

One of the results of this increase in mortality has been a drastic reduction in life expectancy (at birth and other ages). For men, life expectancy dropped from 63.5 years at birth in 1991 to less than 57.3 years in 1994. Men in India, Egypt, and Bolivia have a longer life expectancy. Women's life expectancy has not dropped as much as men's: it was 73.8 years in 1992 and 73.2 in 1993 and has dropped a few tenths of a percentage point in 1994-95. The dismaying aspect of the drop in male life expectancy is that it is due, to a large extent, to an increase in adult mortality, particularly in the age range of forty to sixty. As one observer of the situation has commented, "No country can afford a trend in which the most productive citizens die in huge numbers while they are in their prime."[20] A great deal of that mortality is attributable to sociogenic causes involving violence, disorganization, anomie, and personal frustration—causes such as homicide, suicide, alcohol poisonings, and traffic accidents (often related to alcohol abuse).[21]

Maternal mortality is at least eight to ten times higher than in the West; it may be compared to the level of Tanzania.[22] According to A. S. Kiselev and A. Ye. Ivanova, regional variations in maternal mortality are due, to a large extent, to varying social and economic conditions; there is no increase in this indicator in relatively well-to-do regions. Thus maternal mortality increased in Tomsk and Magadan oblasts, areas that had the most serious social and economic problems.[23]

The average number of children per woman over a lifetime has decreased from 2.2 in 1987 (barely above the replacement rate) to 1.6 in 1992 and 1.3 in 1993.[24] As S. P. Ermakov has pointed out, zero population growth or even a negative rate for some years cannot necessarily be used to confirm the existence of a social crisis or the failure of reform policies. Negative population growths were recorded in the 1980s for Hungary, Germany, and Austria. However, "the considerable rise in mortality rates especially in the working age population is peculiar to the demographic crisis in Russia."[25]

Numerous other statistics indicate that the state of the health of the population is declining. The projection is that by the year 2015, if the current trends continue, only 15 to 20 percent of the newborns will be healthy when they enter the world. There are new cases of hepatitis, encephalitis, scarlet fever, diphtheria (practically nonexistent in the West), typhoid, bacterial dysentery, tuberculosis, whooping cough, bubonic plague, anthrax, and German measles, as well as unconfirmed cases of malaria in Moscow and confirmed cases in St. Petersburg.[26] The morbidity for measles increased by over 300 percent between 1992 and 1993, for diphtheria by 296 percent, for scabies by 132 percent, and for whooping cough 64 percent. But the increase in morbidity among children was far greater: diphtheria, 4.2 times; measles, 3.7 times; scabies, 2.6 times; and whooping cough, 1.6 times.[27] The rates of children's vaccinations are decreasing both because of the shortage of vaccines and because of the parents' (legitimate) fears that their children may become infected by poorly sterilized reusable needles. Failure to vaccinate, for example against rubella (German measles), leads to an increase in birth defects.[28] Pollution is another source of health problems, particularly for children. Food is often poorly inspected, increasing the risk of bacterial and viral infections as well as other digestive problems.

Mounting health problems are a reflection of a deeper "postwar" systemic crisis. An improvement in the health of the population will not come from medical and public health measures alone (as we have seen, they contribute only marginally to health) but from general improvement in the economy, increased political stability, and decreased social tensions. In addition, an important psychological aspect of the problem needs to be addressed. Russian sociologists note the social anomie, pessimism, and despair: there is simply no feeling, among the majority of the people, that it is worth worrying about one's future health.[29]

THE REGIONAL DIMENSIONS

The health crisis is both national and regional, if not local. In dealing with health, the Russian Federation is saddled with its Soviet inheritance of administrative centralization. In the words of Murray Feshbach: "The Soviet bureaucratic legacy of excessive centralization continues to inhibit practical and realistic environmental and health initiatives. Information still flows upward and is rarely shared laterally. Conflicting jurisdictions between ministers and agencies and among center, *oblast*, *raion*, and municipal authorities discourage individual initiative at all levels."[30]

The collapse of the Soviet system has been accompanied by efforts to decentralize the administrative structure of the state and to transfer a great deal of power to the regions and the municipalities. In the area of health care this has meant, among other things, efforts to introduce a system of mandatory medical insurance to be administered locally or regionally and to increase privatization and competition in order to improve the efficiency and efficacy of health care. These efforts have not met with a great deal of success, in light of the economic instability and the lack of adequate financial resources, both at the federal and the local and regional levels.

Regional differences characterize the health situation within the Russian Federation. For example, in European Russia, the number of abortions relative to live births is very high, as it is also in the Far East and Siberia.[31] On the other hand, in regions that have a Moslem-oriented culture, abortions are considerably rarer. In Yaroslavl oblast, the abortion rate is eight times greater than in Chechnya-Ingushetia.[32] Up to 25 percent of cases of maternal mortality are linked to abortions, and the maternal mortality rate is, as mentioned earlier, eight to ten times greater than in Western Europe. In Tuva and Altai republics, the maternal mortality rate "exceeds the indices for African countries."[33]

In 1993, there was a fivefold spread in the cost of a food basket in different regions. By the same token, health problems and the resources to cope with them also show a great deal of variation. For example, infant mortality ranges from less than 12.1/1,000 in Kamchatka oblast to a high of 39.4/1,000 in Tuva republic, a spread of 3 to 1.[34] Underreporting may explain some of the variations, especially for poorly developed and largely rural, low-density population areas. The same variation over the territory of Russia is seen in child morbidity caused by parasitic and infectious diseases, as well as in these conditions for adults and teenagers. One can safely assume that underreporting led to a child morbidity rate for the Chechnya and Ingushetia area half as much as that for Moscow. The proportion of reservoirs and water samples that do not meet minimum standards for bacteriological indicators varies significantly by region. Differences in the adequacy of household and industrial waste disposal show a regional spread of about 2.5 to 1; the availability of sewerage systems varies from a high of 100 percent in Moscow (city) to a low of 36 percent in Tuva.

Table 8.1 provides data on atmospheric discharge and lung cancer deaths for all administrative regions in 1992 and shows a spread, between Kurgan oblast and Dagestan republic, of more than two to one for lung cancer mortality (ages 0–64, urban population); this corresponds to a ratio of nine to one for tons of atmospheric discharge per capita for these two regions. The variability in men and women for seven types of cancer also shows remarkable differences from one region to another. For example, the male morbidity for colon cancer ranged from a low of 9.9/1,000 in the Volga-Vyatka Central region to a high of 23.7/1,000 in the Northwest region, an almost two and one-half spread. For women, the spread was of the same magnitude, also with a high in the Northwest region but with a low in the Central Chernozem region. According to B. A. Revich, E. M. Aksel, and V. V. Dvoryin, lung cancer rates in Tuva republic, Khabarovsk and Altai krais, and Magadan and Sakhalin oblasts are significantly higher than the Russian Federation average.[35] Rates of stomach cancer morbidity and mortality in Tuva republic and in Novgorod, Volgograd, Pskov, Kostroma, Vladimir, and Smolensk oblasts are also significantly above the national average. Reasons for the differences can only be surmised. Natural factors, the ethnic composition of the population, and technogenic variables may all play a role. Although a direct causal relationship between the environment and the level of morbidity and mortality is difficult to establish, some of the data available are suggestive. For example, in Russia in

Table 8.1
ATMOSPHERIC DISCHARGE FROM STATIONARY SOURCES, ATMOSPHERIC DISCHARGE PER CAPITA (URBAN POPULATION), AND DEATH RATES DUE TO LUNG CANCER (POPULATION 0–64), 1992, BY ADMINISTRATIVE REGION

Administrative region	Atmospheric discharge from stationary sources (tons per square kilometer)	Atmospheric discharge (tons per capita, urban population)	Age-standardization death rate due to lung cancer (per 100,000 population, ages 0–64)
Adygey republic	0.01867	0.06454	18.6
Bashkortostan republic	0.05558	0.30662	21.3
Buryat republic	0.00370	0.20634	26.8
Chechen/Ingush republic	0.11267	0.36248	23.7
Chuvash republic	0.04732	0.10714	18.8
Dagestan republic	0.00609	0.03663	16.0
Altai republic	0.00155	0.27787	17.3
Kabardin-Balkar republic	0.00737	0.01909	25.8
Kalmyk republic	0.00070	0.03169	23.3
Karachai-Cherkess republic	0.01771	0.12387	16.3
Karelian republic	0.01368	0.37571	29.4
Khakass republic	0.01810	0.27072	34.7
Komi republic	0.01803	0.82443	27.7
Mari El republic	0.01131	0.05281	20.2
Mordovian republic	0.03199	0.15784	26.2
North Ossetian republic	0.06730	0.11872	20.7
Tatarstan republic	0.07083	0.17675	20.6
Tuva republic	0.00291	0.33420	30.0
Udmurt republic	0.07532	0.27560	21.5
Sakha (Yakut) republic	0.00058	0.24459	29.1
Altai krai	0.02017	0.21418	34.8
Khabarovsk krai	0.00375	0.21090	31.2
Krasnodar krai	0.02694	0.07327	25.4
Krasnoyarsk krai	0.01187	1.27312	31.0
Primorsky krai	0.02109	0.19289	29.5
Stavropol krai	0.02627	0.11221	24.9

Table 8.1 *continued*

Table 8.1 *continued*

Amur oblast	0.00315	0.15969	28.6
Arkhangelsk oblast	0.00885	0.43968	29.8
Astrakhan oblast	0.01253	0.09736	32.7
Belgorod oblast	0.05116	0.15319	22.6
Bryansk oblast	0.02485	0.08629	25.1
Chelyabinsk oblast	0.20610	0.61367	28.7
Chita oblast	0.00549	0.25911	28.1
Irkutsk oblast	0.01161	0.38795	27.6
Ivanovo oblast	0.03212	0.07017	30.2
Kaliningrad oblast	0.04685	0.10048	32.8
Kaluga oblast	0.01420	0.05313	27.6
Kamchatka oblast	0.00130	0.15638	30.9
Kemerovo oblast	0.10673	0.36779	27.3
Kirov oblast	0.01728	0.17287	25.4
Kostroma oblast	0.02229	0.23990	26.7
Kurgan oblast	0.02837	0.33022	36.2
Kursk oblast	0.01778	0.06691	27.1
Leningrad oblast	0.07279	0.43052	28.3
St. Petersburg city	N/A	0.02976	23.9
Lipetsk oblast	0.22696	0.69260	28.8
Magadan oblast	0.00157	0.44859	33.9
Moscow oblast	0.13529	0.07037	22.7
Moscow city	N/A	0.02796	24.9
Murmansk oblast	0.04248	0.58256	26.4
Nizhegorodsk oblast	0.05765	0.14955	28.2
Novgorod oblast	0.01233	0.12656	32.0
Novosibirsk oblast	0.01805	0.15283	29.3
Omsk oblast	0.03039	0.29120	26.1
Orel oblast	0.01528	0.06620	29.0
Orenburg oblast	0.06987	0.60273	31.9
Penza oblast	0.01286	0.05858	26.1
Perm oblast	0.04708	0.31322	24.6
Pskov oblast	0.00617	0.06321	29.8
Rostov oblast	0.05055	0.16495	24.6
Ryazan oblast	0.07966	0.35089	27.8
Sakhalin oblast	0.01752	0.24874	32.6
Samara oblast	0.13590	0.27332	28.8
Saratov oblast	0.02478	0.12386	32.2
Smolensk oblast	0.03385	0.20959	26.5
Sverdlovsk oblast	0.01599	0.50013	27.6
Tambov oblast	0.01664	0.07633	31.7
Tomsk oblast	0.00986	0.44636	29.5
Tula oblast	0.20484	0.34941	30.0
Tver oblast	0.01379	0.09662	29.0

Table 8.1 *continued*

Table 8.1 *continued*

Tyumen oblast	0.01419	0.86557	24.1
Ulyansk oblast	0.03790	0.13491	29.0
Vladimir oblast	0.03493	0.07691	30.3
Volgograd oblast	0.02543	0.14330	31.2
Vologda oblast	0.06154	0.98875	27.3
Voronezh oblast	0.02033	0.06956	24.9
Yaroslavl oblast	0.06991	0.21048	27.5

Source: Murray Feshbach, ed., *Environmental and Health Atlas of Russia* (Moscow: PAIMS Publishing House, 1995), p. xviii.

1989, the overall cancer rate was 268 per 100,000, but in the heavily polluted mining and industrial towns, rates were considerably higher. The rate was 485 in the mining town of Norilsk and 502 in the industrial town of Yekaterinburg.[36]

The availability of health resources, human and material, varies between and within regions, most likely depending on the economic development of the regions. In 1991 budgetary allocations ranged from a high of 574 rubles per capita in Magadan oblast to a low of 149.3 in the area of Chechnya-Ingushetia. There was also a striking difference between the allocation to Moscow (261.6 rubles) and that to St. Petersburg (119.6). The availability of physicians shows a spread of about 2.5 to 1 among the regions, though the spread is even greater when Moscow and St. Petersburg are included.[37] In general, such statistics are a legacy of the failure of the Soviet regime to move significant numbers of physicians to the countryside and rural areas; regional differences in this respect parallel the differences in degrees of urbanization and industrialization. In the countryside, most medical care was provided by paramedical personnel (mainly feldshers and nurses). Regional distribution of paramedical personnel and of hospital beds per capita differs by almost two times. A note of caution should be introduced here: the word *hospital* may connote, in the former Soviet context, a variety of institutions, many of which hardly qualify for that appellation. Many so-called hospitals are often inadequately equipped buildings lacking elementary sanitary and hygienic conditions such as running water and a sewerage system.

Central health authorities in the Russian Federation argue in favor of an equalization of regional conditions through the enforcement of national standards. On the other hand, in reaction to the centralization and bureaucratization of the Soviet period, demands for decentralization and local autonomy are widespread. The Soviet health bureaucracy was far too often incapable of reacting swiftly and decisively in health emergencies, such as in an outbreak of infectious disease or the Chernobyl catastrophe. In theory at least, the devolution of power from the center should allow the regions to shape their health and preventive services toward the specific morbidity and mortality patterns of their areas. Yet hasty efforts to dismantle the overcentralized system in favor of one based on market-oriented principles has, as one former Soviet official from Central Asia expressed it, "destroyed the old house before building (or completing) the new one."[38] This has led to a further worsening of the health system, locally and regionally. The situation is complicated by the fact that both federal and regional governments are unable to collect enough taxes to sustain programs traditionally funded from the state treasury. In the absence of a functional substitute (such as private health care), health care is further deteriorating.

Physicians, most of whom are still on the public payroll, complain bitterly that they are paid less than veterinarians and bus drivers. Some have gone on strike from time to time, carrying placards with warnings such as "A hungry physician (or surgeon) is dangerous to your health!" The average monthly pay in Russia in March 1995 for the economy as a whole was 361,500 rubles; for industry, it was 432,800, and for the oil industry it was 1,082,600. In health care, physical education, and social security monthly pay averaged 238,700 rubles, less than 70 percent of the average pay in Russia.[39] So far, private medicine, supposedly financed at least in part by voluntary health insurance, has not been able to plug the gap. Only a small fraction of the population has access to such services. A system of obligatory medical insurance was passed in 1993, and a medical insurance infrastructure has developed. In 1995 there was 1 federal fund and 88 regional funds, as well as 484 medical insurance organizations involved in insuring the population; some 75 million policies have been issued. These funds are financed from a contribution equal to 3.6 percent of the wage fund of every enterprise, whether public or private.[40] A small part of that amount is sent to the federal fund, but most of it remains at the local or regional level.

GENERAL CONCLUSIONS

Clearly, most of the population in the Russian Federation still expects the state to be responsible for providing medical care, and people are interested more in assurance than in insurance. This expectation was central in the Soviet welfare system, and there is no reason to assume that it has disappeared. But in many instances, regions are too small or impoverished to be able independently to support the necessary services, including training future health personnel, conducting research, producing pharmaceuticals and medical equipment, and providing adequate clinical services. Directors of hospitals are so strapped for funds (eroded further by inflation) that they devote most of the money to pay health personnel, leaving little for capital repairs, maintenance of equipment, food for patients, and so on.

One advantage of centralization was that it provided opportunities (unfortunately, often unused) for economies of scale; at least in theory, the center had the ability to move human and material resources from where they were available to where they were needed. Regionalization removes this advantage; furthermore, many of the health and particularly the environmental problems cannot be tackled from a strictly local or regional standpoint. Epidemics and pollution spread regardless of map boundaries, often at great speed, and require coordinated central controls that override local autonomy. The interaction between the region and the center is thus a delicate matter, requiring a balance of local and national interests and initiatives. In an interview published in *Meditsinskaya gazeta* in the spring of 1995, the head of the Department of Public Health of Primorsky (Maritime) krai detailed the many problems he had to face, including a diphtheria epidemic that affected 70 percent of the administrative districts under his jurisdiction. This was complicated by an increase in the prevalence of hepatitis B (at twice the rate in the Russian Federation overall) and a devastating earthquake. Asked about funds, he answered: "First of all, we have to rely on ourselves, but we cannot get along without help from the center. From the promised 800 million rubles, we have received only a small amount, and obviously in such straits we cannot survive alone."[41] Apparently, the decentralization of the Russian Federation and the greater autonomy granted the regions presents a mixed picture for health services and the protection of the environment. "One can only rejoice," according to L. Smirnyagin, "that people in the regions are coming to understand that the main source of local situations is to be found in the region itself, not in Moscow."[42]

Though the potential of local self-rule, in the long run, may be positive, at the present time the situation has more negative than positive elements, at least in the area of health and the environment. That delicate balance between centralization and decentralization is difficult to establish and maintain in times of uncertainty, economic decline, political instability, and institutional confusion. And as might be expected, the most vulnerable members of the population bear the brunt of this unstable situation: newborns, children, young mothers, adolescents, the sick, invalids, and retirees, among others. Health problems are most acute in the least-developed regions, where the financial resources at the local and regional levels are limited, where the population is scattered in isolated settlements and villages, where the means of communication are poorly established, and where health facilities are often completely inadequate or nonexistent. But the magnitude of the problems, the differences in rates of morbidity and mortality from one region to another, the trend toward separatism, the political and ideological barriers to cooperation, and the lack of money render the health situation in the regions difficult to resolve. Health is a sensitive area. Vectors for the transmission of diseases and epidemics are always lurking and do not necessarily respect regional boundaries; an integrated, national and at times international approach is often mandatory. Such an approach, in many instances, will run contrary to the wishes of regional authorities and their interests in shaping their own health policies. Thus in the area of preventive and clinical medicine, important accommodations (if not concessions) will need to be made to provide the regions with the maximum benefits that state-of-the-art medicine can offer. At the same time, the international community will, we hope, display greater concern for the health of 150 million people than it has for that of Boris Yeltsin and will provide what is essentially humanitarian assistance.[43] However, at the regional as well as at the national level, real and lasting improvements in the health of the people will come, eventually and largely, as a result of an improvement in general conditions (economic, political, social, and cultural). In the absence of such progress, health personnel will continue to fight a rearguard action, and in some instances their efforts may be, particularly for elderly adults, not much more beneficial than a mustard plaster on a dead man's chest.

NOTES

1. Michael Specter, "Plunging Life Expectancy Puzzles Russia," *New York Times*, August 2, 1995, pp. 1, 6.
2. "Russia May Become a Country of Widows," *Segodnya,* July 19, 1995, p. 12, in *Current Digest of the Post Soviet Press* 47, no. 29 (1995): 17.
3. A. Newsholme and J. A. Kingsbury, *Red Medicine: Socialized Health in Soviet Russia* (New York: Doubleday, Doran and Co., 1993); Henri E. Sigerist, *Socialized Medicine in the Soviet Union* (New York: W. W. Norton and Co., 1937); Henri E. Sigerist, *Medicine and Health in the Soviet Union* (New York: Citadel Press, 1947); Gordon Hyde, *The Soviet Health Service: A Historical and Comparative Study* (London: Lawrence and Wishart, 1974).
4. C. Davis and Murray Feshbach, *Rising Infant Mortality in the USSR in the 1970s* (Washington, D.C.: U.S. Department of Commerce, 1980).
5. Mark G. Field, "Soviet Infant Mortality: A Mystery Story," in D. B. Jelliffe and E. F. Patrice Jelliffe, eds., *Advances in International Maternal and Child Health*

(Oxford: Clarendon Press, 1986), pp. 25–65. See David Blane, "Editorial: Social Determinants of Health-Socioeconomic Status, Social Class, and Ethnicity," *American Journal of Public Health* 85, no. 7 (1995): 903–4, and Frank W. Oechsli, "Editorial: Ethnicity, Socioeconomic Status, and the 50-Year U.S. Infant Mortality Record," *American Journal of Public Health* 85, no. 7 (1995): 905–6.

6. See, in particular, the work of Barbara A. Anderson and Brian D. Silver "The Geodemography of Infant Mortality in the Soviet Union, 1950–1990" (paper presented at the Seminar on the Geodemography of the Former Soviet Union, Radford University, Radford, Virginia, August 5–7, 1994), and "Assessing Trends and Levels in Working Age Mortality in the Newly Independent States" (paper presented at the Workshop on Mortality and Disability in the Newly Independent States, Committee on Population, National Research Council/National Academy of Sciences, Washington, D.C., September 8–9, 1994). Also France Meslé, Vladimir Shkolnikov, and Jacques Vallin, "Mortality by Cause in the USSR in 1970–1987: The Reconstruction of Time Series," *European Journal of Population* 8 (1992): 231–308.

7. Roland Pressat, "Une évolution anachronique: la hausse de la mortalité en Union soviétique," *Le Concours Médical*, May 21, 1983, pp. 105, 431.

8. L. Hockstader, "Death and Disease Rates Soar in Russia," *Guardian Weekly* (March 13, 1994), p. 18.

9. Nicholas Eberstadt, "Marx and Mortality," *New York Times* (April 6, 1994), p. A21.

10. For greater detail, see Mark G. Field, "The Health Crisis in the Former Soviet Union: A Report from the 'Post-War' Zone," *Social Science and Medicine* 41, no. 11 (1995): 1469–78.

11. Christopher M. Davis, "Russia's Health Reform: A Complicated Operation," *Transition* (World Bank) 4, no. 7 (September 1983): 1–3.

12. Cited in N. Rimashevskaia, "The Individual's Health Is the Health of Society," *Sociological Research* (May-June 1993), pp. 22–34.

13. *State Report on Population Health in the Russian Federation in 1991* (Moscow, 1992). In Russian.

14. *State Report on the State of the Environment of the Russian Federation in 1991* (Moscow, 1992). In Russian.

15. For more recent data, see Murray Feshbach, ed., *Environmental and Health Atlas of Russia* (Moscow: PAIMS Publishing House, 1995).

16. A part of this decrease may well be a long-term "echo" of the population losses of the Second World War, but the decrease is primarily the result of a decrease in fertility and an increase in abortions.

17. "Abortion Ratio Fell to Lowest Level Since '77," *Boston Globe*, December 24, 1994, p. 7.

18. UNICEF, *Public Policy and Social Conditions: Central and Eastern Europe in Transition*, Regional Monitoring Report no. 1 (November 1993).

19. "Sick Residents of a Sick City," *Segodnya*, May 4, 1995, p. 9, in *Current Digest of the Post Soviet Press* 47, no. 20 (1995): 15.

20. Specter, "Plunging Life Expectancy."

21. See, for example, Michael Ellman, "The Increase in Death and Disease under 'Katastroika,'" *Cambridge Journal of Economics* 18, no. 4 (August 1994): 329–55.
22. A. S. Kiselev and A. Ye. Ivanova, "The Birth-Rate and the Health of Newborns," in Feshbach, *Atlas,* p. 3-1.
23. Ibid.
24. S. P. Ermakov, "Birth Rates, Death Rates, and Natural Population Growth," in Feshbach, *Atlas,* p. 1-5.
25. Ibid.
26. Hockstader, "Death and Disease Rates Soar."
27. V. A. Magnitskiy and A. Ye. Ivanova, "General Morbidity of the Population," in Feshbach, *Atlas,* p. 3-3.
28. Specter, "Plunging Life Expectancy."
29. M. Specter, "Climb in Russia's Death Rate Sets Off Population Implosion," *New York Times,* March 6, 1994.
30. Murray Feshbach, *Ecological Disaster* (New York: Twentieth Century Fund Press, 1995), p. 100.
31. Kiselev and Ivanova, "The Birth-Rate and the Health of Newborns," pp. 3-1 and 3-2.
32. Feshbach, *Atlas,* p. xix.
33. Kiselev and Ivanova, "The Birth-Rate and the Health of Newborns," p. 3-1.
34. Figures for infant mortality, as well as other data in this paragraph, are taken from *State Report on Population Health in the Russian Federation in 1991,* issued by the Administration of the President of the Russian Federation, Ministry of Health of the Russian Federation, State Committee on Sanitary and Epidemiological Inspection, Russian Academy of Medical Sciences (Moscow, 1992). See "Infant Mortality in 1991," p. 15; "Child Morbidity Caused by Parasitic and Infectious Diseases in 1991," p. 44; "Adult and Teenage Morbidity Caused by Infectious and Parasitic Diseases in 1991," p. 46; "Proportion of Water Samples That Do Not Meet Sanitary Standards for Bacteriological Indicators," p. 66; "Sanitary Conditions in Household and Industrial Waste Processing and Disposal Places in Human Settlements in 1990," p. 67; and "Sewerage Systems on Living Premises in Urban Areas," p. 69.
35. B. A. Revich, E. M. Aksel, and V. V. Dvoryin, "Morbidity and Mortality from Malign Neoplasms," in Feshbach, *Atlas,* p. 3-7.
36. A. G. Vishnevsky and S. V. Zakharov, eds., *Naselenie Rossii* (Moscow: Centre for Demography and Human Ecology, 1993), cited in Ellman, "The Increase in Death and Disease," p. 337.
37. Figures for the availability of physicians, as well as other data in this paragraph, are taken from *State Report on Population Health in the Russian Federation in 1991.* See "Number of Doctors in 1991, per 10,000 of the Population," p. 78; "Number of Paramedical Personnel in 1991," p. 79; and "Number of Hospital Beds in 1991," p. 81.
38. Personal communication at the UNICEF Beijing Symposium on safety nets in transitional economies, July 1994.

39. Vitaly Golovachov, "Will We Keep On Sliding Long? The Pay of 30 Million Russians Is below the Minimum Living Standard," *Trud,* May 6, 1995, in *Current Digest of the Post Soviet Press* 47, no. 19 (1995): 16.
40. Lyubov Kalesh, "What Does It Cost to Get Sick? Insured Medicine Is No Panacea," *Izvestiya,* September 16, 1995, p. 2, in *Current Digest of the Post Soviet Press* 47, no. 37 (1995): 23.
41. T. Kozlov, "Its Name Is Region," *Meditsinskaya gazeta* (in Russian), no. 31 (April 21, 1995), p. 5.
42. L. Smirnyagin, "The Heart of the Matter: The Separation of Powers No Longer Exists at the Local Level," *Segodnya,* August 2, 1994, p. 3, as quoted in Elizabeth Teague, "Federalization a la Carte," *Perspectives* 5, no. 2 (November-December 1994).
43. "Mr. Yeltsin's Health," editorial, *New York Times,* February 14, 1995, p. A8.

IV
ETHNIC PERSPECTIVES

9

From the Outside Looking In: Armenians in Western Siberia

Cynthia Buckley

The dissolution of the Soviet Empire in the early 1990s created large diaspora communities nearly overnight. The establishment of fifteen successor states to the former Soviet Union raised serious questions concerning populations that were purportedly "not where they belonged" due to their status as military occupiers, economic migrants, colonial occupiers, or simply "outsiders" because of their language and ethnicity. In the Russian Federation the size of the "new diaspora" varies significantly by region. In this chapter I examine the social position of one specific category of "outsiders," ethnic Armenians in western Siberia.

Within this category, I focus on a particular occupational group—those associated with seasonal construction brigades—in order to explore the interrelationships between ethnicity, social class under the old regime, and the reformulation of ethnic and civic identity. Using previous studies of seasonal construction brigades in Altai krai as well as observational and interview data from a western Siberian village, I argue that the regional economic status associated with a particular ethnic group strongly influences the likelihood of local inclusion or exclusion of a diaspora community during the transitionary period.

A HETEROGENEOUS FEDERATION

Whereas the ethnically Russian population in the near abroad has attracted much attention from scholars and policymakers,[1] within Russia a substantial population ethnically associated with the countries of the near abroad remains unstudied. At the time of the last Soviet census, nearly eight million inhabitants of the Russian Federation were members of a non-Russian titular nationality. Byelorussians and Armenians had the largest proportion of their ethnic groups resident in the Russian Federation (12 percent and 11.5 percent, respectively). The Central Asian and Baltic nationalities exhibited the lowest proportions of their titular nationalities resident in the Russian Federation.

Most of the Armenian population in Russia can be found in just eleven oblasts. Though Armenia is the most ethnically homogeneous of all the successor states, only 66 percent of Armenians in the former Soviet Union reside in Armenia. Armenian diaspora populations are also found in large numbers in North America and Europe. Within the Russian Federation, the distribution of the Armenian population varies significantly, not only in size but also in economic and social characteristics.

In any given region, high correlations between specific occupations and ethnicity will influence the attributes ascribed both to the ethnic group and to the occupation. Whereas age, gender, and educational attainment all influence the perception of an individual's ethnicity and the construction of his or her social identity, occupational patterns (niches) attributed to specific ethnic groups represent an important factor in the prestige and social status of the entire social group.[2] In western Siberian oblasts of the Russian Federation, one specific occupational category, that of seasonal construction worker, is highly associated with Armenian ethnicity, particularly in rural areas. These laborers, *otkhotniki*, have played a historically significant role in the economic development of rural settlements and, in turn, the construction of an Armenian identity in these locations. Although their numerical standing is difficult to quantify with any accuracy, they represent a key element in the regional construction of ethnicity.

SEASONAL LABOR MIGRATION

Seasonal labor brigades, often operating on the edges of organized state labor, have been part of the Soviet labor force for years.[3] The utilization of seasonal labor brigades for construction work intensified noticeably in western Siberia in the 1970s, a time when rural development funds were available but rural labor forces were dwindling.[4] In order for state and collective farms to take advantage of funds available for infrastructure development, contracts were made with traveling work brigades, who completed work in the village but were not categorized as employees of the farms.[5] In the western Siberian case, such construction work typically needed to be completed during the summer months, a period of intensive labor demands in terms of agricultural work.[6]

Seasonal laborers were drawn from many social groups and places of residence, but the practice of seasonal labor migration, particularly for construction and heavy labor, was typically associated with ethnic groups from the Caucasus and, in some cases, Central Asia.[7] In western Siberia, brigades tended to be from Georgia, Armenia, and occasionally Kazakhstan, although some workers were drawn from nearby towns and cities.[8]

The likelihood that ethnic groups from the Caucasus would fill this occupational niche was increased by two institutional elements. First, tendencies toward ethnic segregation in the armed forces often led to conscripts from Central Asia and the Caucasus serving in construction details while in the army, where they obtained new skills or developed preexisting skills.[9] Second, regional employment patterns often reflected a dearth of middle- to high-paying job opportunities in the Caucasus Mountains and Central Asia, particularly for men. Seasonal migration served not only as a means of supplementing rural labor forces but also as a mechanism to alleviate the problems of high rates of regional unemployment.[10]

In addition to taking on ethnic connotations, the occupational niche of seasonal laborers was often accused of negative traits such as shoddy workmanship, a tendency to overcharge, and untrustworthiness. *Shabashniki,* as seasonal laborers were identified, became a necessary evil. Seasonal construction work was required, and there were no other workers for the task.[11] Yet, official toleration and local utilization did not signal their acceptance.[12] Because of their seasonal residence and their exclusion from formal economic and cultural structures, the seasonal migrants were the village strangers, part of the village but always on the outside of village society, looking in.[13]

As outsiders, the seasonal laborers were often subject to negative stereotyping. They were seen as undereducated, lacking in the discipline to maintain year-round employment, and potentially disruptive to village life. Since the brigades consisted of men far from home, the *otkhotniki* were sometimes viewed as a possible danger to village girls.

SEASONAL LABORERS IN ALTAI KRAI: GENERAL TENDENCIES

In an examination of seasonal labor migrants in the Topchika raion of Altai krai, M. A. Shabanova thoroughly illustrates the importance of seasonal labor brigades to local villages. Labor shortages in the region necessitated the use of seasonal brigades for construction. In her region of investigation, four-fifths of the children did not intend to work in the villages. Additionally, of available adults surveyed in the area, the majority were disinclined toward participating in seasonal construction work, citing the difficulty of the work in addition to the long hours required.[14]

The characteristics of seasonal labor migrants in Topchika raion raise several questions regarding the stereotypical portrait of a *shabashnik*. Shabanova found that the majority of the seasonal laborers surveyed had full-time jobs and had completed secondary education. In many cases, the migrants had specific goals (the purchase of a car, the construction of a house, or the wedding of a child) that required large sums of money, and working in seasonal construction brigades was one way to earn the requisite funds.[15] Seasonal migrants from outside the region cited a desire to live in their own region as a barrier to permanent migration (63 percent), whereas brigade participants from the region did not want to live in a village (72 percent).[16]

The majority of the seasonal laborers in Topchika were from neither the Caucasus nor Central Asia; they came primarily from Altai krai.[17] Brigades from Kazakhstan and Armenia were present, and some of the "regional" brigade participants were originally from the Caucasus, but the popular ethnic perception of these brigades was not realistic. However, proportionately more brigade supervisors and organizers did have ties to the Caucasus and Kazakhstan, providing some underpinning for the ethnic perception associated with this occupational niche.

In Topchika few seasonal migrants expressed interest in permanently moving to the village in which they were employed. Even though many workers would return year after year to the same village, often as part of a family network, few would establish permanent residence *(propisat)* in the villages of the raion. By maintaining links to an established home outside of the village, these laborers remained on the periphery of village life. Although ethnicity and language skills may have made interaction with village residents easier for some than for others, the *otkhotniki* typically kept to themselves, working long hours until the construction season ended and they returned home.

In some cases a member of a seasonal construction crew did establish permanent residence in the village in which he worked. Grachuk Sukiasian, the seasonal brigade leader in the village of Shabanova, was one such case.[18] Yet even though Sukiasian established permanent residence in a village where he had worked for many seasons (as had his father before him), his Armenian ethnicity and his nontraditional occupation niche worked together to reinforce his status as an "outsider" in the village.

A CASE STUDY

Grachuk Sukiasian, his wife, and his children have been residents of the village of Shabanova near Leninsk-Kuznetski in Kemerovo oblast for seven years. Previously, Grachuk had maintained an official residence in

Armenia while spending the majority of his time in Shabanova. Like his father before him, he operates a seasonal construction crew working on contract to Zaria, the collective farm (kolkhoz) in the area. In 1988, tired of the long absences of her husband, Sveta Sukiasian brought their children to live in western Siberia, registering as an official inhabitant of the village and establishing a permanent home there.[19]

Initially, the Sukiasians were the only Armenian family in Shabanova, although two men from the construction crew stayed in the village intermittently during the winter. In spite of language difficulties for the children in school and pressures from Sveta's in-laws to return to Armenia, she and the children remained in Shabanova. That spring, the wife and the daughter of another crew member arrived, doubling the number of Armenian families resident in the village.

Their ethnicity set them apart from the Slavic population of the village, a uniqueness dramatically accentuated by their occupational choices. The Armenian men were not official employees of Zaria, which employed nearly everyone of working age in the village. The Armenian women cooked and cleaned for the work crews in the summer, in addition to taking care of domestic and child-care responsibilities. Their lack of official association with the collective farm in the village, the center for village life, left them in a curious position in the "company town" atmosphere that Shabanova shared with many other western Siberian villages.[20]

Like many of the other villages in western Siberia, Shabanova was subject to large-scale out-migration during the 1970s due primarily to a lack of economic diversity and poor infrastructural development. From the early 1970s to the present, Zaria has maintained an informal relationship with the Sukiasian construction brigade, first run by Grachuk's father. Although out-migration has slowed in recent years, many of the young people still move out of the village, leaving a labor shortage for summer construction.

I collected data on Zaria during the winter of 1989–90, during the fall of 1990 through the summer of 1991, and during 1992 and 1993 by way of interviews, participant observation, the local press, kolkhoz records, and village registries. These main periods of data collection have been supplemented by letters from village inhabitants and by visits to the village in 1993 and 1994.[21] In addition, several interviews, both formal and informal, were conducted with the Sukiasian family concerning their position in the village. Although the goal of this research was not a specific examination of the interaction between occupation and ethnicity in the village, data relating to this topic appeared throughout the field records. By examining the direct and indirect statements, we can better appreciate the history and local mythology relating to this family and the importance of regional variations in occupational patterning.

SOCIAL NETWORKS

"Grachuk, he's one of ours," remarked the current director of the joint-stock company that replaced Zaria (although the basic structure has remained the same and the current director is the former president of the kolkhoz). "I remember when he first came to us, as a boy with his father," the director recollected in 1992. While listing the construction jobs that the Sukiasian crew has completed in the village, he repeated that every year there was something for the crew to do. The director was pleased that Sukiasian moved to the village permanently, believing it expedited the summer construction projects. He can often be found at the Sukiasian household, watching videos and occasionally partaking of Grachuk's home brew *(samogon)*. He claims, however, that their friendship and their working relationship are completely separate entities.

The Sukiasians are integrated into two basic social networks in the village. The first network is that of the village elite: the chief economist, the engineer, and (until the post was abolished) the local party secretary and their families are those villagers with whom the Sukiasians are most likely to interact. A secondary network, of Armenian families in the area, provides a mechanism for dissemination of information concerning conditions in Armenia, news of relatives, and summer work brigades and job opportunities. Though the Sukiasians feel they are on friendly terms with many of the villagers, these two networks cover the vast majority of their social interactions.

A third type of network, primarily one of unequal exchange, became clear from observing the Sukiasian household. Grachuk is the primary producer of high-quality *samogon* in the village, as well as the owner of a car. These two attributes motivate several of his neighbors to ask for assistance. Requests have ranged from that of a neighbor who wanted a *banki* of *samogon* for a birthday celebration to that of another, elderly neighbor who needed a ride to Easter church services. Typically such requests come only from those villagers living near the Sukiasian household. I observed Grachuk refuse a request only once, when an obviously intoxicated neighbor asked for a second liter of *samogon*. Such requests were seldom directed toward the director of the joint-stock company or the chief economist (both of whom also used the Sukiasian *samogon* equipment and also possessed cars). As one neighbor, a *skotnik*[22] on the farm, remarked: "Grachuk is a simple man and willing to share what he is lucky enough to get. He has a lot of things he obtained one way or another and makes his money off the kolkhoz. He knows he should help us, us, *kolkhozniki*" (male, age forty, February 1991).[23]

Whereas Grachuk was most definitely not viewed as "one of us" by the *kolkhozniki*, he was more approachable than the local leaders. His position as a contract worker for Zaria provided a sense of entitlement for the *kolkhozniki,* who more often than not found themselves at the Sukiasians' door when need struck.

SOCIAL PERCEPTIONS

Even though the Sukiasians established social networks and attempted to integrate themselves into exchange networks in Shabanova, for many residents of the village they remained "outsiders," in both passive and active modes of attribution.

During 1991–92, when movement toward privatization was taking place in urban Russia as well as in Armenia, local leaders often asked me if I had heard Grachuk discuss a possible return to Armenia. Such queries were repeated when news coverage of the Nagorno-Karabakh conflict increased. Though typically followed by statements of remorse at the thought that the Sukiasians might leave (they belonged to the same social network), these inquiries carried a passive message of exclusion: the idea that the Sukiasans were not truly integrated into the village and that they really belonged elsewhere. Yet even though the Sukiasians often expressed concern over the situation in Armenia and worried about their parents in Armenia, they did not seriously consider leaving. Rather, in the spring of 1992 they began the construction of the second story of their house. Likewise, the other Armenian family in the village had a second child, sending for the grandparents to come to Shabanova rather than returning to Armenia themselves.

Villagers outside of the Sukiasians' social network were more active in their pronouncements of exclusion. One tractor driver remarked on the car, videocassette player, and other trappings of wealth he thought that Grachuk possessed: "It is impossible to have all those things without working all winter. It can't be honest. Armenians get wealthy no matter where they go. Not Russians" (male, age thirty-four, May 1992).

But as this statement indicates, much of the active exclusion of the Sukiasians from the village incorporated issues of wealth and labor more directly than ethnicity. Even in one of the most negative ethnic statements found in my transcripts, the main focus is on economics: "Why do we pay the Armenians, 'the construction brigade,' thousands and thousands? The people he hires just take the money back to Armenia. It is our money. Kolkhoz money" (pensioner, male, age sixty-two, June 1992).

This statement not only emphasizes economics but also reveals a catch-22 for seasonal laborers. They are not expected to stay in the village, but they are rebuked for taking their earnings outside the community.

PROFITS, LIES, AND VIDEOTAPES

Much of the animosity toward Grachuk reflected popular interpretations of the profits generated by his work brigade. In an interview explaining the methods used in establishing a price with the kolkhoz, Grachuk explained it this way: "I look at the project the kolkhoz needs done and then offer a bid at a specific amount per square meter. I hire men to do the work [at] a lower amount per square meter, but I run around and get all of the materials. . . . The farm would rather work with me because I can do the work faster and three or four times cheaper than Goskomstroi" (November 1990). Although the kolkhoz president was quick to point out that the farm often assisted in obtaining materials for the construction brigade, he confirmed that Grachuk was able to complete projects faster and at less cost than Goskomstroi. But he differed substantially on the savings incurred, claiming a more modest 40 percent savings.

The local mythology in the village was that the construction brigade seriously overcharges the kolkhoz for all projects. Although construction funds typically came out of oblast money specifically targeted for infrastructure development, some residents claimed, "They are taking the money right out of our pockets." Charges of speculation were often levied against the construction brigade by small groups of villagers. The kolkhoz drivers, who had seen their relative wages fall during the early 1990s, were often involved in such discussions.[24]

Claims that Sveta was making over fifteen times the average kolkhoz wages for her work with the brigade also drifted through the village in early 1991, even though most villagers agreed that Sveta worked extremely hard, cooking and washing for the entire brigade. The rumor that she charged the kolkhoz 25,000 rubles for her services was fantastical. Questions regarding her pay rate (which she was unable to quote) indicated that her husband did not include her labor in his bids for construction jobs but instead paid her indirectly from his profits. Nonetheless, from 1991 to 1993, villagers were quick to believe that the Sukiasians were extracting huge and, more important, unjustified sums from the kolkhoz.

The Sukiasians did not enjoy the highest standard of living in the village, yet their possessions were a point of contention among some villagers. Their videocassette player, for example, was one of seven in the village but was nearly always the first one mentioned when discussing the "rich households." Even though the Sukiasians inhabited a house that was still under construction and lacked indoor plumbing until 1994, they were viewed as extremely wealthy. Their employment status outside the typical farm structure was sometimes used as a means of implying that their wealth was ill deserved, again pointing to the class element in their exclusion from the village and their role as outsider. Their failure to fill a specific place in the official economy provides opportunity to highlight their ethnic otherness, generating a situation in which "differentness" becomes compounded.

ON THE OUTSIDE OF REFORM

The seasonal construction brigades of western Siberia, such as the one described, represent potential entrepreneurial experience and ability. In the case of the Sukiasian family, these attributes were not rewarded in the early stages of privatization, either in Armenia or in western Siberia.

Plans to divide kolkhoz assets in Shabanova, in accordance with governmental priorities, center on the division of assets among kolkhoz employees.[25] Although construction brigades were in the employ of the collective farms, the construction workers were individual contractors, not employees. Therefore, brigade leaders such as Grachuk will not share in the distribution of assets from Zaria (assuming that decollectivization takes place). Since his residency is registered in Russia, he will also not receive stock options, land, or animals in the privatization process taking place in his home village in Armenia. In terms of the reform process, individuals such as Grachuk are on the outside looking in, both in western Siberia and in Armenia. As "outsiders" both at home and away, they fit quite well into contemporary conceptualizations of diaspora populations.[26]

The example used here illustrates the interaction between occupational niche and ethnicity in the construction of social identity. This interaction can inform the processes through which regional ethnic relations are to be determined, not only in western Siberia but also in other regions of the federation. The occupational patterns of the post-Soviet diaspora populations, both those within and those outside of Russia, have played an important role in the local conceptualizations of ethnic identity. Such attributes will play a significant part in orienting these identities to a post-Soviet context.

CONCLUSION

This chapter has attempted to present an analysis of the position of one particular outsider group, the Armenian diaspora, in the Russian Federation, by focusing on a specific element within that population: those laborers involved in seasonal migration. Both regional survey data and village evidence from rural western Siberia indicate that the ethnic patterning observed in seasonal construction brigades—in combination with issues of class, income, and labor—keep not only seasonal migrants, but also those who choose to establish permanent residence, on the outside of rural society.

NOTES

1. See, for example, Iu. Avdeev, "Migratsionnaya politika na etape perestroiki," in Kalev Katus, ed., *Podkhody k upravleniiee migratsionym razvitiem* (Tallin: Valgus, 1989), and G. Morozova, "Sovremennye migratsionnye iavleniia: Bezhentsy i emigranty," *Sotsiologicheskie Issledovannia* 3 (1992): 34–40.
2. See G. Lenski, *Power and Privilege: A Theory of Social Stratification* (New York: Armonk Publishers, 1966); D. Featherman and R. Hauser, *Opportunity and Change* (New York: Academic Press, 1978); and especially, V. Radaev and O. Shkaratan, *Sotsial'naya Stratifikatsiya* (Moscow: Nauka, 1995).
3. Seasonal migration has long been recognized as an important part of the overall labor strategy in the Soviet Union. See "O kooperatsii v SSSR: Proekt zakona soiuza sovetskikh sotsialisticheskikh kadrov v narodnom khoziaistve," *Postanovlenie Ts.K. KPPS,* Sov. Min. 13 1117 (December 1979), and A. F. Bockkov, "Nekotorye voprosy pravavago regulipovaniia truda sezonnykh robotnikov sovkhozov," *Voprosy sovetskogo prava i zakonnosti na sovremennom etape* (Minsk: Akademy nauk BSSR, 1965). The ethnic aspect of some migrational streams has also been discussed: I. V. Bromlei and O. Skaratan, "Natsional'nye trudovye traditsii-vazhnyi faktor intensifikatsii prozvodstva," *Sotsiologicheskie Issledovanni* 2 (1983): 43–54.
4. On the specific case of western Siberia, see M. A. Shabanova, *Sezonnaia i postoannais migratsiia naseleniia v sel'skom raione* (Novosibirsk: Nauka, 1990). Information concerning the interaction between labor shortages and the availability of regional construction funds can be found in *Regional'nye problemy naseleniia trudovye resursy SSR* (Moscow: Statistika), and S. Maniakin, "Stabilnost' ekonomicheskogo i sotsial'nogo razvitiia sibirskogo sela," *Mezhdunarodnye Selekh Khozaistva Zhurnal* 5 (1985): 24–28.
5. See O. Latsis, "Individual'nyi trud v sovremnoi sotsialisticheskoi ekonomike," *Kommunist* 1 (1987): 79–82, and also "Rabotnik minitsii i 'shabashnik': esli skazat' otkrovenno," *Izvestiya,* June 16, 1985.
6. See D. V. Chernykh, "Mezhsezonnye rezervy truda: Kakikh ispol'sovat'," *EKO,* no. 9 (1983), pp. 100–106, and also "Ob uporiadochenii organizatsii i oplata truda vremennykh stroitel'nykh brigad," *Postanovlenie Soveta Ministrov SSSR ot 15 Maya 1986 C.P. SSSR* (otdel pervyi) (Moscow, 1986) no. 23, Ct. 134.
7. S. A. Karapetian, "Kak izuchali 'shabashnika,'" *Izvestiya,* April 15, 1986, p. 3. See also V. Galichenko, "Zhitie odnogo shabashnika," *EKO,* no. 3 (1987), pp. 100–136.
8. See Shabanova, *Sezonnaia i postoannais migratsiia naseleniia v sel'skom raione.*
9. See E. Jones, "Minorities in the Soviet Armed Forces," *Comparative Strategy* 3, no. 4 (1982): 285–318, and E. Wimbush and M. Alexiev, "The Ethnic Factor

in the Soviet Armed Forces: Preliminary Findings," Rand Note, N1486-NA (May 1980).
10. Patterns of regional unemployment and regional labor shortage were often exacerbated by institutional regulations concerning the official registration of residence. Individuals not residing in their registered place of residence were often denied access to social services and social guarantees. Seasonal migration crews provided a way to increase local labor power without requiring additional social services (housing, schools, etc.). See C. Buckley, "The Myth of Managed Migration: Migration Controls in the Soviet Period," *Slavic Review* 54, no. 4 (1995): 896–916.
11. See A. Brovin, "Sezonnye brigady: Plusy i minusy," *Sotsialnaya truda* 10 (1983): 77–84.
12. See L. Fedorov, "Shabashnik': blaga ili elo?" *Stroitel'naya gazeta*, December 4, 1985, p. 1, and A. Gal'tsov, "Chego khochet shabashnik," *Sobesednik*, no. 48, (1985): 13.
13. This conceptualization of the stranger as a social type can be found in G. Simmel, *On Individuality and Social Forms*, ed. D. Levine (Chicago: University of Chicago Press, 1971). See also the description of diaspora nationalism in E. Gellner, *Nations and Nationalism* (Ithaca: Cornell University Press, 1983).
14. See Shabanova, *Sezonnaya i postoannais migratsiia naseleniia v sel'skom raione*.
15. Ibid., p. 146.
16. Ibid., p. 124.
17. Ibid., p. 67.
18. Though confusing, the similarity between the name of the village and the family name of the researcher M. A. Shabanova is purely coincidental.
19. Originally they rented a home from Zaria. After one year they began to build their own home in the village, moving into the basement while the house was still in progress.
20. On the difficulties associated with the interface between the social and economic responsibilities of collective farms, see T. I. Zaslavskaya, V. D. Smirnov, and A. N. Shaposhnikov, *Metodologiia i obshche kontury konseptsii perestroiki upravleniia agranom sektorom sovetskogo obshchestva* (Novosibirsk: IEOPP Preprint, 1987).
21. During the last two data collection periods, I lived in a construction trailer (a former railway car) on the Sukiasian property. Since my primary research objective at the time did not concern attitudes toward the Sukiasians, the effect of my residence on the expressed opinions of the residents was not considered. In retrospect, as the relational data was culled from the field record, I realized that some villagers might have been reluctant to express to me negative opinions toward the Sukiasians, since I was living on their property. However, as the recorded remarks indicate, several villagers were not reluctant to share negative opinions toward the family or toward Armenian seasonal migrants in general.
22. A *skotnik* is a person who works with the livestock. In the village of Shabanova, this was a fairly low-status and low-paying occupation.
23. Village respondents ouside the Sukiasian family will not be identified by

name. The subject of this chapter emerged from a review of field notes after I had completed my observations. Whereas I was able to contact the Sukiasians for permission to openly use their information for this chapter, I could not do so for all respondents. The main focus of my reserach while in Shabanova was the social effects of agrarian reform. Although the subject of this chapter is related to that focus, I feel the identities of respondents not informed of this specific topic should remain masked.

24. The similarities in economic positions of the drivers and the *skotniks* and in their opinions toward the construction brigade were not coincidental. Their lower status in the community, as well as the relative decline in their wages during the period of observation, helped generate negative feelings toward those in the community who were not seen as suffering economically.

25. See C. Buckley, "Between Consumption and Production: Boundary Issues on a Siberian Kolkhoz," in S. Kotkin and D. Wolff, eds., *Rediscovering Russia in Asia* (New York: M. E. Sharpe, 1995).

26. See J. Clifford, "Diasporas," *Cultural Anthropology* 9, no. 3 (1994): 302–38. See also E. Hobsbawm, *Nations and Nationalism since 1790* (Cambridge: Cambridge University Press, 1990).

10

A Tale of Two Villages: A Comparative Study of Aboriginal-State Relations in Russia and Canada

Greg Poelzer

For modern states, the status of aboriginal peoples represents one of the greatest challenges to regional integration. Russia is no exception. For sixty years the Soviet state sought to transform the way of life of the aboriginal peoples of the Russian north and to incorporate them into the social fabric of the dominant society. The state collectivized hunting and reindeer-herding economies, repressed shamanism and other spiritual practices, and educated aboriginal children in boarding schools away from their parents. In the late 1980s, however, during the period of *glasnost* and *perestroika*, aboriginal leaders and concerned scholars alike began to assess critically the consequences of Soviet policy for aboriginal peoples.[1] The Khanty writer Yeremei Aipin drew national attention to the destruction that resource exploration and development had wrought on lands traditionally used for hunting and reindeer herding.[2] Others pointed out the startling decline in aboriginal language retention. And in the provocative article "The Big Problems of the Small Peoples," A. Pika and B. Prokhorov's portrayal of aboriginal life contrasted sharply with the official line that the social conditions of aboriginal peoples in Soviet Russia were markedly better than those of their counterparts in other industrialized countries, such as Canada or the United States.

In Canada, for instance, the life expectancy for an Indian person was forty-three years of age; deaths due to violence, accident, or suicide were three times the national average; and only 25 percent of homes on reserves had indoor plumbing.[3] In Russia, social indicators were almost identical: the life expectancy for an aboriginal person was forty-five years, the suicide rate was three times the national average, and less than 1 percent of aboriginal homes had indoor plumbing.[4]

Faced with the question of their survival as distinct peoples, aboriginal leaders in Russia began to mobilize politically at the national and regional levels. In 1988, a group of prominent aboriginal writers led by Vladimir Sangi wrote to Mikhail Gorbachev asking that the government address the serious situation of aboriginal peoples.[5] At the same time, aboriginal leaders at the regional level organized Native associations throughout the Russian north. These efforts culminated in the founding of the Association of the Small Peoples of the North (the equivalent of the Assembly of First Nations in Canada) in March 1990. Today, the twenty-six officially recognized "Small-Numbered Peoples of the North" are seeking greater self-determination within the Russian state.[6] Whether the newly emerging political order can accommodate the goals and aspirations of aboriginal peoples will determine to a significant extent whether the state can successfully extend its rule from its central territorial domains to its most distant, peripheral districts.

This chapter draws a comparative historical analysis of two aboriginal communities, one in Russia and the other in Canada. The origins and outcomes of contemporary struggles for aboriginal self-government are highlighted. Tyanya, an Evenk community in eastern Siberia, and Gift Lake, a Métis community in northwestern Canada, serve as the comparative referents. Adopting a comparative historical approach has the advantage of explaining social phenomena that are both historically grounded and generalizable beyond the cases studied.[7] Notwithstanding very different social and political legacies, struggles for aboriginal self-government in both countries are rooted in the particular course of aboriginal political development resulting from modern state-building. Further, in contrast to most other aboriginal political studies, which tend to focus at the macrohistorical level of analysis,[8] this comparative study, based on fieldwork conducted in the two communities, proceeds at the microhistorical level. Charles Tilly explains: "At the *macrohistorical* level, we seek to account for particular big structures and large processes [for example, state-building] and to chart their alternate forms. At the *microhistorical* level, we trace the encounters of individuals and groups with those structures and processes, with the hope of explaining how people actually experienced them."[9] By wading in at the microhistorical level, we can gain a more intimate understanding of the challenges that aboriginal-state relations pose to the regional integration of the state, a problem shared by Russia and Canada.

WHY TYANYA AND GIFT LAKE?

In the real world there are no perfectly paired cases, of course, yet Tyanya and Gift Lake lend themselves well to comparative analysis, for several reasons. Tyanya and Gift Lake are both relatively isolated and traditional compared with aboriginal communities lying closer to major population and industrial centers. The two communities engage in the same or similar traditional economic pursuits (both communities hunt moose and geese, for instance), since they are located in boreal forest (taiga) regions at comparable latitudes (Tyanya is approximately two degrees north of Gift Lake). In terms of population, the communities are very similar in size, between five and seven hundred people. And importantly, they both recently achieved self-government.

Tyanya is located in the Olekminsk district, in the southwestern corner of Sakha (Yakutia) republic, 280 kilometers south of the district administrative center of Olekminsk (pop. 11,000). Tyanya is the population center of the Tyansky soviet, which has a total area of 23,994 square kilometers. Nestled among the pines and larch of the taiga forest, Tyanya sits on the left bank of the Tyanya River, not far from its confluence with the Tokko River. From the other side of the Tyanya River, a small mountain overlooks the village, completing the postcard setting. The settlement is accessible from Olekminsk during the summer only by air or river and during the winter by air. The Tyanya and Tokko Rivers serve as the primary local transportation routes during the summer. Since Tyanya is located in southern Sakha, the winters are markedly warmer than in the capital of the republic, Yakutsk: when it is fifty degrees (centigrade) below zero in Yakutsk, it is only thirty degrees below in Tyanya, though the temperature can fall to forty degrees below. Most of the present-day community members of Tyanya are descendants of the Evenk clans of southwestern Sakha, who inhabited the basin of the Tokko, Torgo, and Cheruoda Rivers—a group referred to as the Tokkinsky Evenk by Russian (Soviet) anthropologists. According to oral tradition, the first families of the Tokkinsky Evenk came to the Tyanya area between 1850 and 1860.[10] By 1931, it was estimated that some sixty Evenk families, numbering about 300 people, were living in the Tokko-Tyanya River Basin.[11] In 1991, the population of the settlement was 557, 70 percent of whom were Evenk; the rest were predominantly Yakut.

Gift Lake Métis settlement is located in northern Alberta, northwest of Lesser Slave Lake, and has a total area of 840 square kilometers. Most of its residents live in the settlement village extending out from the eastern shore of the lake that gives the settlement its name. The land is dominated by rolling hills and is treed by spruce, poplar, birch, and larch. A number of small lakes and ponds dot the territory of the settlement, and a large lake, which used to support a vibrant commercial fishery, abuts its eastern border. Of the eight Métis settlements in Alberta, Gift Lake is one of the most remote. It is accessible from the major town in the area, High Prairie (pop. 3,000), by a secondary highway that cuts through the settlement (and that was paved only in the last decade). The summers are quite warm, but in winter the temperature can drop to forty degrees below zero. Most of the residents of Gift Lake settlement are descendants of Cree and Cree-speaking Métis families who lived in the area north of Lesser Slave Lake.[12] Although Métis people have lived in this general area for some time, the first Métis to settle continuously in the Gift Lake area arrived in 1878.[13] By the 1920s other families began to settle there as well, and by 1942 six families were living at Gift Lake. In 1993, the population of the settlement was 697, almost all of whom consider themselves Métis.

ABORIGINAL LIFE ON THE EVE OF MODERN STATE-BUILDING

At the beginning of this century, neither Tyanya nor Gift Lake existed as aboriginal settlements. Tyanya was a small trading post inhabited by a half dozen Yakut families, and Gift Lake was inhabited by only a couple of Métis families. Tyanya and Gift Lake, like many other contemporary aboriginal settlements, came into existence only as a result of the momentous changes precipitated by modern state-building. To understand the profundity of these changes, we need first to examine Evenk and Métis life on the eve of modern state-building.

At the time of the Russian Revolution, the Tokkinsky Evenk, like other indigenous peoples of the Russian north, still lived a tribal way of life. Commenting on the situation in Sakha in the early 1920s, M. P. Sokolov wrote, "With few exceptions they [the Evenk], up to now, have not changed their indigenous ways of life and almost all are nomadic trappers."[14] The Tokkinsky Evenk were primarily hunter-gatherers and, in contrast to the Evenk who lived on the tundra, did not practice intensive reindeer breeding. Small herds of reindeer were kept but were limited to the purposes of transportation, clothing, milk, and a supplemental meat supply. Instead, the taiga Evenk primarily hunted wild reindeer, moose, and elk, fished char and trout, and gathered berries, mushrooms, and other edible plants. This way of life, based on hunting-gathering and pastoralism, required the Evenk to live in small, nomadic social collectivities. These collectivities, or clans, were patriarchical and often consisted of only one or two families, rarely more than several. The Metanka clan, for example, one of the original clans to locate in the Tyanya area, consisted of one father and the families of his four sons.[15] Given the small size of Evenk social collectivities, there were no formal, authoritative decision-making structures. To the extent that decisions had to be made within a clan or among clans, they were traditionally reached by consensus or mutual understandings. It is also important to note some significant intercultural exchanges resulting from the northern migration of the Yakut people into territories inhabited by the Evenk, several centuries before Russian colonization. One of these was the adoption of the Yakut knife (which had a metal blade) as a standard piece of hunting equipment. More significant was the adoption of the Yakut language for trade and, eventually, for everyday use by many Evenk.[16] In one district of southern Sakha, it was reported in the early 1930s: "Every single one of these nomadic Evenk knows the Yakut language. Most of these nomadic Evenk have forgotten their native Evenk language.... it is clear although they are 'nomadic' the Yakut language has become their native language."[17] Despite these cultural changes, the Evenk sociopolitical organization endured.

In the early part of this century, the Métis of northern Alberta also still lived a nomadic, tribal way of life. Most Métis hunted moose and deer, harvested whitefish, gathered berries and other bush food, collected herbs and roots for medicine, and trapped fur to exchange for supplies such as flour and ammunition. Even as late as the 1930s, these traditional activities persisted as the primary economic pursuits of northern Alberta Métis. In his petition to the Alberta provincial government requesting free and unrestricted access to trapping, the prominent Métis leader J. F. Dion noted: "The Métis and non-Treaty Indians being by nature of a transient and migratory disposition, trap over very large areas carrying their equipment by dog team and establishing progressive camps as they travel through the country. Moreover, the Métis and non-Treaty Indians depend almost entirely for their livelihood upon their trapping activities."[18] Along with nomadism, the northern Alberta Métis shared other important elements of social organization with the Evenk. Crucially, the primary unit of social and political life was the family clan. Beyond the family unit, social organization was fluid, and there were no formal decision-making structures. Families set up camp wherever they chose, and trapping areas were acknowledged by mutual respect. In these regards Métis life was similar to the traditional way of life of the Indians of the Canadian boreal regions, such as the Cree and the Dene, with one exception. As a result of the mixed heritage of the Métis people, Christianity—not shamanism—provided the primary basis of spirituality for many Métis. This distinction is still evident today.

Why were the Evenk and the Métis able to maintain traditional ways of life into the first part of this century? Before modern state-building, tsarist Sakha and pre-Confederation Alberta[19] were what Anthony Giddens calls primary settlement frontiers, "regions where a state is expanding outwards into territory previously either having virtually no inhabitants, or populated by tribal communities."[20] Frontiers are areas "on the peripheral regions of a state (not necessarily adjoining another state) in which the political authority of the center is diffuse or thinly spread."[21] Subject to limited control by premodern political orders, the Evenk and the Métis were able to carve out considerable political and cultural autonomy. This situation changed dramatically, however, with the development of modern states in Russia and Canada.

STATE POLICY AND ABORIGINAL POLITICAL DEVELOPMENT

Despite obvious differences in the nature of their polities and economies, the modern states that emerged in Russia after the October Revolution in 1917 and in Canada after Confederation in 1867 displayed critical similarities. In contrast to the political orders that preceded them, the modern states in Russia and Canada possessed both a universalizing political logic and an organizational capacity to pursue this logic. The organizational capacity was manifest in the creation of highly centralized, bureaucratic administrative organs. The universalizing political logic was reflected in, among other things, the creation of universal citizenship and in the efforts by Canadian and Soviet state-builders to transform frontier areas into bordered territories. This latter undertaking required establishing effective surveillance and internal pacification over the entire territorial expanse of the state, including its most remote regions and populations. From this perspective, aboriginal peoples represented an exceptional challenge. The nomadism of many indigenous peoples made surveillance and internal pacification difficult, if not impossible. The perceived "backwardness" of indigenous peoples precluded their immediate incorporation as equal members of the body politic. Exceptional challenges demanded exceptional measures: in the eyes of the state, tribal ways of life had to be eliminated.

In the Yakut ASSR,[22] "the Native question" became a central concern of state policy following the creation of the Committee of the North at the federal level in 1925. This committee was the primary state organ charged with developing and overseeing state policy toward aboriginal peoples. The directives of the Committee of the North were, first, to address the social crisis confronting many aboriginal peoples in the Russian north as a consequence of the devastation wrought by the Revolution and the Civil War, especially the decimation of reindeer herds and of fur-bearing animals, and, second, to develop a strategy to incorporate the "Small Peoples of the North" into the new political order. Although aboriginal policy was developed by the central government, its implementation was carried out by regional administrations. In 1925, the

Yakut ASSR created the Committee for the Affairs of the Small Native Peoples to oversee implementation, marking the beginning of a concerted effort to tackle the Native question.

Change in all other dimensions of aboriginal life depended, first, on addressing the political dimension. If the state was to maintain effective surveillance and internal pacification over aboriginal populations, nomadism and egalitarianism had to be checked and transformed. Accordingly, aboriginal peoples were organized into a succession of territorial-administrative units. These successive changes were, in part, a consequence of general changes in the structural organization of the state, but they were also a result of the increasing control exercised by the state over indigenous peoples. Before 1925, the clans that made up the Tokkinsky Evenk fell within the administrative jurisdiction of the Charo-Olekminsky raion of Aldansky okrug.[23] In 1925, the raion was transferred to Olekminsky okrug. At that time, the Tokkinsky Evenk, along with three other clan groups, were organized into *clan soviets* within the raion.[24] As administrative units, clan soviets simply reflected existing Evenk sociopolitical organization and thus were not new forms of political organization. Moreover, clan soviets were not fixed *territorially;* rather, they were mobile political *administrative* units within the raion-level territorial administration. Importantly, the nature of clan soviets underscored the limited power of the Soviet state over its frontier regions.

With the rise of Joseph Stalin, the power of the center waxed and the state began to consolidate its rule in the regions. This change was reflected in territorial-administrative changes in the regions and among aboriginal communities. At the district level, okrugs were eliminated in the late 1920s as a meso-order of administration within the Yakut ASSR; Olekminsky okrug became Olekminsky raion on January 9, 1930,[25] and for the next seven years the Evenk remained under the jurisdiction of Olekminsky raion. In 1937, Tokkinsky raion, which was composed overwhelmingly of Evenk and Yakut, was created from two raions: Olekminsky and Tommotsky (the latter now part of Aldansky raion).[26] For nearly two decades, the Evenk of Tyanya fell within the jurisdiction of this territorial-administrative unit, dominated by aboriginal peoples.

At the local level, political change was felt more directly. In the 1930s, clan soviets were abolished, and the state started denomadizing the Evenk and began building institutions of local government. No other changes in Evenk life would be as radical. The Evenk were organized into the Tokkinsky Village Soviet, modeled along the lines of village soviets throughout rural Russia. However, the soviet—like the neighboring Kindigirsky Village Soviet—retained its clan name, thus maintaining its aboriginal identity. The Evenk were encouraged to live in one of two settlements within the soviet: Tyanya or POS (Trapping and Hunting Station), which was south of Tyanya on the Tokko River. The results of this process were not instantaneous, however: by 1940, at Tyanya only eighteen of forty-six households and at POS only three of thirty households lived in permanent dwellings; the rest still lived a nomadic way of life.[27] Nevertheless, the Evenk were now unambiguously subject to the authority of the local soviet council. From this time forward, decisions affecting community life were made authoritatively, not by consensus. In 1949, near the end of Stalin's regime, Tyanya and POS continued to exist as two separate settlements of roughly similar size. At that time, the population of Tyanya was 136 and POS 117, about 74 percent and 78 percent of whom were Evenk, the rest being mainly Yakut.[28]

During the period of Nikita Khrushchev, the Evenk experienced further significant changes, marking the end of a nomadic way of life. At the district level, Tokkinsky raion was consolidated in 1953 with Olekminsky raion, which had a substantial Russian population.[29] More dramatic were the changes that occurred at the local level, especially the process of "villagization" in which smaller, often seminomadic communities were amalgamated into a single, larger settlement. Villagization was seen as pivotal to the accelerated assimilation of aboriginal peoples into Soviet society. It also made surveillance and internal pacification easier to accomplish. As a consequence, POS was disbanded and its residents were moved to Tyanya. Further, all residents at Tyanya were settled in permanent dwellings. Between the 1960s and early 1990s, other than the change in the name of the soviet from Tokkinsky (after the clan) to Tyansky (after the village), the administrative and territorial organization of the Evenk of Tyanya changed very little. By 1967, the population of Tyanya was 398.[30]

At the same time that the Evenk were experiencing dramatic changes in their lives, so too were the Métis people of northern Alberta, a third of the way around the world. As progeny of European and Indian cultures, many Métis people reflected the way of life of both worlds, and the lifestyle of many Métis was largely indistinguishable from that of Indians. This was particularly true of the Métis of northern Alberta. At the time of Confederation, however, the Canadian government chose not to recognize the Métis as aboriginal peoples and, thus, did not assume legal responsibility for their affairs.[31] As a consequence, unlike Canadian Indians, the Métis across Canada did not acquire separate, territorial-administrative bases. As T. C. Pocklington has noted, "By far the most important difference between the Indians and the Métis is that the former acquired, at least legally, a secure land base while the latter did not."[32] But because the federal government chose not to recognize the Métis people, it left the door open for provincial governments to assume jurisdiction over them. In the 1930s, the Alberta government did just that. Importantly, the assimilationist and segregationist policies pursued by the provincial government toward the Métis people thereafter strongly paralleled the Soviet policies directed toward the Evenk.

The Métis people were drawn to the attention of the provincial government of Alberta in the early 1930s. At that time, Alberta was engaged in provincial state-building, having entered the Canadian federal state in 1905. Alberta had decided to open forest reserves to agricultural settlement, and soon the federal government would transfer jurisdiction over natural resources to the province. Since many Métis were squatters on these lands, their way of life was seriously threatened, but their leaders in Alberta were especially effective in mobilizing Métis people to meet this challenge. In 1932, the Métis Association of Alberta was formed to advance Métis interests, particularly claims for separate Métis land bases for access to free hunting and fishing and claims for social entitlements such as education. At the same time, politicians jockeyed for the Métis vote in provincial elections, enabling the Métis to find receptive ears within the provincial state. Finally, the Great Depression was especially hard on the Métis, whose living conditions were markedly worse than those of the neighboring Indian populations. As a result, the government of Alberta established a royal commission, known as the Ewing Commission, in 1934 to investigate the situation of the Métis and to provide policy recommendations. Hearings were held throughout the subsequent year. In early 1936, the commission produced its report, and in 1938 the provincial government acted on the report by passing the Métis Population Betterment Act.

The imperatives underlying the recommendations of the Ewing Commission and subsequent government policy—the imperatives of well-being and assimilation—had uncanny parallels to those guiding the Soviet policy in the Russian north. Like Russia confronting the social devastation left by the Revolution and the Civil War, the government in Alberta recognized that measures had to be taken to address the desperate social conditions resulting from the depression. The government observed that the population expansion into and the development of hitherto frontier regions of the province had undermined the capacity of the Métis to use traditional economic pursuits to provide a means of livelihood, "creating conditions of extreme privation and rendering their occupations precarious even in the remote and wholly unsettled districts."[33] As a consequence, many Métis were living in shacks on the fringes of Indian reserves and along road allowances, in conditions conducive to the spread of communicable diseases such as tuberculosis. "It is common practice, even in the settled areas, for large families (in some cases as many as ten or twelve person [*sic*]) to live in a one room shack without any ventilation or any regard for the protection of their health."[34] In addition to poor health and housing, the high level of illiteracy among the Métis population also worried the government. One Métis leader, Malcom Norris, commented on his fellow Métis, "If you know the half-breed element at all, you will know that they are extremely illiterate and therefore inarticulate."[35] However, the government's concern with Métis education and literacy was not entirely altruistic but was also conscious of the "stigma which attaches to any civilized country that permits a large number of children to grow up within its boundaries without the slightest elementary education."[36] To fail to incorporate the Métis into the social fabric of the dominant society was to fail as a *modern* state.

Government assimilationist goals and Métis aspirations for a land base coincided, and on November 22, 1938, the Métis Population Betterment Act was passed into law. The cornerstone of this legislation was its provisions for the creation of settlements (originally called colonies) for the Métis people of northern Alberta. Of the original Métis settlements, two were subsequently terminated by the provincial government (one settlement was unoccupied, and the residents of the second were moved to other settlements); still other settlements were amalgamated and split. As a result, eight settlements exist today, one of which is Gift Lake.

In 1939, in accordance with the Métis Population Betterment Act, a Métis Settlement Association, which officially denoted the members of a given settlement, was established at Settlement Area No. 3, Utikuma Lake (later renamed Gift Lake), by the Métis people of the Gift Lake area. In 1940, 32 families numbering 149 people were approved as belonging to the settlement association.[37] Of these families, 13 were living on the settlement while the other 19 were waiting to move onto it.[38] Less than three decades later, in 1967, the population had grown to 404 as other Métis families moved onto the settlement from the surrounding area.[39]

In contrast to Tyanya, Gift Lake did not experience numerous territorial changes. But Gift Lake, along with the other Métis settlements, did undergo very important administrative changes, each one waxing the power of the province vis-à-vis the settlement and, thus, increasing the provincial surveillance and internal pacification capacities in the frontier. An important 1940 amendment to the Métis Population Betterment Act eliminated the phrase "that the ways and means of giving effect to such recommendations [of the Ewing Commission] should be arrived at by means of conferences and negotiations between the Government of the Province and representatives of the Métis population of the Province."[40] Other amendments in 1940 gave the minister and the cabinet sweeping powers over the settlements, severely reducing local political autonomy.

In 1952, amendments concerning the governing boards further increased the power of the provincial state. Whereas previously the board for each settlement had consisted of up to five elected members of the respective settlement association, each board now consisted of a supervisor appointed by the government, two settlement association members appointed by the government, and only two members elected by the settlement population. Between 1952 and 1990, governance of Métis settlements changed very little. The changes in 1940 and 1952 were inconsistent with democratic principles of the polity of Alberta. However, they were similar to the pattern of aboriginal-state relations that emerged in Tyanya. As the power of the state grew, so did its domination of aboriginal communities, regardless of whether the regime was authoritarian or democratic.

For the Evenk of Tyanya and the Métis of Gift Lake, modern state-building meant fundamental and irrevocable change. In each case, the state created aboriginal settlements to serve as crucibles within which Evenk and Métis lives would be transformed. Nomadism was replaced by life in permanent settlements with delimited territorial boundaries, and membership in the community became permanent. Local structures of government replaced traditional, consensus decision-making. In the process, important elements of Evenk and Métis life were lost. Nevertheless, others endured. Kinship, for instance, remained central to political life within the communities. Traditional activities such as hunting and fishing also remained important in everyday life. The very creation of aboriginal settlements segregated these communities from dominant Russian and Canadian societies and had the unintended consequence of melding strong, aboriginal collective identities. It is these collective identities that provided the foundation for the quests for self-determination in Tyanya and Gift Lake.

THE PATH TO SELF-GOVERNMENT

On November 1, 1990, the provisions of the Alberta Métis Settlements Accord negotiated between the Alberta Métis Federation and the government of Alberta became law; as a result, the Métis of Gift Lake, along with the Métis of the seven other settlements, became self-governing within the Province of Alberta. On December 23, 1992, the Supreme Soviet of the Republic of Sakha passed "The Law Concerning Nomadic Clan Communities of the Small-Numbered Peoples of the North"; as a consequence, the Evenk of Tyanya, along with other aboriginal communities of Sakha, also formally entered the era of self-government. These agreements represent firsts for aboriginal peoples in both countries. The Alberta Métis remain the only Métis in Canada to have a secure land base and are also one of the few aboriginal groups to have achieved self-government. Sakha republic was the first jurisdiction in Russia—and remains one of only two such jurisdictions—where aboriginal peoples can, by law, organize self-governing communities.

These self-government agreements were the consequence of the particular course of aboriginal political development precipitated by modern state-building. This course of development represents a radical break with crucial elements of traditional social and political life. To be sure, basic elements of aboriginal culture have endured and are crucial to defining contemporary aboriginal identity. Others, though, have irrevocably changed. The processes by which the state attempted to eliminate tribal ways of life and, thus, transform frontier regions into bordered territories created the foundations for politicized aboriginal communities. But as resource mobilization theorists remind us, "The passage from condition to action [is] contingent upon the availability of resources and changes in the opportunities for collective action."[41] Together, the assimilationist and segregationist policies created the *condition* of politicized aboriginal communities and provided the *resources* for those communities to engage in struggles for greater political autonomy. Broader changes in state and society, as well as in the international community, provided the *opportunity* for aboriginal collective action. This analysis turns now to a discussion of condition, resources, and opportunity.

The condition of politicized aboriginal communities assumes the existence of both interests and organization. *Interests* refer to the grievances of groups engaged in collective action. For the Evenk and the Métis, the primary goal of their political struggles was self-government: securing a collective land base and acquiring decision-making authority over the people and territory of that land base. As early as 1969, in a letter to the premier of Alberta, the Métis Settlement Associations raised the issue of self-government: "We would respectfully submit the Government should give immediate consideration to incorporating the concept of self autonomy in the Métis Betterment Act in order to permit the Métis Settlement Associations to more effectively govern their own affairs."[42] The political autonomy of the Métis settlements was advanced throughout the 1970s; however, the most detailed articulation of this autonomy appeared in the 1982 federation document that outlined the bases of Métis aboriginal rights, including the right to self-government. The Evenk, along with the other aboriginal peoples of Sakha, formally expressed their claims to self-determination for the first time in the 1990 decree that founded the Association of the Small Peoples of the North.[43]

Organization reflects the degree of collective identity and the extent of intragroup ties. Evenk and Métis identities, as already argued, were fundamentally shaped by the segregationist policies of the state. The loosely connected, nomadic social collectivities of the various Evenk and Métis family units living near Tyanya and Gift Lake, respectively, were brought together into more or less permanent communities. From the perspective of collective action, these local-level settlements are the fundamental unit of political community and group identity. Unlike many modern nations, in which the strongest political attachment lies with the national rather than the regional or local community, contemporary aboriginal peoples find their strongest political attachment in the local-level community. The development of Evenk and Métis political organization reflected this reality.

Formal structures of group organization at the local level were already institutionalized by the time the Evenk and the Métis embarked on their quests for self-government: the village soviet in the case of the Evenk; the settlement in the case of the Métis. Group organization, however, was not limited to the local level. The experiences of state policies that the Evenk of Tyanya and the Métis of Gift Lake shared with other aboriginal peoples fostered a pantribal identity. The development of a literate aboriginal population, courtesy of the state, as well as the usage of a single common language (Russian or English) among aboriginal peoples, made this possible. Pantribalism served as a surrogate for nationalism among disparate aboriginal peoples. For the residents of Gift Lake and Tyanya, the most important pantribal organization was at the regional level. Although there are also district-level and national-level organizations, these have played a secondary role. In 1989, the Association of the Small Peoples of the North of Yakutia (Sakha) was created through the efforts of members of the aboriginal intelligentsia in the Yakut ASSR. The association has an ambiguous status, since it was only semiautonomous from the state. It was created and is still funded by the state; yet the goal of the association is to represent groups challenging the state. In 1975, the Alberta Federation of Métis Settlement Associations was created by the leadership of the eight Métis settlements. In contrast to the association in Sakha, the federation was incorporated as a nonprofit society, independent of the state. Both of these organizations played central roles in advancing the collective interests of the Evenk of Tyanya and the Métis of Gift Lake.

For groups to pursue their interests, they must possess resources. Compared with the dominant state and society, the Evenk and the Métis are relatively resource-poor, especially in terms of numbers and money. But they are not without resources. Many of the resources available to the Evenk and the Métis were provided or generated unintentionally by the state. Among the most important of these are land, administrative apparatuses, skilled leadership, money, and access to media. If the struggle for self-government is viewed not simply as bringing pressure to bear on the state but also as collecting those elements that make for self-government, then the Evenk and the Métis are resource-rich in critical areas. One has only to compare, for instance, the Alberta Métis with the Métis in other provinces of Canada, who do not have territorial-administrative units, to see the resource advantages of the Alberta Métis.

The occupancy of territory claimed by the Evenk and the Métis was perhaps their most important resource. Another important asset was the possession of institutions of local government. If nothing else, governments can organize other resources, including people, for political struggle. The occupancy of territory and the possession of institutions of local government, however, significantly lowered the threshold to acquire self-government in both cases. Land did not have to be set aside, and institutions did not have to be built from scratch. Rather, self-government was mainly a question of the transfer of authority from the state to the aboriginal communities.

The resolution of this question required bringing other resources to bear on the state. Leadership and media—and to a lesser extent, money—played a much greater role, and the Evenk and the Métis were especially well served by skilled political leaders. At the regional level in Yakutsk, Evenk aboriginal leaders, many of whom were apparatchiks under the Soviet system, were able to steer aboriginal interests carefully through the legislative processes. This feat is remarkable given that aboriginal peoples make up less than 5 percent of the population of Sakha. At the local level, effective leadership was just as critical, not only in mobilizing local support for self-governing communities but also in dealing with district-level administrations, which had a considerable impact on the process. Without the tireless leadership of Mikhail Bagaev, Tyanya might not have been one of the communities in Sakha to achieve self-government. In Alberta, the fate of Gift Lake depended more on the leadership of the federation collectively than it did at the local level. In both cases, the media was a very important tool in bringing pressure to bear on the state. The newspaper press in Sakha devoted considerable attention to the situation of aboriginal peoples, particularly their living conditions and the vulnerability of their cultures. In Alberta, the media was also useful, even when not used. In 1989, when negotiations in self-government were stalling, the Métis threatened to run a caravan into the provincial capital just before the election, which would have embarrassed the government. An agreement was reached before the election.[44] Finally, money cannot be ignored as a valuable resource. Conducting meetings, printing policy positions, and distributing promotional paraphernalia among the rank and file all required funding. Sakha and Alberta are comparatively resource-rich, and as a consequence, the amount of money available to the aboriginal organizations from the respective states was comparatively high.

Although politicized aboriginal communities and the possession of resources were necessary conditions for successful struggles for self-government, they were not sufficient. An opportunity to act was also needed. Struggles for self-government could not take place without critical changes within state and society. The emergence of a dissent-permitting society and national attempts at constitutional change were crucial in this regard. Without such conditions, the mobilization of collective resources and the articulation of group interests is difficult, if not impossible.

CONCLUSION

The process of collective action to acquire self-government by the Métis of Alberta, starting in the late 1960s, took much longer than did this process for the Evenk, whose action started in 1988 with the tumultuous changes accompanying the collapse of the Soviet order. But in both cases, collective action bore fruit: Gift Lake, in 1990, and Tyanya, in 1992, became self-governing communities. In both cases, self-government agreements enable modern states and aboriginal peoples to coexist. Self-government represents the two sides of aboriginal-state relations. On the aboriginal side, self-government represents the recognition by the state of some degree of political autonomy for aboriginal peoples to make decisions affecting the well-being of their political communities. On the state side, self-government represents success in the regional integration of its rule.

The successful struggles for self-government in Tyanya and Gift Lake are still exceptions in both Russia and Canada. Some communities are poised to achieve self-government in the near future, but for most, the struggle will continue for some time. Until the state accommodates the aspirations of all aboriginal communities, the integration of the state—from its central domains to its most peripheral regions—will remain incomplete.

NOTES

1. See, for instance, V. Sangi, "Mnenie ob ostroy probleme otchuzhdenie," *Sovetskaya Rossiya*, September 11, 1988; Margaita Lomunova, "Sever Stavit Problemy," *Literaturnaya Rossiya*, April 22, 1988; and V. Komorov, "U Narodnostey Severa," *Sel'skaya zhizn'*, October 27, 1988.

2. Yeremei Aipin, "Not by Oil Alone," *Moscow News Weekly*, no. 2 (1989), as published in *IWGIA Newsletter*, no. 57 (May 1989).
3. Don Carmichael, Tom Pocklington, and Greg Pyrcz, *Democracy and Rights in Canada* (Toronto: Harcourt Brace Jovanovich, 1991), p. 179.
4. A. Pika and B. Prokhorov, "Bol'shie problemy malykh narodov," *Kommunist*, no. 16 (1988), pp. 76–83.
5. "Native Northerners Eye Their Rights," *Current Digest of the Soviet Press* 42, no. 29 (1990).
6. Several terms are used to refer to those peoples who lived a tribal, nomadic way of life at the time of first contact with the Russians, following the Yermak expedition of 1581. Today, the total aboriginal population stands at just over 180,000 people. The twenty-six officially recognized "Small-Numbered Peoples of the North" are the Aleut, Chukchi, Chuvan, Dolgan, Ents, Eskimo, Evenk, Even, Itel'men, Ket, Khant, Koryak, Mansi, Nanai, Negidal, Nenets, Nganasan, Nivkh, Orochi, Orok, Saami, Sel'kup, Tofalar, Udege, Ul'chi, and Yukagi.
7. Theda Skocpol, *States and Social Revolutions: A Comparative Analysis of France, Russia, and China* (Cambridge: Cambridge University Press, 1979), p. 6.
8. Some excellent works concerning aboriginal politics in Russia and proceeding at a macrohistorical level of analysis include the following: James Forsyth, *A History of the Peoples of Siberia: Russia's North Asian Colony, 1581–1990* (Cambridge: Cambridge University Press, 1992); Gail Fondahl, "Siberia: Native Peoples and Newcomers in Collision," in Ian Bremmer and Ray Taras, eds., *Nations and Politics in the Soviet Successor States* (Cambridge: Cambridge University Press, 1993); and Yuri Slezkine, *Arctic Mirrors: Russia and the Small Peoples of the North* (Ithaca: Cornell University Press, 1994).
9. Charles Tilly, *Big Structures, Large Processes, Huge Comparisons* (New York: Russell Sage Foundation, 1984), p. 61. Tilly further argues that if "the work is historical, it need not be grand. When it comes to understanding proletarianization, for example, much of the most valuable work proceeds at the scale of a single village. Keith Wrightson and David Levine's study of Terling, Essex, from 1525 to 1700 tells us more about the creation of a propertyless underclass than do reams of general essays about capitalism" (p. 14).
10. Interview with Evenk elder, November 1991.
11. "Proizvodstvenno Finansovy Plan Tokkinskogo Okhotsovkhoza Yakutgostorga na 1931 god," Central State Archives of the Yakut ASSR, F. 55, Op. 4, D. 1.
12. As a legal-racial category, the Métis people are one of the three aboriginal peoples recognized by the Canadian constitution (the other two are the Indian and the Inuit peoples). In its broadest meaning, "Métis" refers to anyone who is of mixed Indian-European ancestry and who is not a legally defined, status Indian. Sometimes, "Métis" more narrowly refers to the people of mixed Indian (usually Cree) and Scottish or French ancestry who are the descendants of the Red River community of Manitoba during the last half of the nineteenth century. Métis people lived in northern Alberta long

before the arrival of settler populations, the founding of the Canadian state, or the eruption of the Riel Rebellions in the 1880s.
13. David May, ed., *Mud Roads and Strong Backs: The History of the Métis Settlement of Gift Lake* (Edmonton: Friesen Printers, 1984), p. 1.
14. M. P. Sokolov, *Yakutia po Perepisi 1917 goda* (Irkutsk: Izdanie Yakutskogo Statisticheskogo Upravleniya, 1925), p. xxvi.
15. Interview with an Evenk elder, November 1991.
16. By the turn of the century, it is estimated, as many as half of the Evenk in Sakha spoke Yakut as their native language. (At the same time, Evenk words had made their way into Yakut: an estimated 4 percent of the words of the Yakut language are Evenk in origin.)
17. "Dokladaya Zapiska o Kochevykh Evenkov Aldano-Mayskogo Raiona," Central State Archives of the Yakut ASSR, F. 50, Op. 1, D. 3794.
18. "To the Honourable George Hoadley, Minister of Agriculture," Provincial Archives of Alberta, Accession No. 70.414/1417.
19. At that time, northern Alberta was the District of Athabaska.
20. Anthony Giddens, *The Nation-State and Violence* (Berkeley: University of California Press, 1987), pp. 49–50.
21. Ibid., p. 50.
22. The Yakut Autonomous Soviet Socialist Republic was founded in April 1922 as a constituent unit of the Russian Soviet Federated Socialist Republic.
23. "Proekt Ekonomicheskogo i Administrativnogo Paoonirovaniya Olekminskogo Okruga," Central State Archives of the Yakut ASSR, F. 70, Op. 1, D. 1055. During the 1920s, okrugs existed as middle-level territorial-administrative units, between the republic and the raions.
24. Ibid.
25. Nikolai Nikolaevich Tikhonov, *Meri po Bozrozheniyu Kochevoy Rodovoy Obshchiny Tokkinskikh Evenkov Etnicheskoi Gruppy "Cheroda"* (Yakutsk: n.p., 1992), p. 12; See *Statistichesky Spravochnik Yakutskoy ASSR* (Yakutsk: Izdanie Gosplana i UNKhU YaASSR, 1941), p. 56.
26. "Opisanie Tokkinskogo Raiona Yakutskoi ASSR [1951]," Olekminsk State Archives, F. 23, D. 15, Op. 1.
27. "Dokladnaya Pereselenchesky Otdel pri SNK YaASSR tov. Borisovu S.Z.," Yakut State Archives, F. 52, Op. 18, D. 292.
28. "Tokkinskiy Raion Fiziko-Geograficheskiy Obzor," Olekminsk State Archives, F. 23, D. 14, Op. 1.
29. "Otchetnaya Vedomost'," Olekminsk State Archives, F. 56, D. 18, Op. 1.
30. Olekminsk State Archives, F. 3, D. 331, Op. 1.
31. Only in the 1982 Canadian constitution were the Métis finally recognized as aboriginal peoples, along with the Indian and the Inuit peoples.
32. T. C. Pocklington, *The Government and Politics of the Alberta Métis Settlements* (Regina: Canadian Plains Research Center, 1991), p. 6.
33. "Report of Activities in Connection with the Settlement of the Métis, Period January 1st, 1939, to January 31st, 1940," Provincial Archives of Alberta, Accession No. 70.414/File 1937.
34. Ibid.

35. "Evidence and Proceeding, Half-Breed Commission," Provincial Archives of Alberta, Accession No. 75.75, Box 2, #9.
36. Government of Alberta, *Report of the Royal Commission Appointed to Investigate the Conditions of the Half-Breed Population of Alberta, 1936* (Edmonton: Government of Alberta, 1936), p. 14.
37. "Report of Activities in Connection with the Settlement of the Métis."
38. Ibid.
39. "Progress Report: All Colonies, November 30, 1966–November 30, 1967," Provincial Archives of Alberta, Accession No. 79.333/2.
40. Government of Alberta, *An Act Respecting the Métis Population of the Province* (Edmonton: Government of Alberta, 1938).
41. Eduardo Canel, "New Social Movement Theory and Resource Mobilization: The Need for Integration," in William K. Carroll, ed., *Organizing Dissent: Contemporary Social Movements in Theory and Practice* (Toronto: Garamond Press, 1992), p. 24.
42. "To the Honourable Harry Strom, Premier of Alberta, and the Honourable Members of the Executive Council," Provincial Archives of Alberta, Accession No. 76.502, Box 20.
43. *Ustav Assotsiatsii Narodnostey Severa Yakutii* (Yakutsk, 1990).
44. Pocklington, *Government and Politics*, pp. 149–50.

11

The Tatarstan Model: A Situational Dynamic

Nail Midkhatovich Moukhariamov

The republic of Tatarstan has occupied a central place in recent years in virtually every discussion of the federative structure of Russia and its likely path of evolution. Reasons for this attention derive as much from the republic's innovative role in Russian economic reform and cultural complexity as from Tatarstan's important strategic location at the heart of Eurasia. Located at the intersection of the main latitudinal pivot of Russia and the great Volga River, the republic's boundary intersects four navigable rivers and two main rail lines linking the central part of the country with the Urals and Siberia. This geographic centrality is complemented by the presence of substantial energy reserves in the region, making it a republic with great economic potential.

Tatarstan's complex ethnic map also makes it an important arena for evaluating the linkages between ethnic dynamics and emerging center-republic relations. After Russians, Tatars form the second-largest ethnic community in the Russian Federation, accounting for just under 4 percent of its population. Within their own republic, Tatars account for 48.5 percent of the population (1.8 million people), and Russians are a close second, composing 43.2 percent of the republic. However, only a quarter of all Tatars live in the republic: a further 3.8 million live in various regions of the Russian Federation.[1] The most significant concentrations are found in Moscow city and oblast, in Udmurtia, and in Ulyansk, Samara, Orenburg, Perm, Sverdlovsk, Chelyabinsk, and Tyumen oblasts; more than one million reside in the neighboring republic of Bashkortostan. Although approximately 80 percent of all Tatars are concentrated in the Volga-Urals region, beyond Russia more than one million Tatars live in Central Asia and Kazakhstan,[2] and compact groups of Tatars are found in the Baltic countries, Poland, China, Turkey, Romania, and Finland.

Tatarstan is thus the focal point for a substantial ethnic diaspora concentrated principally in Central Russia and Asia.

The historical experience of the Tatars has produced a centuries-old legacy of ethnic identity that includes statehood: Volzhskaya (Volga) Bulgaria, which in A.D. 922 adopted Islam; the Turkish Golden Horde; the Kazan Khanate, which was formed in 1445 and which in 1552 was united "by iron and blood" with the Russian state by Ivan Grozny, with the mass of its population subjected to forced baptism on pain of agonizing death. The Tatars are one of very few Russian nations whose past provided not even the slightest cause for official Soviet festivals marking "voluntary" entries into Russia.

The Tatar component dominated in the Moslem world of the Russian Empire, and at the beginning of the twentieth century it enjoyed political and ideological hegemony, predominating in all Moslem fractions of the prerevolutionary State Duma, at all congresses of Moslems of Russia up to 1917, and afterward in the membership of the Moslem Socialist Committee, in the Moslem Office of Narkomnats (People's Commissariat for Nationalities), and at congresses of Communist Organizations of the Peoples of the East. This situation was always a source of dissatisfaction to Joseph Stalin, who only reluctantly abandoned plans for the deportation of the Kazan Tatars by tried and tested methods. During the years of the Revolution and the Civil War, various fractions of the Tatar national movement actively generated ideas for a national state structure (a Volga-Urals state in extraterritorial and territorial variants, or the plan for a Tatar-Bashkir republic). The creation in 1920 of the Tatar autonomous republic provided the Bolsheviks with a testing ground for the experimental development of Soviet federalism.

In addition to its distinctiveness, the Tatar element is an integral part of the Slavic-Turkic and Christian-Moslem historical and cultural synthesis, which over the centuries has formed Russia's unique civilization. Without such an intensive fusion of Slavic, Turkic, and Moslem languages, social structures, traditions, political culture, and martial experience, Russia would not be what it is today. Tatar influences can be seen everywhere from place-names and genealogies of the elite to architecture and clothing. The design and decoration of St. Basil's Cathedral on Red Square in Moscow is clad in images from the Kul-Sharif Mosque, which was destroyed by Grozny's armies on the territory of the Kazan kremlin (where, up to the present day, one can find coins minted in both the Russian and the Tatar languages). The symbol of Russian sovereignty, the Cap of Monomakh, is styled in a typical Tatar manner but crowned with a cross. Only vulgar prejudice from both sides permits the past to be viewed exclusively in terms of a "yoke," a "conquest," or a forcible conversion to Christianity.

Contemporary relations between Russians and Tatars in Tatarstan are closely interwoven in the course of their synchronous modernization and in the virtual elimination of signs of cultural divisions of labor, ethnic stratification, and similar impediments to social mobility. In terms of its potential, by the beginning of the 1990s the republic of Tatarstan had one of the highest integral indicators of economic development of all Russia's autonomous regions. Tatars were until quite recently fond of saying that in terms of gross national product, the republic outstripped Armenia, Tadzhikistan, Moldova, Turkmenistan, and even all three of the Baltic republics combined. Tatarstan has in many respects monopolized the production of freight vehicles, synthetic rubber, polyethylene, thermoplastic piping, magnetic tape, and cinematographic and photographic film.

The most important structural peculiarity of the republic is that it simultaneously holds the leading position in all three defining branches of the Russian economy as a whole: the fuel and energy, the military-industrial, and the agrarian complexes. The oil and petrochemical industry has been developing there since 1943, and the combined volume of oil extracted is close to three billion metric tons.[3] Military aviation enterprises, capable of producing Blackjack and Backfire strategic bombers and multipurpose helicopters, are located next door to instrument-making factories and producers of ammunition and antisubmarine vessels. Finally, Tatarstan's agricultural sector has avoided the precipitous drops in gross production that typify the current economic crisis in Russia. Hence, the special route chosen by the leaders of Tatarstan has naturally received increased attention from others seeking to emulate its experience.

At the same time, the political processes unfolding within and around the republic over the last few years have not reflected a smooth, unidirectional transition from "the old order" to a new order. Rather, there has been a sequence of qualitatively independent phases, during which an essential reorientation of Tatarstan's policy has taken place. Complicating this period has been a pronounced alteration in the key macro-level factors affecting republican policy: an all-Union context was rapidly transformed into an all-Russian one, leading to new economic conditions accompanied by growing political demands for national-state status.

Finally, and most important, this reorientation process has unfolded on two levels. The first is connected with problems relating to producing a workable distribution of resources of power, influence, and control and with the emergence of a decision mechanism maintaining the balance of interests within the republic, as well as within its relations with Moscow. This is the level—largely implicit—at which the actual "rules of the game" between political actors are established. The second, explicit level deals with the means by which the new "rules of the game" combine with symbolic manipulation, the mobilization of public opinion, and the conflicting interests of ruling and nonruling elites to produce concrete policies under the new conditions.

The difficulty in unraveling the activity at these levels is compounded by the fact that the composition of active participants on the political stage in Kazan and Moscow during these years has not been constant, nor have their positions remained static. In particular, a cardinal restructuring of the very idea of "the center" has occurred, with the result that interpretations of key problems in center-republic relations have constantly been changing. Nevertheless, it is possible to delineate several qualitatively distinct phases in the most recent history of relations between Tatarstan and Moscow (see table 11.1).

The initial stage—"Pre-Sovereignization"—lasted from 1987 to August 1990, when Tatarstan issued its "Declaration of State Sovereignty." The essence of the initial changes was a review of the traditional autonomous national-state status of Tatarstan. This was not directed at Russia as such but toward the institutions of *Soviet* rule. The role of the center was therefore played first and foremost by Soviet Union structures, and a strictly Russian factor remained in the background, given the extent to which party-*nomenklatura* rule had suppressed Russian identity. Thus, the first secretary of the Tatar Regional Committee of the Communist Party of the Soviet Union (CPSU) was, according to custom, a member of the Central Committee and simultaneously a member of the Presidium of the Supreme Soviet of the USSR. In the field of economic administration, around 80 percent of industrial output was produced in Tatarstan at enterprises subordinate to the Soviet Union, 18 percent at those subordinate to Russia, and 2 percent at those subordinate to the republic. In short, Kazan was accustomed to interacting almost entirely with Soviet Union structures, a situation that first had to be addressed before the republic could attack the problem of developing a meaningful autonomy.

On a macro level, party-administrative hypercentralization was gradually delegitimized, and the Soviet regime's claims of a productive national policy and of a resolution of the national question in the Soviet Union were rejected by the Tatarstan elite. In 1989 a parliamentary opposition appeared, shielded by the authority of Andrei Sakharov, whose radical views on national self-determination were widely publicized; and in 1990, opposition to the Soviet Union authorities acquired a more vocal and assertive form. The future of Tatarstan was seen by the republican authorities and the public in the rather limited economic terms of regional self-accounting and self-financing. Tatar policy at this stage therefore sought to emulate aspects of the Baltic economic experience, but without the separatist connotations of that region.

Table 11.1
POLITICAL EVOLUTION OF THE "TATARSTAN MODEL"

Chronology
1987–88 to August 1990 "Pre-Sovereignization" 1990 to 1993 "Sovereignization" After February 15, 1994 "Post-Sovereignization"
Macropolitical Environment
Democratization Beginning of conflict "Russia-Union" August putsch, 1991 Breakup of the USSR October events, 1993 Elections in federal organs of power
Economic Course
Regional autonomy Self-financing "Soft entrance into markets" From moderate reform to competitive economics
Status Claims
Union republic in USSR Sovereign state, associated with Russia, subject to international law Special status in treaty and "asymmetrical" federation
Rhetoric
Criticism of Stalinist autonomization Criticism of unitarism and "imperial" center Criticism of the plan of the "gubernization" of Russia

National claims during "Pre-Sovereignization" varied from "leveling" the rights of all subjects of the federation to granting Tatarstan the status of a union republic. The national movement, most significantly the Tatar Public Center *(Tatarsky obshchestvennyi tsentr),* initially adhered to this strategy—an outgrowth of democratization as understood by the CPSU—as being the most daring and farthest reaching. At that time, the principal targets of national criticism were Stalinist chauvinism, the Soviet principle of "autonomization," and the "four-tiered" federal structure of the USSR. Under no circumstances, however, was Russian imperialism the object of Tatar rancor. The task of overcoming the region's socioeconomic inadequacies and ethnic cultural-linguistic limitations inherited from the Soviet era was, during this period, framed exclusively in terms of elevating Tatarstan's status to that of a union republic.

The republic's mass media began an unprecedented, energetic campaign to discuss the "blank spots" of national history and the hidden pages of spiritual heritage. This was reflected in the attention paid, for example, to the epic literature of the republic of Adygeya and to *Gayaz Iskhaki*, the classic of prose, drama, and social and political literature, dedicated to ideological auto-da-fé. Most important, though, was the explosion of popular dissatisfaction with the dissemination and adoption of the Tatar language and its functions. This was a reflection not simply of changes already begun but also of powerful new (or newly resurfaced) catalysts of ethnonational identity. As a result, the politicization of Tatar ethnicity and the legitimization of nationalist discourse were given a strong linguistic impulse.

National consciousness was also boosted during these years by the arrival in the republic of Boris Yeltsin, recently elected chairman of the Supreme Soviet of the RSFSR. It was in Kazan that, enthused by the adoption of the "Declaration of State Sovereignty" and, most likely, impressed by rallies for democracy and by growing criticism of the Soviet Union's center, he uttered the phrase that was to become famous: "Take as much sovereignty as you can swallow."[4]

The culmination of this stage was the adoption on August 30, 1990, of the "Declaration of State Sovereignty" by the republic of Tatarstan. The parliament of Tatarstan, which had shortly beforehand been elected without monopoly control on the part of the party, was not the first in Russia to declare sovereignty. However, it was the first to do so without indicating its subordination to any federation, whether the Soviet Union or the Russian Federation. This decision was the result of an ad hoc compromise and became possible due to the energy of national-radical deputies, among whom Fauziya Bairamova, leader of "Ittifak," the Tatar party of national independence, stands out as particularly active.[5] As a whole, the document allowed for a wide range of interpretations and appeared carefully balanced. Both Russian and Tatar were, significantly, declared official languages of state. This was the key factor impeding the resolution of conflicts between Russians and Tatars and thereby contributed to the emergence of a sentiment of ethnic parity in the republic.

The next phase—"Sovereignization"—saw the escalation of confrontation with Moscow and lasted from the adoption of the declaration (August 1990) until the end of 1993. Tatarstan's movement toward a separate course began to acquire still greater momentum after August 1991. Two factors account for this change. First, the days of the Moscow putsch by the State Committee on the Extraordinary Situation (GKChP) allowed

Tatarstan's leadership to adopt a more independent position. Second, its efforts to become involved on an equal footing in the Novo-Ogarevo negotiations—which were held between the center and the union republics and which discussed the "reformed Union," with quite different results in the form of the Belovezhsky agreement of December 1991—created, in principle, a new configuration in the relations between Kazan and Moscow.

A vital factor in the unfolding situation was the bilateral nature of Tatarstan's relations with the center; such bilateralism was rapidly becoming a distinguishing feature of the Russian Federation. Added to this new dimension of Moscow-Kazan relations was a complicating factor: the previous gap between Soviet Union and Russian political structures was now eclipsed by a widening split between the branches of presidential, governmental, parliamentary, and judicial power *within* the Russian government. This left Tatarstan's leaders with considerable room for political maneuvering in their dealings with Moscow. President Mintimir Shaimiev succeeded in translating this maneuverability into solid political achievements, as the following examples reflect:

- On March 21, 1992, in spite of an official ban by the Moscow authorities, a referendum was held in Tatarstan in which 62 percent of voters responded positively to the following question: "Do you agree that the Republic of Tatarstan is a sovereign state, a subject of international law, which builds its relations with the Russian Federation and other republics and states on the basis of equal agreements?"
- On March 31, 1992, the Tatarstan leadership refused to take part in signing the Federative Agreement, which would have encroached on the sovereignty recently declared by the republic and approved by referendum.
- On November 6, 1992, the Supreme Soviet of Tatarstan adopted a constitution, Article 61 of which contained the following claim: "The Republic of Tatarstan is a sovereign state, a subject of international law, associated with the Russian Federation and Russia on the basis of an Agreement on the reciprocal delegating of plenary powers and subjects of authority."
- On April 25 and December 12, 1993, insufficient voter turnout made it impossible to hold two Russian referenda and elections to the Federal Assembly of the Russian Federation, each of which would have brought Tatarstan's policy more in line with that of other subjects of the federation.[6]

At least three parallel and closely intertwined processes characterized the evolution of Moscow-Kazan relations and revealed the growing political stakes attached to Tatarstan's sovereignization. First, a delicate political and legal confrontation between republic and center unfolded, with Moscow attempting to diminish or invalidate Kazan's status before the republic took major steps in the direction of autonomy. Several days before the March 1992 referendum, for example, the Russian Constitutional Court declared invalid two articles in the republic's "Declaration of State Sovereignty," several changes in its constitution, and the resolution on carrying out a referendum concerning the status of a "subject of international law." Hence a key aspect of the "Tatarstan model" was the ability to preempt Moscow's crucial legal decisions that could have derailed the process of sovereignization. The referendum therefore had to be carried out, without fail, *before* the signing of the Federative Agreement in Moscow (which it was); and Tatarstan's constitution had to be adopted *before* the Russian constitution came into force. Agility in navigating Moscow's treacherous legal waters thus contributed to Tatarstan's success.

A second feature of the period ending in 1993 was an intensification of the "war of words," with statements from Moscow acquiring a more threatening and inflammatory tone. In the lead-up to the referendum, the chairman of the Constitutional Court, Valery Zorkin, anticipated "seas of blood," whereas Vice-President Alexander Rutskoi proposed inclusion in the criminal code of an article "to imprison for 10–15 years national-careerists and separatists, otherwise we shall be left with Dudaevs and Shaimievs."[7] The Speaker of the Russian Supreme Soviet, Ruslan Khasbulatov, was equally harsh in his pronouncements on the Tatarstan issue. There was a corresponding heightening of tone in the mass media of both camps: from the Russian side came irate accusations of "national separatism," "Islamic fundamentalism," and "ukrainization of the economy" and of the republic's being "a little island of communism" and an "ethnocratic Bantustan"; from the Tatar side could be heard no less energetic epithets and predictions of the inevitable collapse of the "chauvinistic empire" and "neighboring state" of Russia.[8]

The atmosphere of rising political and ideological passions and mounting conflicts was ameliorated by a third feature of the Moscow-Kazan relationship: a line of pragmatism that grew in importance and proved crucial for a breakthrough in the tension. The interaction of executive powers in Russia and Tatarstan developed over time a kind of "bureaucratic market" in which political elites realized that state action to maximize economic benefits, and not idealistic pronouncements, provided the greatest guarantee of political stability and economic growth. As early as January 1992, this pragmatic dimension resulted in a series of negotiations between Yegor Gaidar and the prime minister of Tatarstan,

Mukhammat Sabirov; the talks culminated in the signing of the "Agreement between the Government of the Russian Federation and the Government of the Republic of Tatarstan on Economic Cooperation."[9] This was an important first step in developing a distinctive set of "rules of the game" for the changing macroeconomic and macropolitical environment. The central economic issue on the agenda was, of course, oil. Tatarstan and Moscow ultimately decided to divide the overall volume of oil extracted in 1992 (approximately twenty-five million metric tons) equally between Russia and Tatarstan, leaving five million metric tons as an export quota for the republic. This share was increased in subsequent years, up until the cancellation of quotas. The revenue these exports provided Tatarstan was crucial in providing a base from which the republic could implement its proclaimed policy during the first three years of economic reforms: a "soft entry into the market." In short, the republican authorities utilized part of the oil revenue stream as social shock-absorbers, particularly for subsidizing food prices to create the safety net essential for the transitional period.

In the summer of 1993, specific intergovernmental agreements consolidated this trend, including a package of accords regulating relations between the republic and the center in such key areas as ownership, sale, and transportation of oil and petrochemical products, branches of the defense industry, support and control of higher education, and environmental protection. A parallel agreement on customs was viewed as a serious failure on the part of the republic: customs duties levied on products entering the republic—an important source of revenue for the republican budget—remained wholly under the jurisdiction of Moscow.

In other words, the harsh rhetoric and legal maneuvering on constitutional issues proved little more than a smoke screen masking intensive activity based on mutual agreement between the ruling elite in Kazan and that in Moscow on spheres of interest and responsibility. Emotions expressed in newspapers and the electronic mass media continually sounded alarms, yet on the elite level the picture was quite different—that is, significantly more rational and calm. The triumph of pragmatism makes sense of developments that cleared the way for both sides to sign, on February 15, 1994, the treaty between the Russian Federation and the republic of Tatarstan "On the Demarcation of Subjects of Jurisdiction and on Mutual Delegation of Plenary Powers between Organs of State Authority of the Russian Federation and Organs of State Authority of the Republic of Tatarstan."[10]

This event marked the beginning of a new stage in relations between Moscow and Kazan: "Post-Sovereignization." This was a first and, in many ways, experimental step, which subsequently led to the conclusion of similar agreements between Moscow and the other subjects of the Russian Federation. A distinguishing characteristic of the "founding" agreement between the center and Tatarstan—a result unprecedented in the practice of Russian federalism—was its origin as a political compromise between federal and republican elites. Broad political agreement permitted economic issues to be treated as the subject of specific intergovernmental agreements. In addition to the packet of agreements signed in 1993, new documents tackled the division of political authority in the areas of banking, finance and credit, and foreign currency policy. Other agreements attempted to demarcate plenary powers in the field of foreign economic affairs, as well as to establish the all-important budgetary relations between the Russian Federation and the republic of Tatarstan. Finally, a separate agreement was concluded on the coordination of the fight against crime and other infringements of the law.[11] In contrast to agreements reached later between Russia and its other individual subjects (including many agreements with oblasts), the agreement with Tatarstan chiefly concerns the distribution of republican and federal powers, not merely the region's obligations for maintenance of the social sphere.

Further, the February 1994 treaty demonstrates a complex tension between the two sides' political will and legal authority. The preamble to the agreement states, "The Republic of Tatarstan is as a state united with the Russian Federation by the Constitution of the Russian Federation, by the Constitution of the Republic of Tatarstan and by the agreement on demarcation of subjects of influence and by mutual delegation of plenary powers."[12] But this does not resolve the legal collision between the two constitutions. The Tatarstan constitution endows the republic with the right to "independently determine its state-legal status" (Article 69) as "a sovereign state, a subject of international law, associated with the Russian Federation" (Article 61). The Russian constitution, however, extends sovereignty to all territory of the Russian Federation (Article 4), based on "state unity, a single system of state power," with equal rights between the subjects of the federation (Article 5). The text of the 1994 agreement explicitly avoided terms that could arouse objections from the two sides—terms such as "sovereignty" and "association"—preferring instead "unification." The agreement thus reflected a compromise that, at least provisionally, avoided serious conflict: significant economic independence was promised to Tatarstan (with the exception of customs regulation) in exchange for legal loyalty to the center. Although this was not a permanent resolution of key issues, it permitted a reduction in the critical acuteness of conflicts.

Finally, the agreement on division of jurisdiction does not detail, as would many later agreements between Russia and other subjects of the federation, the problem of distribution of expenditures in the social sphere. Consequently, the steps taken by Yeltsin and Shaimiev were principally political and symbolic, demonstrating their desire to resolve the crisis without resorting to force. They succeeded in shifting the situation from the brink of a precipice and defusing interethnic anxieties. Each side gained something and sacrificed something. Russia demonstrated that potential or actual separatism was an extraordinary and peripheral problem that could be resolved—albeit provisionally—through dialogue. In less than a year, the "Tatarstan model" would become the promising alternative to the Chechen debacle and would serve as evidence of Moscow's capacity for flexibility. Tatarstan, on the other hand, obtained the center's consent to forfeit its monopoly on budgetary questions and foreign economic policy. Economically, Tatarstan also gained important advantages: the republic successfully created and consolidated its sphere of exclusive competence in foreign economic affairs as reflected, for example, in its authority to conclude trade and economic agreements with foreign states and the right to attract credits under its own guarantees. This was paralleled by a broadening of Tatarstan's independence in the spheres of taxation and banking. Tatarstan found for itself a special, and to a certain extent privileged, status in its articulation of a "diluted" interpretation of its sovereignty, an interpretation that did not challenge the center.

Yet, important unaddressed issues remain: the fact that the republic unconditionally delegated to the center such functions as the judicial system, the office of public prosecutor, criminal procedure and investigation, amnesties and pardons, and civil legislation while it reserved for itself the regulation of administrative and social relations, environmental protection, and use of natural resources reveals Tatarstan's accomplishments as very much a work-in-progress. The powers delegated by Tatarstan to the center are in many respects identical to those delegated by other subjects of the federation, yet Tatarstan's bilateral agreement allowed it to deal with Russia on an equal footing, in contrast to the remaining eighty-eight subjects of the federation. Consequently, "sovereignty" or "jurisdiction of the republic" has acquired an ambiguous and increasingly relativistic meaning in the Russian Federation.

For some, this step in the direction of a novel type of federation was an indication of the breakup of Russia; for others, it was a healthy sign of political flexibility and creativity in reducing the level of interregional suspicion and fear. Opponents' arguments, based on anything from mere unpleasantness to serious legal expertise, span a range of opinions from "soft" doubts to outright negativism. Vladimir Lysenko, for example, noted: "In no single state in the world (including federative ones) does the whole conclude agreements with its parts. . . . It is necessary to put a stop to 'agreement creation' before it is too late."[13] But today no state in the world is the same type of federation as the Russian Federation, with its national-state character and its prehistory to present-day problems.

In reality, sufficient information has not yet accumulated to produce a fair assessment of whether the Tatarstan model will prove to be disintegrative or constructive to the Russian Federation. But this has not prevented the agreement's detractors from challenging its constitutional basis. Pavel Russkikh wrote: "The Constitution does not require that such agreements be observed by citizens, society and state organs. In other words, internal Russian agreements do not entail legal consequences, do not establish a legal norm that is binding for all, legally indestructible."[14] But this overlooks the fact that constitutional interpretation in the Russian Federation is as yet undeveloped and inconclusive, especially on the issue of demarcating powers between the federation and its subjects.

Some of the harshest critics, such as Vladimir Zhirinovsky, continue to stick to images of catastrophe and threats to the unity of Russia and actively put forward plans for *gubernizatsiya*[15] as a desirable type of political structure for Russia.[16] There are also geostrategic schemes that emphasize the confessional factor, whose distinguishing feature is the thesis of the "Orenburg isthmus," a narrow strip of land that is several tens of kilometers in length and that divides the Tatar-Bashkir "outposts" from the rest of the "Islamic world," effectively bringing the south and east of the Moslem world into the heart of Russia through Central Asia and Kazakhstan.[17] This argument is problematic, as anyone familiar with the sociocultural conditions in the Volga and Urals regions of Russia knows well. The extensive Islamic revival in this region is not aimed at abolishing the centuries-old traditions of Tatar-Russian interaction that constituted the basis for a political compromise.

Another contentious point in discussions about Tatarstan concerns the republic's image as a persistent defaulter in payment of taxes to the federal budget. Leaving aside the fact that nonpayment is endemic in Russia, affecting all parts of the country's economy to varying degrees, several facts are relevant to the case of Tatarstan. A special agreement dating from 1994 requires the republic to make payments to the federal budget on the basis of the following norms and agreements: (1) profit tax, 13 percent; (2) personal income tax, 1 percent; (3) value-added tax, determined annually by the Russian and Tatarstan Ministries of Finance.[18] In accordance with these same agreements, the republican budget retains excises on spirits, vodka, liquor-vodka products, oil and gas, land payments, and income from privatization, as well as a special tax for financial support of key branches of the economy. Tatarstan's position in this system of budgetary federalism is shown in tables 11.2

and 11.3. As indicated by the information in these tables, the claims that Tatarstan is a little island of prosperity are inaccurate at best. The republic's per capita budget expenditure is moderate, and its level of federal subsidies is among the lowest in the entire federation.

Because the economic content of the "Tatarstan model" awaits more precise definition, the republic's image has fluctuated in the public consciousness. For some, it is a "new Kuwait," flourishing because of its oil; for others, it is an "agricultural republic," supplying its own food and exporting the surplus to neighboring regions; for yet others, the republic is a nascent "high-tech center." But the State Program of Economic and Social Progress—the official manifesto of Tatarstan's current strategy, adopted by parliament in 1996—proceeded from a developmental thesis that, although vague, lays down the basic elements of future Tatar economic policy: "The Tatarstan model is a model of a socially oriented economy, set in motion by outside investments and competing due to high value added taxes (VAT) on goods and services."[19] The principal factors involved in guaranteeing the effectiveness of the strategy are Tatarstan's possession of oil reserves as state property, the training of qualified specialists in key economic sectors, and the region's strategic geographic position.

Finally, a reassessment of the terminology used to describe and classify the "special case" of Tatarstan is appropriate. In particular, categorizing the situation as a conflict between nationalities, or as an issue of "national-separatism" or "nationalism," is inaccurate. In general, terms such as "inter-national relations," "inter-national marriages," and "inter-national conflicts" appear to be inadequate conceptual tools in explaining Tatarstan's unique status. Since ethnic communities are unlikely to be the direct subjects of relations, it is more useful to focus on the behavior of elites who claim to represent ethnic groups or peoples. Thus, speaking about conflict between Tatars and Russians in the republic and beyond its borders does not advance our understanding of the Tatarstan model. In reality, the high point of national-radical influence in the republic was reached in 1992, when the protoparliament of Milli Medzhlis (the National Assembly) laid claim to the legitimate realization of the Tatar people's national sovereignty. However, after the republic's ruling elite coopted the initiative and pushed through an agreement with Moscow, the active role of practically all those in the national movement—the Tatar Social Center, the Ittifak Party, Milli Medzhlis—steadily diminished. Mass mobilization based on nationalist sentiments proved unsuccessful in the Tatar environment as local elites failed to galvanize ethnonational responses and as analysts and commentators overestimated the role of this variable in the Moscow-Kazan relationship.

Table 11.2
RUSSIAN FEDERATION REPUBLIC BUDGET FIGURES FOR THE FIRST HALF OF 1995

	Budget Expenses per Capita (1,000 rubles)	Federal Subsidies as a Percentage of Republic Budget Revenues	Share of Taxes Assigned to Regional Budget (%)
Average	635	9	61
Adygey republic	346	39	75
Altai republic	489	68	71
Bashkortostan republic	739	0	73
Buryat republic	561	21	83
Dagestan republic	323	62	82
Ingush republic	455	92	23
Kabardin-Balkar republic	304	34	83
Kalmyk republic	553	64	69
Karachai-Cherkess republic	313	26	76
Karelian republic	657	19	64
Komi republic	1,165	16	54
Mari El republic	425	24	79
Mordovian republic	392	16	79
North Ossetian republic	369	51	78
Tatarstan republic	620	2	74
Tuva republic	867	66	84
Udmurt republic	444	15	58
Khakass republic	522	8	70
Chuvash republic	438	11	72
Sakha (Yakut) republic	1,973	0	99

Source: Rossiiskie regioni nakanune vyborov—95 (Moscow: Yuridicheskaya Literatura, 1995).

The most persuasive evidence of this is electoral behavior in those Tatarstan regions, mainly rural, with an absolute majority of Tatars. Electoral returns from the federal list of candidates from unions and blocs in the December 17, 1995, elections for deputies to the State Duma reveal that in these rural districts, the "Our Home Is Russia" movement received more than 43 percent of votes, whereas "Nur" (Light), the all-Russian Moslem movement, received 6.25 percent. In urban districts,

Table 11.3
SUBJECTS OF THE FEDERATION BUDGET FIGURES OF REGIONAL STATUS IN 1995

	Share Received from Federal Budget in Budget Revenues of the Region (%)	Share of Taxes "Left" to the Region (%)	Provisional Balance of Financial Supply to One Person, 1,000 Rubles
NON-SUBSIDIZED			
Bashkortostan	0.2	74	597
Tatarstan	0.9	77	469
Krasnoyarsk krai	1.0	65	1,038
Lipetsk oblast	1.1	60	967
Nizhnegorodskaya oblast	1.1	52	1,056
Samara oblast	1.2	52	1,478
Sverdlovsk oblast	2.1	57	1,128
Yaroslavl oblast	2.9	52	1,137
Moscow city	6.7	54	2,817
St. Petersburg city	0.4	55	1,237
Khanty-Mansiisk AO	0.4	40	9,297
Yamal-Nenets AO	1.2	45	9,480
SLIGHTLY SUBSIDIZED			
Sakha (Yakutia)	9.0	100	-295
Belgorod oblast	7.1	58	800
Vladimir oblast	9.2	58	594
Volgograd oblast	4.8	60	688
Vologda oblast	7.8	66	625
Irkutsk oblast	4.8	64	885
Kursk oblast	7.4	63	428
Leningrad oblast	10.0	60	660
Moscow oblast	7.3	51	1,096
Orenburg oblast	9.0	58	627
Perm oblast	5.7	53	1,114
Ryazan oblast	3.7	59	608
Tyumen oblast	8.0	65	840
Chelyabinsk oblast	4.2	62	812
SUBSIDIZED			
Karelia	15.2	67	295
Komi	16.4	58	1,046
Udmurtia	14.5	62	469
Khakassia	13.0	76	221

Table 11.3 *continued*

Table 11.3 *continued*

Chuvashia	20.0	68	144
Krasnodar krai	10.8	61	455
Primorsky krai	17.9	61	519
Arkhangelsk oblast	12.0	70	345
Voronezh oblast	15.7	61	358
Kaliningrad oblast	15.5	63	437
Kirov oblast	16.0	64	307
Murmansk oblast	12.8	64	701
Novosibirsk oblast	16.9	67	395
Omsk oblast	18.6	64	469
Rostov oblast	15.8	59	418
Saratov oblast	13.3	62	375
Smolensk oblast	10.7	64	381
Tver oblast	16.3	60	437
Tomsk oblast	12.4	57	1,181
Tula oblast	11.7	63	443
Ulyansk oblast	13.8	59	486
MODERATELY SUBSIDIZED			
Adygeya	42.7	66	-100
Buryatia	34.6	78	-248
Kabardino-Balkaria	44.6	77	-318
Karachaevo-Cherkessia	45.1	66	-131
Mari El	29.5	73	-266
Mordovia	33.3	72	-159
Northern Ossetia	39.5	66	-345
Altai krai	38.7	73	-164
Stavropol krai	25.3	59	306
Khabarovsk krai	23.7	65	332
Amur oblast	28.5	67	86
Astrakhan oblast	26.0	63	238
Ivanovo oblast	28.9	64	141
Kaluga oblast	21.8	62	316
Kamchatka oblast	34.4	74	-311
Kemerovo oblast	25.5	74	107
Kostroma oblast	44.0	61	-90
Kurgan oblast	20.9	70	141
Magadan oblast	26.4	67	-137
Novgorod oblast	23.2	66	208
Orel oblast	34.8	60	134
Penza oblast	27.1	65	129
Pskov oblast	29.0	68	74
Sakhalin oblast	29.0	71	4

Table 11.3 *continued*

Table 11.3 *continued*

Tambov oblast	25.3	65	115
Chita oblast	23.5	72	98
Nenets AO	30.9	70	42
Taimyr AO	20.3	73	341
Evenki AO	47.7	79	-2,725
HIGHLY SUBSIDIZED			
Altai	74.4	67	-791
Dagestan	64.4	79	-659
Kalmykia	66.1	57	-702
Tuva	78.8	75	-1,245
Evresky AO	55.7	77	-535
Aginsk-Buryatia AO	69.4	80	-425
Komi-Permyak AO	56.3	77	-427
Koryak AO	81.6	68	-6,677
Ust-Ordinsk Buryat AO	70.6	73	-778
Chukotka AO	50.7	69	-2,285
Russian Federation	12.4	59	765

Source: Rossiiskie vesti—Spetsialn'i vypusk, no. 2 (April 1996).

Nur did not even rank among the top five electoral blocs, and the nationalist-Moslem vote in the republic as a whole was only 5.13 percent. This compares with republic-wide returns of almost 30 percent for Our Home Is Russia and just less than 16 percent for the Communist Party. Nur managed to take second place in only four of the more than forty rural districts, with a maximum vote of 15 percent in one district. Clearly, this low level of support is insufficient to sustain mass ethnic or confessional mobilization in the Tatar political environment.[20]

National-radical circles in Tatarstan were understandably dismayed with the result, but in the presidential elections they proposed little more than joining forces with the Communists. This helps explain—at least in part—the strong showing of Communist leader Gennady Zyuganov in the republic, but it also testifies to a profound ideological and political crisis in the ranks of a movement that not long before had tried to claim a dominant political position in the republic.

The muted appeal of ethnonationalism was also reflected in the public statements of the leadership. In a message to the State Council of the Republic in early 1996, President Shaimiev noted: "It remains a priority of Tatarstan's domestic policy to strengthen international and civil accord, which is fundamental to political stability. . . . Sometimes in the political heat of the moment there are those who attempt to exploit the most varied devices and methods, including the ethnic question. In accordance with the Constitution of the Republic of Tatarstan, we are building a multiethnic, multicultural society, in which the main priority is citizenship, not ethnic affiliation."[21] These and similar pronouncements from Tatar leaders indicated that the ethnic factor was receding in the discourse and symbolism associated with political legitimacy.

In concluding, several points emerge as especially noteworthy. First, the "Tatarstan model" represents a pragmatic solution to a crisis resulting from a complex of overlapping disintegrative and centrifugal tendencies pressing on the Russian Federation and its constituent regions. This crisis, which has often been misinterpreted as an "inter-national" conflict, in reality consists of an accumulation of political and economic contradictions in the ethnoregional context embedded in the Soviet system. The sources of mounting tension in this case are not factors stimulating mass mobilization but are rather the actions of political elites at the center and in Kazan. Accordingly, the Tatar experience indicates the need to establish crisis-management tactics with the aim of articulating political instruments of stabilization in the initial stages of post-Soviet breakdown.

Second, the Tatarstan model possesses a highly dynamic nature. The alignment of structural elements of, and participants in, the crisis—whether central or regional, democrat or nationalist—is of an extremely changeable, mobile character. Even such seemingly constant values as the "center" and "power" are prone to exceptionally abrupt and unexpected change in their contours and positions. Thus, methods for regulating centers of conflict and passing through crisis phases should be just as flexible. By contrast, stubbornly clinging to ideological principles or rigid political formulas risks producing an impasse and raises the probability of social instability.

Third, the experience of recent years shows that the Russian Federation must not approach the problem of state integrity from stereotypical or traditional perspectives. This means that under no circumstances must federal authorities adopt one single "model" and attempt to apply it across a broad spectrum of subjects of the federation. It would be just as much of a mistake to spread the same type of threats and challenges to the prospects of Russian federalism as were created by the "renewal of the Soviet Union" in its day. Within the USSR and Russia, there were and are mechanisms for approaching regional issues that have much in common, but many regions possess highly specific elements related to cultural and historical bases of unity. Hence, what succeeded in Tatarstan might not be viable in Vologda oblast, Sakha republic, Primorsky krai, or elsewhere.

Future Russia-Tatarstan relations are not guaranteed to be free from problems. Presently, a serious source of potential conflict is the psychological discomfort of many of the other regional elites in light of the greater political influence acquired by Tatarstan and the high rating of its leaders. Many are inclined to link this to the republic's artificially created "most favored nation" status. A reflection of this is the exhausting struggle by the center and some regional elites to equalize the status of all subjects of the federation, to bring into line with the constitution of the Russian Federation all legal acts of its subjects or agreements concluded with them. This effort is quite distinctly traceable in the halls of the State Duma. The most complicated and immediate problem for Russia and Tatarstan, however, is finding painless methods for moving into an epoch that may provisionally be called the "post–Yeltsin and Shaimiev" era, when the political personalities that created the Tatarstan model are replaced by entirely different elites. This will be the ultimate test of the viability of Tatarstan's unique position in the federation—a test that may arrive sooner than anticipated.

NOTES

1. *Tatari i Tatarstan: Spravochnik* (Kazan: Tatarskoe knizhki, 1993), pp. 21–32.
2. Ibid.
3. M. R. Mustafin and R. G. Khuzeev, *Vse o Tatarstane. Ekonomiko-Geograficheskii spravochnik* (Kazan: Tatarskoe knizhki, 1994), pp. 18–21.
4. This is a statement that Boris Yeltsin repeatedly confirmed during his last trip to Kazan. *Kommersant-Daily*, February 5, 1994; *Segodnya*, May 31, 1994.
5. This compromise reflected a balance between two parliamentary flanks: the national-radicals ("Ittifak") and the national-moderates (the "Tatarstan" deputies group), on the one hand, and the democratic-federalists (the groups "Consent" and "People's Power"), on the other hand, with Shaimiev playing the role of moderator; *Tatari i Tatarstan*, pp. 94–97.
6. *Obreteniye suvereniteta: Khronika sobytii*, nos. 7–8 (1992), pp. 13–18, and no. 8 (1993), pp. 9–12; F. Kh. Moukhametshin, *Respublika Tatarstan: Ot referenduma do dogovora* (Kazan, 1995).
7. *Moskovskie novosti*, March 22, 1992.
8. For example, see: *Nezavisimaya gazeta*, March 1, 1994; *Utro Rossiya*, March 17–18, 1994; *Molodezh' Tatarstana*, April 28, 1995; *Tatarstan*, no. 9 (1991), p. 27; *Sovetskaya Tatariya*, April 11, 1992.
9. *Belaya kniga Tatarstana: Put' k suverenitetu (Sbornik ofitsial'nikh dokumentov), 1990–93* (Kazan, 1995), pp. 20–22.
10. Ibid., pp. 58–63.
11. Ibid.
12. Ibid., p. 58.
13. *Rossiiskaya gazeta*, July 2, 1995.
14. *Nezavisimaya gazeta*, January 26, 1995.

15. *Gubernizatsiya* refers to the type of structure found in the prerevolutionary state system of the Russian Empire, one based on a fundamental administrative-territorial unit, the *gubernia*. The subsequent abolition of republics is seen, in this perspective, as a means of minimizing ethnic separatism.
16. *Nezavisimaya gazeta*, March 23, 1995.
17. D. V. Dragunsky, *Etnopoliticheskiye protsessi na postsovetskoi prostranstve i rekonstruktsiya Severnoi Evrazii* (Polis, 1995), pp. 40–43.
18. "Soglasheniye mezhdu Pravitel'stvami Rossiiskoi Federatsii i Respubliki Tatarstan o biudzhatnykh vzaimootnosheniyakh mezhdu Rossiiskoi Federatsiei i Respublikoi Tatarstan," *Belaya kniga Tatarstana*, pp. 51–52.
19. *Vremya i dengi*, March 26, 1996.
20. This is according to data received in the central election of the republic of Tatarstan.
21. *Poslaniye prezidenta Respubliki Tatarstan M.M. Shaimieva Gosudarstvennomu Svetu* (Kazan, 1996), p. 3.

Conclusion

Democracy and Federalism in the Former Soviet Union and the Russian Federation

Robert V. Daniels

The health—political, economic, social—of the Russian constituent regions is one of the most crucial questions for the future of the Russian Federation. Have the provinces and republics really become significant now that the old empire has surrendered the former union republics of the USSR? What vitality can be found in the regions for practical political and economic reform when the imperial center is floundering between liberal utopianism and Third World degradation? What are the prospects for federalism as a solution to the regions' troubled relationship with the Russian center? These are the defining questions addressed and elucidated by the present collection of inquiries into the nature and condition of Russian regionalism. The answers—or persisting uncertainties—may hold the key to Russia's future, economic as well as political, and to the nation's capacity for mobilizing both its human and its natural resources in the struggle to become what Moscow hopes will be a "normal" country.

Politically, the centerpiece of this problem is the question of federalism. In any very large country, meaningful federalism, as an alternative to bureaucratic centralism or chaotic particularism, is crucial to a genuinely functioning democracy. By distributing power, federalism curbs arbitrary rule, both at the center and locally. It decentralizes responsibility while providing a mechanism to restrain potential local conflicts and abuses. It provides a school of democracy, and it quite literally brings government closer to the people.

These propositions hardly require any substantiation for Canadians and Americans, whose political traditions and experience have made the principles of federalism second nature, if not always problem-free.

Indeed, we know that federalism ensures institutionalized tension between the various levels of government, but we also know that this tension is good for vigorous democracy. Elsewhere, unfortunately, federalism may be equally desirable but may nevertheless lack a firm basis either in principle or in practice. Western Europe has seen a long struggle between particularism and state-building, culminating in the hypertrophy of the national state. Only in the last few decades has the central authority been tempered in some European countries by the institution of genuine democratic powers at the regional level. Constitutions that bow verbally to federalism are not enough; in Latin America, federal constitutions copied from that of the United States failed to avert either national dictatorships or the concentration of a country's economic and cultural life at the center.

Russia—that is, the Russian Empire, its Soviet reincarnation, and Russia today—is an extreme case. The land is huge in area and in population, and both geographically and ethnically it exhibits the most extreme diversity. As Don K. Rowney shows in his treatment of the historical background, the Russian state has been held together and expanded over the course of five centuries only under a harsh tradition of centralism.

Russian centralism has left no space for democracy, no chance for people to acquire democratic experience at the local level and in face-to-face relationships (other than in the premodern village community). The only exception to this rule was the experimentation with provincial councils *(zemstva)* during the period of limited reform between 1861 and 1917, the era that Edward Keenan calls an "aberration" in the despotic Russian tradition.[1] In Russia, democracy has been more a threat to national unity than a support for it, above all when it has been accorded to the ethnic minorities conquered by the empire in the course of its long expansion from the sixteenth century to the nineteenth. In Russian political culture, centralism is one of the deepest instincts of rulers and ruled alike. Given these historical and cultural considerations, the question of Russian regions and Russian federalism has to be addressed in the larger context of the Soviet Union and the circumstances of its breakup.

The Revolution of 1917 showed all too clearly the disintegrating effect of democratization in a formerly centralized, multiethnic autocracy. With the formation of the revolutionary soviets—local workers' councils—political power temporarily devolved to provincial and municipal entities, whether or not they were based on ethnic minorities. This was one of the main factors undermining the Provisional Government. To reconstitute an effective revolutionary government, the Bolsheviks needed to address the centrifugal forces of regionalism and ethnicity by abandoning Lenin's prerevolutionary concept of in-or-out self-determination, which allowed only for independence from or acquiescence in central rule. Instead, as Joan DeBardeleben explains in her overview of Russian federal development, they instituted an elaborate system of pseudo-federalism to mask the reimposition of bureaucratic centralism on both Russian and non-Russian regions. Neither the formal powers assigned to the constituent units of the USSR nor the boundaries arbitrarily drawn to define these units made much difference as long as all effective authority was concentrated in the leading organs of the Communist Party in Moscow. (In a few instances, where central control was not challenged, this framework made possible some positive steps toward modern statehood, as Greg Poelzer finds in the case of the indigenous peoples of Siberia.)

With the coming of *perestroika* and the loosening of Communist Party rule in the late 1980s, the dummy federalism of the USSR, as well as the dummy democracy embodied in the hierarchy of soviets—local, regional, and central—began to come alive. But as this new life infused the old Stalin-Brezhnev constitutional structures, it highlighted some of the weaknesses that had been concealed in the formal Soviet system.

First of all, Soviet federalism was conceived on ethnic lines, defined in practice as linguistic affiliation, rather than being based on geographically or economically natural regions or even on historic traditions. Although citizenship was union-wide, every inhabitant of the USSR was legally classified according to nationality, that is, ethnolinguistic parentage, independently of residence in a particular region.

Thanks to the ethnic principle, Soviet federalism was grossly unbalanced. The Russian republic, comprising over half the population and three-quarters of the area of the Soviet Union, occupied a place administratively analogous to the overweening position of the former Kingdom of Prussia within the German Empire and the Weimar Republic. At the same time, ethnic traditions as diverse as those in the old Austrian Empire made Russia's hegemony unacceptable to the non-Russians of the Soviet Union.

Given these conditions, no workable federal democracy was possible in the Soviet Union: if Russia were represented by population, it would overwhelm the minorities; if it were represented equally to the other republics, it could be absurdly outvoted by much smaller populations. The bicameral Supreme Soviet, resembling the congressional setup in the United States, could work only as long as the legislative function was merely a rubber stamp. If, on the other hand, there had been no government for the Russian republic as such but rather a number of Russian regional entities comparable to the other union republics (instead of the one, monolithic Russian union republic), the representational problem would have been eased. Furthermore, if there had been no alternate authority in Moscow, the government of the Soviet Union could not have been dispensed with as it was in 1991.

The Union's structure, combined with the ethnic identification between citizens and republics, made it impossible to draw satisfactory boundaries between the units of the Soviet federal system. Due to ethnic intermixture, minorities were bound to be left on both sides of any boundary, potentially condemned to be second-class citizens or noncitizens in their own homes if the respective regional entity became genuinely autonomous or independent. An extreme example of irrational boundaries drawn in the 1920s is the cotton-growing Fergana Valley in Central Asia, where the rim of the valley is in Kyrgyzstan, the mouth is in Tadzhikistan, and the middle is in Uzbekistan (virtually cut off from the rest of that republic), all without solving the cross-border minority problem. The large Russian populations bounded off into eastern Ukraine and northern Kazakhstan are another case in point. Further, ethnically based entities were arbitrarily classified, between those belonging directly to the Soviet Union and those subordinated to some larger ethnicity (usually Russia). The Soviet principles of federalism guaranteed a situation of ethnic crisis if or when the Soviet Union was democratized.

For the non-Russian subjects of the USSR, democratization was bound to unleash a struggle to realize the potential statehood embalmed in the Soviet federal structure. It is extraordinary how the boundaries of convenience that Moscow set among the ethnicities became real political obsessions once democratization gave local leaders the opportunity to assert their national demands. This extended even to Ukraine's claim of suzerainty over the Crimea, despite its Russian majority and the casual history of Nikita Khrushchev's reassigning the peninsula to Kiev as an anniversary present in 1954. On the other hand, as separatism began to threaten the integrity of the Soviet Union, a backlash by Russians who identified the USSR with Russia became a serious prospect. Minority nationalism was the Achilles' heel of democratization in the Soviet realm, as the events of 1991 showed.

President Mikhail Gorbachev went a long way toward addressing the problem of federalism in his Union Treaty of March 1991, as noted by DeBardeleben. The treaty—scheduled to be formally signed the day after the August coup intervened—was intended to replace the coercive treaty of 1922 that had created the USSR and to provide the basis for a new constitution. Its language leaned heavily to the rights of the republics, "sovereign states" that possessed "full state power" and retained "the right to the independent resolution of all questions of their development." But it left the assignment of powers between the Union and the republics agonizingly vague and confusing. As John F. Young observes, this was paralleled by an equally ambiguous delineation of authority between regions and municipalities. The draft specified the logical central responsibilities—defense, state security, foreign policy, communications, the space program—but promised the republics a share in formulating policy for all these areas, while it put the bulk of governmental responsibilities for the economy and social policy in the hands of "the USSR . . . in conjunction with the republics." Then, as though to compensate, it declared, "Republic laws have supremacy on all questions, with the exception of those falling within the Union's jurisdiction." The new Constitutional Court was supposed to sort all this out if disputes arose.

The actual dissolution of the Soviet Union was not an inevitability, at least not until the August putsch and its unforeseeable consequences. Gorbachev's concessions to the republics, by reducing the Soviet Union from a federation to a confederation, might have satisfied all but the Baltic states. However, these proposals were anathema to the Communist conservatives and Russian nationalists; the 1991 coup plotters, in their "Appeal to the Soviet People," inveighed against "the confrontation between nationalities and the chaos and anarchy that is threatening the lives and security of the citizens of the Soviet Union and the sovereignty, territorial integrity, freedom and independence of our fatherland. . . . A mortal danger threatens our homeland . . . , the breakup of the state."[2]

Ironically, the coup attempt and its failure served to discredit the central authority altogether and allowed the union republics to assert de facto independence. Boris Yeltsin, as president of the Russian republic, merely delivered the final blow to the confederal compromise when he conspired with President Leonid Kravchuk of Ukraine and President Stanislav Shushkevich of Belarus in December 1991 to declare Gorbachev's government liquidated. This was the real coup, cutting the remaining republics loose from the Union center—whether they wanted to be or not.

Yeltsin's curious role in the dissolution of the Soviet Union is the key to the apparent contradiction in his attitudes toward federalism in the Soviet Union and in Russia. Until Moscow's standoff with Chechnya erupted into violence in 1994, it was not fashionable in the West to find fault with Yeltsin's record as the great democratizer, but the reality has been less attractive all along. Ever since 1987, evidently, Yeltsin had been motivated by a passion for revenge against Gorbachev, starting when the latter failed to promote Yeltsin to full membership in the Politburo at the June plenum of that year even though his position as party boss of Moscow entitled him to that rank. This snub (probably a temporary concession by Gorbachev to the Communist conservatives) led to Yeltsin's denunciation of the whole leadership and his consequent humiliation and demotion in the fall of 1987. Nevertheless, Gorbachev allowed Yeltsin to become a rallying point for the most ardent democratizers and to be elected first as a deputy to the People's Congress and Supreme Soviet in 1989 and then as chairman of the Russian republic's Supreme Soviet in 1990.

From this power base, Yeltsin campaigned against Gorbachev by adopting the most radical reform positions: to end the power of the Communist Party, to privatize the socialized economy, and to uphold the sovereignty of the republics against the Union, despite the paradox in this last position. Russia was the core of the Soviet Union, and the Soviet Union, as the reincarnation of the empire, was essentially Russia writ large. So under Yeltsin, Russia was declaring independence against itself, a move that made sense only as the creation of a second, allegedly more legitimate power center in Moscow. The real issue, at that point, was which leader, commanding which government, would prevail. To defeat Gorbachev, Yeltsin was willing to pay the price that his separate power base in the Russian republic implied, namely the independence of the other fourteen republics from Moscow. But the evident motive, it is important to remember, was one not of principle but rather of personal politics. If any final token is needed, it was Gorbachev's exclusion from the list of dignitaries, including all the other defeated presidential candidates, at Yeltsin's second-term inauguration in August 1996.

The year before, Gorbachev was asked (by Italian television reporters) why he had allowed Yeltsin to work against him in this ultimately fatal way. His reply was poignantly revealing: "I should have listened to those who begged me to send Yeltsin as an ambassador to Africa. But I wanted to give a signal of change, to show that even in our country dissenters could stay in politics. With Yeltsin I ended up as a victim of my own principles."[3]

Nevertheless, the outcome was not wholly catastrophic. The Soviet Union/Russian Empire did not collapse; it merely decolonized, in the manner of the French overseas empire under President Charles de Gaulle. It did so voluntarily and only to the extent of the Communist-created union republics. Once Yeltsin became master in Moscow, the instincts of a Russian centralizer unmistakably reasserted themselves with respect to both the Russian and the non-Russian regions of the surviving state.

The breakup of the Soviet Union had some practical consequences of a decidedly negative nature. The disruption of the economic unity of a highly integrated continental trading area was one of the main causes of the post-Communist economic crisis throughout the former Soviet Union. The liquidation of union-wide citizenship created potentially devastating tensions between newly privileged majorities and newly underprivileged minorities everywhere in the fourteen non-Russian republics. The Soviet Union had experienced extensive ethnic integration through migration and mixed marriages, as a U.S.-style melting pot cooked down nationality differences in the urban sector of society. In consequence, with the demise of the Soviet Union, millions of families were left stranded or divided. Cynthia Buckley cites a curious example of the problem with Armenian construction workers in Siberia. Politically, in many non-Russian republics, the tender shoots of democracy emerging in the late 1980s withered in the climate of nationalist authoritarianism and interethnic hatred, leaving the field more often than not to ex-Communist despots in nationalist colors. In Russia itself, the psychic blow of the sudden loss of empire heightened the potential for authoritarian nationalism and stiffened resistance to any further concessions to minorities who happened to find themselves still within the borders of the Russian Federation.

Federalism as the basis of democratization within the old USSR failed with the breakup of the Soviet Union. This left open the equally pertinent question of federalism within the residual Russian republic. As of this writing, there are still no conclusive answers—only a multitude of questions.

Within the Russian republic, it is important to bear in mind, there were two kinds of pseudo-federalism inherited from the Soviet regime. One was the ethnically based distinction of autonomous republics, autonomous oblasts, and national okrugs, a distinction drawn in the 1920s on the same principles as the union republics except that the former groups were administratively subordinate to the Russian republic or to krais and oblasts thereof. For the most part, these entities were less populous than the union republics and had more Russians among their inhabitants (in some cases, majorities), with much more ethnic integration. However, Joseph Stalin's criterion for the distinction was disingenuous: to be a union republic, an entity had to be located on a border of the USSR so that it could exercise its "right" of secession should it so choose!

After the breakup of the USSR, there was no historical or constitutional principle keeping the lesser ethnic entities within the Russian Federation, except the Soviet government's assignment of a lower status to them in the 1920s and their subordination to Russia under Soviet federalism. Not surprisingly, when the union republics won independence, some of the autonomous republics—including Chechnya in the North Caucasus—wanted it for themselves as well. Here is the root of the tragedy in that region and of the embarrassment of foreign governments as they tried to take a position on Moscow's intervention against the Chechen secession.

The second category of sham federalism in the Russian republic was the hierarchy of administrative units in the solidly Russian areas of the country—oblasts or krais, raions, cities, industrial settlements, and villages—all with their respective soviets and executive committees, all controlled by the centralized apparatus of the Communist Party. Like the ethnic entities in the Russian republic and in the Soviet Union at large, these representative institutions began to come alive under *perestroika*, especially after the quasi-democratic local elections of the spring of 1990. True, the renovated soviets were dominated more often than not by Communist apparatchiks, but these were apparatchiks learning the techniques of democratic politics as they jockeyed for power within their respective entities and as they dealt with the center. Ironically, conservative resistance to Gorbachev's reforms contributed significantly to emerging pluralism in the USSR, quite the contrary of traditional Communist principles.

The breakup of the Soviet Union served the interests of local democracy little better in Russia than in the former union republics. In the wake of the August putsch, Yeltsin moved immediately to tighten his own central control over the Russian oblasts, in the name of extirpating Communist Party influence. Without any constitutional authority to do so, he appointed chiefs of administration in many provinces and personal representatives to oversee the administrators in each region.

These moves shifted Russian regional government from the nominal parliamentary principle of the Soviet constitution, with executives responsible to their respective councils, to the American or French form of independent executive, paralleling Gorbachev's change in the Union constitution in 1988–89 and Yeltsin's own reorganization of the Russian republic's government in the spring of 1991. Since late 1991, consequently, government at the oblast level has been chronically torn between the local legislative bodies (often dominated by Communist conservatives under new labels or none), the local executive (hard-pressed by the center), and the center itself. The irony of politics reversed everyone's position: the radical democratizers became partisans of centralism and executive supremacy in order to fight the provincial Communists, whereas the latter often became stalwarts of federalism and of legislative rights to protect their power. Until the crisis of September-October 1993, regional politics thus mirrored the standoff between the president and parliament in Moscow.

The events in the fall of 1993 only accentuated constitutional contradictions at the local level. Yeltsin took his victory over the parliamentarians as the occasion to tighten central authority over the oblasts and krais, which he viewed as a base of sympathy for his parliamentary enemies. He intervened against local governors who had defied his will—some of whom he had appointed himself, some of whom had defiantly been elected.

Simultaneously with the submission of his new federal constitution to popular referendum, Yeltsin decreed the abolition and replacement of all regional and local legislative bodies, on the curious ground that as "soviets"—mere "councils"—they were relics of the Communist regime. This argument betrayed the peculiar literalism of the untutored, taking the word for the reality. Obviously lost on Yeltsin and his supporters was the irony that they were using extraconstitutional central authority, Communist-style, to extinguish legislative bodies that—whatever their labels—were actually beginning to function in a democratic and federalist manner for the first time since the Russian Civil War.

Through all this, the "autonomies"—former autonomous republics and regions, now calling themselves "republics"—remained in limbo, enjoying much more de facto self-government than the oblasts and krais and often disputing the center's right to exercise any authority at all over them. DeBardeleben recounts how in March 1992 Yeltsin put forth a Federal Treaty, which was agreed to by most of the republics though not by Tatarstan or Checheno-Ingushetia. Nail Midkhatovich Moukhariamov examines the factors that allowed Tatarstan to reach a unique and exceptional compromise with Moscow a year later, a result that stands in sharp contrast to Chechnya's continued defiance and rejection of federation citizenship. The 1992 treaty and subsequent agreements were based on a strange concept: understandings between the federal government and a favored few of its own member states, promising them an undefined "sovereignty." Here again, straightforward federalism was skewed by the ethnic principle and by the preponderance of the Russians within the ethnic framework. Yeltsin did not attempt to appoint governors or presidential representatives in the autonomies, though all were subject to the dictate to abolish their "soviets" and elect new (usually smaller) legislative bodies.

The Federal Treaty signed by Moscow and the autonomies was supposed to be incorporated into the new federal constitution of 1993. However, the concept was hobbled by unresolvable contradictions. The republics wanted—and were promised—broad powers of genuine self-government, on the lines of American states and Canadian provinces. The oblasts and krais demanded constitutional equality with the republics in their rights of self-government. But Yeltsin was firmly against easing the central hold over these Russian jurisdictions. In the end, as DeBardeleben and Moukhariamov show, the issue of equality among the regions was fudged. Over the protests of most republics, the Federal Treaty was omitted as a formal part of the constitution. The republics and the oblasts or krais were treated on essentially the same basis, with equal representation for each "subject" in the new Council of the Federation. To be sure, this arrangement finally did resolve the impediment to federalism represented by Russian preponderance, by federalizing ethnically Russian territory on the same basis as that of the minorities.

Unfortunately, the new constitution allowed the demarcation of powers and responsibilities between the center and the regions to be clouded over by a vast gray zone of "joint jurisdiction." In the case of the republics, this vagueness was complicated by contradictions between the federal constitution and their own constitutions, which claimed the right to nullify federal laws. In the actual practice documented by the chapters in this collection, the real distribution of powers, central and local, was left up to political maneuvering and the effectiveness of local leadership.

This looseness has created the possibility—now a reality—of vast differences in the autonomy exercised by individual regions, differences among various republics and oblast-krais as well as between the two categories. The disparities have been exaggerated, as Peter J. Stavrakis, Aleksander A. Galkin, and D. J. Peterson emphasize, by great inequality in natural endowment and economic survivability among the subjects of the federation. The ability to hold up against Russia's general economic collapse since 1991 has varied significantly among the regions, those based on extractive industries faring best. Control of natural resources has therefore become crucial to the practical autonomy of self-assertive regions.

Like so many other matters in today's Russia, the implementation of federalism depends on extralegal defiance of a feeble yet intransigent center, and the success of such resistance depends in turn on local bargaining power or political obstreperousness. Decentralization, under these chaotic conditions, is not necessarily to the good. Its effect on public services is likely to be more negative than positive, as Mark G. Field observes in the health sector. In the economy, as Carol Clark and Darrell Slider suggest, regional and local power means the perpetuation of provincial elites and the obstruction of free-market reform. In the face of all these centrifugal forces, central weakness is qualified only by the willingness to use brute force in extreme situations, exemplified by the impasse in Chechnya.

The tragedy in Chechnya was the culmination of all the ambiguities in Russian federalism. An ethnic region, arbitrarily assigned to the Russian republic, claimed the same right of self-determination as that achieved by the union republics. A local strongman took power through his own coup and asserted sovereign independence from Moscow. For three years the center, unsure of its grip over the other ethnic autonomies, put off a resolution of this defiance. When the response finally came, it took the form of military force, on the grounds that Russia was an integral state that could not tolerate separatism in any form.

Given the background of ethnicity and self-determination in the Soviet Union, the initial responses of most Western governments to the outrage in Chechnya defy comprehension. How could outsiders calmly endorse the breakup of the Soviet Union yet swallow the myth that the Russian Federation was more an integral state than its predecessor? At least there was consistency in this inconsistency: the same foreign powers quickly recognized the breakup of Yugoslavia yet allowed their subsequent policies to be hobbled by the fiction of Bosnia as an integral state.

Chechnya, of course, is an extreme instance in the relations between Moscow and its regions. However, it serves as a warning that federalism may fail in the Russian republic just as it failed in the Soviet Union as a whole, ground up between the millstones of imperial centralism and ethnic particularism. In the case of the Soviet Union, federalism failed as the ethnic principle triumphed. In the case of the Russian Federation, federalism faces the opposite danger, that of reflexive centralism, in which even the autonomy of the ethnically Russian regions is at risk if autonomy for the minority regions is not respected. If either extreme prevails, the prospects for democracy in Russia will turn dim indeed.

NOTES

1. Edward Keenan, "Muscovite Political Folkways," *Russian Review,* April 1986.
2. *Pravda* and *Izvestiya,* August 20, 1991, translated in *Current Digest of the Soviet Press* 43, no. 33 (September 18, 1991): 1–2.
3. RAI, March 3, 1995, reported in *La Repubblica,* March 4, 1995.

EDITORS AND CONTRIBUTORS

LARRY BLACK is Professor of History and Director of the Centre for Research on Canadian-Russian Relations at Carleton University in Ottawa. He has authored, edited, or coedited nineteen books on Russian and Soviet history. The most recent is *Into the Dustbin of History: The USSR from Coup to Commonwealth, 1991* (Academic International, 1993). He also is the editor of the annual, two-volume *Russia and Eurasia Documents Annual* (Academic International).

CYNTHIA BUCKLEY is Assistant Professor of Sociology at the University of Texas at Austin. Her research focuses on demography and rural development. She has written on decollectivization, pension reform, and migration issues in the former Soviet Union and the Russian Federation. Her current work centers on social issues relating to population aging in the Russian Federation.

CAROL CLARK is Assistant Professor in the Department of Economics at Trinity College in Hartford, Connecticut. Her research interests include the post-Communist economic transition in both East-Central Europe and the former Soviet Union. Currently, she is working on a project examining the transformation of enterprise-level institutions in Russia and the emergence of different models of post-Soviet labor relations in individual enterprises.

ROBERT V. DANIELS is Professor Emeritus of History at the University of Vermont. Born in Boston in 1926, he received his Ph.D. from Harvard University in 1951 and has specialized in Soviet political history. He was a Kennan Institute Fellow in 1985 and president of the American Association for the Advancement of Slavic Studies in 1992. His most recent books are *The End of the Communist Revolution* (Routledge, 1993) and *Soviet Communism from Reform to Collapse* (Heath, 1995).

JOAN DEBARDELEBEN is Professor and Director of the Institute of Central/East European and Russian-Area Studies at Carleton University in Ottawa. She has written several articles on Soviet-Russian politics and environmental issues. She is the author of *The Environment and Marxism-Leninism* (Westview, 1985) and *Russian Politics in Transition* (Houghton-Mifflin, 1997) and is the editor of *To Breathe Free: Eastern Europe's Environmental Crisis* (Woodrow Wilson Center Press and Johns Hopkins University Press, 1991) and coauthor, with John Hannigan, of *Environmental Security and Quality after Communism* (Westview, 1995). She received her Ph.D. in political science from the University of Wisconsin—Madison and previously taught at McGill University and Colorado State University.

MARK G. FIELD is Emeritus Professor of Sociology at Boston University; Adjunct Professor, Department of Health Policy and Management, School of Public Health, and Associate in the Davis Center for Russian Studies, Harvard University; and Assistant Sociologist, Department of Psychiatry, Massachusetts General Hospital, Boston. He holds the A.B., A.M., and Ph.D. from Harvard University. He is the author, coauthor, and editor of ten books and over 125 articles or book chapters in the professional literature. His major interests are health conditions in the former Soviet Union and comparative health care systems.

ALEKSANDER A. GALKIN is Professor and Doctor of History at the Russian Academy of Sciences. His field of research is contemporary history and political science. He is currently an adviser for the Foundation of Socio-Economic and Political Studies at the Gorbachev Foundation and a leading researcher at the Institute of Sociology, Russian Academy of Sciences. He has been a fellow of the Russian Academy of Sciences for more than three decades. He has written books on political behavior and mass political movements.

NAIL MIDKHATOVICH MOUKHARIAMOV is Associate Professor of Political Science at the University of Kazan. He has written numerous books and articles on nationalism and ethnic relations in the republic of Tatarstan and in the former Soviet Union as a whole. One of his current areas of research is the transition to democracy in multiethnic societies as a theme for the theory of ethnopolitics.

D. J. PETERSON is a postdoctoral fellow at the University of California, Los Angeles, and a resident consultant for the International Studies Group at the RAND Corporation in Santa Monica, California. He has authored over twenty-five articles on domestic social, economic, and environmental affairs in Russia and the former Soviet Union, and he wrote the RAND-sponsored book *Troubled Lands: The Legacy of Soviet Environmental Destruction* (Westview, 1993).

GREG POELZER is Assistant Professor in the Political Science Programme of the University of Northern British Columbia. He has conducted extensive fieldwork in Sakha (Yakutia) republic and Chukotka and has published articles and presented papers in the areas of aboriginal-state relations and northern development. He is a coeditor of *Polar Geography and Geology,* an interdisciplinary journal on the Russian and circumpolar north.

DON K. ROWNEY is Professor of History and a member of the Graduate Program in Policy History at Bowling Green State University. His research interests focus on the history of Russian state administration and, more recently, on the history of the state-economy relation in Russia and the former USSR. He is also editor of the *Policy History Newsletter.*

DARRELL SLIDER is Associate Professor of Government and International Affairs at the University of South Florida in Tampa. He is coauthor, with Stephen White and Graeme Gill, of *The Politics of Transition: Shaping a Post-Soviet Future* (Cambridge, 1994). His many articles on Soviet and post-Soviet politics have been published in such journals as *Slavic Review* and *Post-Soviet Affairs.*

PETER J. STAVRAKIS is Deputy Director of the Kennan Institute for Advanced Russian Studies of the Woodrow Wilson International Center for Scholars and Associate Professor of Political Science at the University of Vermont. He has written numerous articles on contemporary Russian politics, the effectiveness of U.S. foreign assistance, and bureaucratic reform and state-building in the Soviet successor states, and he is the author of *Moscow and Greek Communism, 1944–1949* (Cornell, 1989). Other recent publications include an analysis of the 1995 Russian parliamentary elections and a critical examination of the U.S. Agency for International Development. His current research interests include the development of bureaucracies in the Soviet successor states and an examination of U.S. assistance to the newly independent states.

JOHN F. YOUNG is Assistant Professor at the University of Northern British Columbia and recently completed his doctorate in political science at the University of Toronto. His research interests include the quest for local self-government in Russia and municipal-regional relations.

INDEX

aboriginal peoples, in Russia and Canada, 195–209
abortion, 168, 170
administration: local, 24; preindustrial, 15–17. *See also* government
administrative units, Soviet, 58
Agrarian Party, 63, 67
"Agreement . . . on Economic Cooperation" (Tatarstan), 221
agriculture: and economic restructuring, 160; in northern European region, 153; in southern European region, 158–9; in Type III regions, 66; in Type IV regions, 67–9
Aipin, Yeremei, 195
Aksel, E. M., 171
Alberta, Canada, 195–209
Alberta Federation of Métis Settlement Associations, 207
Alberta Métis Settlements Accord, 205
alcoholism, 168–9
Alexander I, reforms of, 16–17
Alexander II, and Great Reforms, 27
Altai krai, 171; seasonal workers in, 185–6
Altai republic, 170–1
Amur oblast, 108
Andrews, Jo, 8n5
anomie, social, 169–70

AOs. *See* joint-stock societies
"Appeal to the Soviet People" (1991), 237
appointment: of governors, 50–1; power of, 89, 91–2
Arkhangelsk oblast, 153
armed forces, ethnic segregation in, 185
Armenia, 184
Armenians, in western Siberia, 183–92
Association of the Small Peoples of the North, 196, 207
associations, regional, 127
Astrakhan oblast, privatization in, 111
attitudes, electoral, and regional typology, 70–8
authoritarianism, decentralized, 5
authority, and power, 82–3
automobiles, and environmental pollution, 154
autonomy: of aboriginal peoples, 205–9; cultural, 52–3; of "despotic" state, 23–4; economic, 54; enterprise, 123–4; ethnic, 52–3; of local governments, 90; regional, 52–3, 86–7, 130; state, 26; of state elites, 24–5; of Tatarstan, 220

Bagaev, Mikhail, 208
Bairamova, Fauziya, 218

bankruptcy procedure, lack of, 110
banks, privatization and, 110–11
Barabanov, V. A., 95
Bashkortostan, 63–4; bilateral treaty, 48–9; privatization in, 107, 110
behavior, political, 57–79; and regional typology, 60; in Type I regions, 61–4; in Type II regions, 64–6; in Type III regions, 66–7; in Type IV regions, 67–9. *See also* attitudes, electoral
Belgorod oblast, 51
Belyaev, Sergei, 109
"Big Problems of the Small Peoples" (Pika and Prokhorov), 195
bilateralism, 219–20
bilateral treaties, 48–50, 107, 221–3
birth rate, 168
Black Earth area, 158–9
borders, nationalities and, 36. *See also* frontiers
branch unionism, 120–1, 131, 135; neopaternalism and, 125–6; regionalism and, 122, 143n74
Bratsk, 157
Buckley, Cynthia, 7, 239
budget: health care, 166, 174; local, 89–90, 92–3; regional, 86; of republics, 226
Burkov, Sergei, 114–15, 117n54
Buryatia, 107; bilateral treaty, 48–9

Catherine the Great, 18
center, 11–28
center-periphery relations, 11–28; Tatarstan and, 216, 219–20
Central Chernozem Region, 171
centralism, 234
centralization, 15, 17, 24–7
charters, regional, 48, 94
Chechnya, 45, 53–4; conflict in, 39, 54, 158, 242–3
Chechnya-Ingushetia, 38, 53, 170, 174
Chelyabinsk oblast, 156

Chepelev, V. A., 95
Chernomyrdin, Viktor, 49
children, health of, 169–70
Christianity, Métis and, 199
Chubais, Anatoly, 107–9
Chukotka autonomous okrug, 40
Chuvashia, 54, 113; bilateral treaty, 48–9
cities, 149, 164n40
citizenship, universal, 200
clans, among Tokkinsky Evenk, 198–9
clan soviets, use of term, 201
Clark, Carol, 6, 242
cold war, impact on health, 166–7
Committee for the Affairs of the Small Native Peoples, 201
Committee of the North, 200
Committee on State Property, 126
Communist Party of Russian Federation (CPRF), 3, 5, 63, 67, 229
Communist Party of the Soviet Union (CPSU), 35; Tatar Regional Committee, 216
comparative history, 195–209
concessions, state, to regional elites, 106–7
Confederation of Labor, 136, 137n2, 143–4n77
conscription, military, 19–21
constitutional court, 48, 220; and Federation Council dispute, 51
constitutional referendum (December 1993), 39–40
Constitution of 1993, 39–47, 96, 222, 241–2; Article 72, 84; Article 73, 47; Article 77, 46; Article 85, 47; Article 90, 47
constitutions, of republics, 44, 48, 94; Tatarstan, 219–20, 222
Council of Heads of Republics, 51–2, 54
Council of the Federation, 96
coup attempt of 1991, 237
court system, 47

crime: organized, 53; in Type I regions, 64; in Type II regions, 66; in Type III regions, 67; in Type IV regions, 69
Crowley, Stephen, quoted, 139n14
cultural exchange, among aboriginal peoples, 199
"currency corridor," 62

Dagestan, 114, 171
Daniels, Robert, 7
DeBardeleben, Joan, 6, 235, 241
decentralization: of health care, 174–5; state attempts, 27–8
"Declaration of State Sovereignty" (Tatarstan), 218, 220
Decree No. 239 (Yeltsin), 95–6
defense industry, 112
Delo newspaper, 138n4
democracy, attitudes toward, 71, 74–5
democratization, 234–6
depopulation, 157. *See also* population decline
de-statification. *See* privatization
Dion, J. F., quoted, 199
discrimination, in federal structure, 50
division of powers, 37–8, 46
Dudayev, Dzhokhar, 53
Dvoryin, V. V., 171

Eberstadt, Nicholas, quoted, 166
ecology: and regional typology, 58; in Type III regions, 67; in Type IV regions, 69
economic development, 13–14
economic divisions, 58–60
economic perceptions, 190–1
economic policies, 119; regions and, 126
economic trends, 146–50; regional views of, 71, 73
economy: global, 150; postindustrial model, 145–6, 152; and power of state, 21; of Tatarstan, 215, 221; of Type I regions, 61–2; of Type II regions, 65–6; of Type IV regions, 67–8
egalitarianism, aboriginal, 200–5
elections: federal, 51–2; of governors, 50–1; local, 40, 94; of 1993, 62–5, 67–9; of 1995, 2, 5, 70–8, 226–9; of 1996, 2–3; regional, 40, 85
elites: local, 106; regional, 2, 126–7; state, 15–17, 24–6; of Tatarstan, 216, 221; village, 188
emigration, 157
employment, 130, 134. *See also* management, enterprise; workers
energy use, 162n8
enterprises: control of, 109–10; neopaternalism and, 119. *See also* management, enterprise
environment, 145–61. *See also* pollution, environmental
equality, in Russian Federation, 47
Ermakov, S. P., quoted, 169
ethnic conflict, 69, 114
ethnicity, 4, 7; and administrative structure, 36–7; and occupation, 183–92; and regional typology, 58, 63–4, 67–9; and separateness, 187. *See also* identity, ethnic
ethnonationalism, Tatar, 225–30
European Union (EU), TACIS Program, 2
events, controlling, 15
Ewing Commission (Canada), 203–5
exchange rate, dollar-ruble, 62
exports, 147–8, 152, 157, 159, 162n7

favoritism, in federal structure, 50
federalism, 35–55, 83–7, 233–4; ad hoc, 48–50; asymmetrical, 48–50, 83–4, 97n1; Soviet, 35–7, 235–6. *See also* pseudo-federalism
federal relations, 39–40; shift in, 85–6. *See also* bilateral treaties; trilateral treaty

Federal Treaty (1992), 37–9, 44–5, 84, 96, 98n6, 241
Federation Council, 51–2
Federative Agreement, 219–20
Federatsiya Nezavisimaya Profsoyuzov Rossii (FNPR), 118–19, 124–6
Feshbach, Murray, quoted, 170
Field, Mark, 6–7, 242
finance capital, concentration of, 110
finances, local, 90, 92–3
financial-industrial groups (FPGs), 111–12
Fish, M. Steven, 8n5
food supply, 88, 170–1
FPGs. *See* financia-industrial groups
frontiers, 199–200

Gaidar, Yegor, 106, 220–1
Galkin, Aleksander, 6, 242
geography, and regional typology, 58–60
Giddens, Anthony, quoted, 199
Gift Lake (Alberta, Canada), 195–209
GKI. *See* State Committee on Property
GMPR. *See* Mining and Metallurgy Trade Union of Russia
Gorbachev, Mikhail, 37
government, local, 81–90, 99n15; aboriginal peoples and, 208; and *gubernatorzatsiia*, 93–5; soviets as, 88; strategies for, 95–7
government, regional, 88–90
government control, privatization and, 114
governors, 51, 99n10; appointment of, 85; dismissal of, 98n9; and power of appointment, 89, 91–2; selection of, 50–1
Great Depression, 203
gubernatorzatsiia, and local government, 93–5

health care: budget, 166, 174; current situation of, 167–70; decentralization of, 174–5; Soviet model, 165–6, 174–6; universal, 165
health crisis, regional dimensions of, 170–7
heavy industry, decline of, 128
Hockstader, Lee, quoted, 166
holding companies, privatization and, 108
homicide, 168–9
hospital, use of term, 174
human rights, under Constitution of 1993, 46
hunting-gathering, 198–9

identity, ethnic: of aboriginal peoples, 207; Armenian, 183–92; and Soviet federalism, 235–6; Tatar, 213–14, 218, 225–30. *See also* ethnicity
illiteracy, aboriginal peoples and, 204
income, per capita, 2
income disparity, regional, 160
independence: Chechnya and, 53–4; in 1917–18, 28. *See also* autonomy
Independent Trade Union of Miners (NPG), 119, 125, 136
index of loyalty, 62, 64, 67
index of oppositionism, 62, 64, 67
industrialization, 21–4; and power of state, 12–13; Soviet model, 128; state role in, 22, 24; in Type II regions, 64–6
industrial output, decline in, 146–7
industrial structure, Soviet, 127–8
industry. *See names of industries*
inequity, economic, 2–3, 48
inflation, under Catherine the Great, 18
information, control of, 91
infrastructure: and environmental pollution, 148–9, 154; human,

19–21, 23; oil transport, 155; and role of state, 14, 17–24; urban, 158
insiders, local, privatization and, 106
institutions: and economic development, 13–14; federal, 51–2; and power of state, 21; state elites and, 27
insurance, medical, 170, 175
integration, ethnic, 239
intergovernmental agreements, 221
intergovernmental relations, 81–97; in Omsk, 90–3
intervention, federal, 95–6
investment: foreign, 111–12, 114; private, 105
Irkutsk oblast, 49, 56n24
Islam, Tatars and, 214
Ittifak, 218
Ivanova, A. Ye., 169

joint authority, under Constitution of 1993, 46
joint jurisdiction, 96, 242
joint-stock societies (AOs), 107–8, 132

Kabardino-Balkaria, 107; bilateral treaty, 48–9; privatization in, 109–10
Kahan, Arcadius, 19–21; quoted, 19
Kaliningrad oblast, 49, 153
Kamchatka oblast, 171
Kankrin, Yegor, quoted, 22
Karachaevo-Cherkessia, 97–8n4
Karamzin, N. M., 16; quoted, 18–19, 21–2
Karelia, "green belt," 153
Keenan, Edward, 234
Kemerovo oblast, 112, 127, 134–5, 156
Khabarovsk krai, 171
Khanty-Mansiisk autonomous okrug, 45; electoral attitudes in, 70–8
Khasbulatov, Ruslan, 220

Kiselev, A. S., 169
Komi, 107, 152, 163n36; bilateral treaty, 48–9
Kostroma oblast, 171
Kotlas paper mill, 153
krais, 36, 58; autonomy of, 52–3; response to Chechnya war, 54; status of, 48–50
Krasnoyarsk Aluminum Plant, 114
Krasnoyarsk krai, 45, 156
Kravchuk, Leonid, 237
Kurgan oblast, 171
Kuznetsov, Andrei, quoted, 140n32

labor institutions, 118–37
labor relations, 118–19, 141n39; cooperative model, 132–3
labor shortage, regional, 193n10
landownership rights, 112
land sales, to enterprises, 112–13
land use patterns, in northern European region, 153
language: Russian, 44, 218; state, 44; Tatar, 218; Yakut, 199, 211n16
"Law Concerning Nomadic Clan Communities of the Small-Numbered Peoples of the North," 205
"Law on Krai and Oblast Soviets of People's Deputies and Krai and Oblast Administrations," 38
Law on the State Enterprise (1987), 123
leadership, political, aboriginal peoples and, 208
lease agreements, enterprises and, 113
legislation: environmental, 161n2; for FPGs, 112; for local government, 88, 96
legislature, bicameral, 51
Lehmann, Susan, 8n5
leopard, Amur, 151
levers *(rychagi)*, 82; and center-regional relations, 84–6

Liberal Democratic Party of Russia (LDPR), 62–4, 67
liberals, 62–3
life expectancy, 168–9
lifestyle, traditional, of aboriginal peoples, 198–200
logging industry, 163n25; in Far East region, 150–1; in northern European region, 152
Luzhkov, Yuri, 107–8, 113
Lysenko, Vladimir, quoted, 223–4

macroeconomics, 4
Magadan oblast, 169, 171, 174
Magnitogorsk, 156
management, enterprise, 162n5; strength of, 119–20; as union leaders, 140n31; and union membership, 133; worker identification with, 140n32
Mann, Michael, 17–18; quoted, 12–13, 28n2
mayors, dismissal of, 91–2, 95–6
media: aboriginal peoples and, 208; in Tatarstan, 218, 220–1
Meditsinskaya gazeta, 176
metallurgy, 128, 130, 156–7, 164n39
Métis Association of Alberta (Canada), 203
Métis people (Canada), 195–209, 211n31; status of, 202; use of name, 210–11n12
Métis Population Betterment Act (Canada), 203–4
Métis Settlement Association (Canada), 204, 206
microhistory, 195–209
migration: of aboriginal peoples, 199; seasonal labor, 184–5, 192n3; from western Siberia, 187
militarism, early twentieth-century decline of, 22
military, 17–21; "professional," 24
military spending, 18, 22–3
miners, 125, 127

Mining and Metallurgy Trade Union of Russia (GMPR), 121, 126, 128–36
mining industry, 61–2, 128–35, 156
ministerial model, 17, 27
Ministry of Foreign Economic Relations, 111
mobilization, political, of aboriginal peoples, 196, 205–9
monopolism, 128
morbidity, 167, 169; child, 171
mortality, 165–74; wartime, 20–1
Moscow, 2–3, 99n14, 112–13, 168, 174; administrative status of, 36–7; as center, 11, 96–7, 162n10; privatization in, 107–8
Moukhariamov, Nail Midkhatovich, 7, 241
Mukha, Vitaly, 98n9
municipalities, and waste management, 148–9, 154
Murmansk oblast, 112

nationality, and administrative structure, 36–7
national principle, 35–7
Native associations, in North, 196
"Native question, the," 200
Natives. *See* aboriginal peoples
natural resources, 52, 145–61; control of, 242; ownership of, 161; in Tatarstan, 221; in Type I regions, 60–4
Nemtsov, Boris, 113
neopaternalism, 119–20, 123–6, 134; and branch unionism, 120–1, 125–6
newspapers, 91, 138n4
Nizhni Novgorod oblast, 49, 51, 171; electoral attitudes in, 70–8; land sales in, 113
nomadism, 198–205
nonpayments, economic effects of, 62
Norilsk, 157, 174
Norris, Malcom, quoted, 204

North, Douglass C., quoted, 13
North Caucasus, 114; regional wars in, 69
North-Western Region, 171
Novokuznetsk, 137n2, 156; Zapsib Metallurgical Combinat, 134–5
Novo-Ogarevo negotiations, 219
Novosibirsk oblast, 51
NPG. *See* Independent Trade Union of Miners
Nur, 226, 229

oblasts, 36, 58; autonomy of, 52–3; response to Chechnya war, 54; status of, 48–50
oblasts, autonomous, 36–7
occupation, and ethnicity, 183–92
officials, regional, privatization and, 106–15
oil industry, 61–2, 155; in Tatarstan, 215, 221
okrugs, 58
okrugs, autonomous, 36, 44–5; in Russian Federation, 40; status of, 48–50
Olekminsk, 197
Olekminsky okrug, 201
Olekminsky raion, 201
Omsk, 101n33; oblast-municipal relations in, 90–3
Orel oblast, electoral attitudes in, 70–8
Orenburg oblast, 49, 51
organizations, in institutional framework, 14
Our Home Is Russia, 226, 229
"outsiders," ethnic Armenians as, 183–92

pacification, internal, 200, 202, 204
pantribalism, 207
paper industry, 152–3
parties, political: and regional voting behavior, 70–8; in Type I regions, 62–3; in Type II regions, 64–5. *See also names of parties*
partnerships, company, 133–4
pastoralism, 198
path dependence, 14; reforms and, 16
peasantry, 16; and military conscription, 20–1
periphery, use of term, 11
Perm oblast, 49, 153
personal income tax, 86
Peterson, D. J., 6, 242
physicians, 175; availability of, 174
Pika, A., "Big Problems of the Small Peoples," 195
Pintner, Walter M., 22–3
poaching, 151
Pocklington, T. C., quoted, 202
Poelzer, Greg, 7, 235
Polevanov, Vladimir, 108–9
Polezhaev, Leonid, 91
policy, and outcomes, 15, 27
political development, aboriginal, 200–5
poll tax, 18; abolition of, 23
pollution, environmental, 147–9, 170; agriculture and, 159; automobiles and, 154; coal industry and, 156; control efforts, 148; in Far East region, 151; logging and, 150–1; and lung cancer mortality, 171–4; metallurgy and, 157; oil industry and, 155; paper industry and, 153; in southern European region, 158; steel industry and, 156; in urban areas, 153–4
population: aboriginal, 210n6; of Chechnya, 53; of Far East region, 150–1; heterogeneity of, 183–4; of Omsk, 90; of Russia, 162n11; of Siberia, 157; of southern European region, 158; of Tyanya, 197
population decline, 165, 168–9
POS settlement, 202

power: and authority, 82–3; devolution of, 83, 106; division of, 82–7; organization of, 81; regional, 95–7
pragmatism, and Tatarstan model, 220–1, 230
president, powers of, 46–7, 50, 85
presidential representatives, 99n10
presidents, of republics, 89
Pressat, Roland, quoted, 166
price of land, 112–13
Primorsky krai, 51, 176
privatization, 89–90, 105–15, 123; early stage, 107–8, 114; methods of, 105, 108–10; and neopaternalism, 124; and regional elites, 126–7; and seasonal construction brigades, 191; second stage, 108–10, 114; terms of, 106
privatization checks, 107; investment funds for, 108; in Tatarstan, 107
profit tax, 86
Prokhorov, B., "Big Problems of the Small Peoples," 195
property, state, 109; levels of, 105–6. *See also* privatization
Property Funds, 126
property rights, 161
property tax, 89
protectionism, regional, 127
provinces, "undergoverned," 17
provincial councils, 234
pseudo-federalism, 235; of Russian republic, 239–40
Pskov oblast, 171
public health problems, 158

rationalization, and state administration, 15–16
real estate, privatization and, 112–13
recentralization, 5
referendum of April 1993, 61–2
reform, economic, 16, 121–3, 145–6
refugees, 158
region, use of term, 97n1

regional councils, 51
regionalism: labor and, 118–23; rise of, 126–7; variations in, 4–5
regionalization: and branch unionism, 143n74; environmental, 145–61; and health crisis, 170–7; and industrial restructuring, 127
regional-local relations, 81–97
regions: central and northern European, 152–4; eastern Siberia, 150–2, 195–209; economic, 58; European, 170; Far East, 150–2, 170; privatization and, 106–15; Rust Belt, 160–1; selection of governors, 50–1; southern European, 158–9; southern Siberia, 154–7; Urals, 154–7. *See also* oblasts
regions, typology of, 57–61, 69–70; and electoral attitudes, 70–8; Type I, 60–4; Type II, 60–1, 64–6; Type III, 61, 66–7; Type IV, 61, 67–9
reindeer, 198
renationalization, 109
rents, and preindustrial state power, 19–21
republics, 58, 84; autonomy of, 52–3; budgets, 226; powers of, 47; privatization and, 107; response to Chechnya war, 54; status of, 40–4, 48–50
republics, autonomous, 36–7; and breakup of USSR, 37; under Federal Treaty, 38; as periphery, 38
residence: official, 193n10; permanent, 186
resource mobilization theory, 206–9
resources, natural. *See* natural resources
resources, of aboriginal peoples, 207–9
restructuring: economic, 145–7, 152,

159; industrial, 127–8
Revich, B. A., 171
Reynolds, Scott, 144n77
Rossel, Eduard, 56n27, 98n9
Rowney, Don, 5, 234
Ruble, Blair, 8n5
Russia: as despotic autonomous state, 17–18; Tatar influence on, 214
Russian Academy of Science (RAN), 62
Russian Federation: composition of, 38, 40–5; division of powers in, 37–8, 46; equality in, 47; heterogeneity of, 183–4; regional budgets, 227–9; vertical dimension of, 81
Russian Health Ministry, 165
Russian Soviet Federated Socialist Republic (RSFSR). *See* Russian Federation
Russia's Choice, 62
Russkikh, Pavel, quoted, 224
Rutskoi, Aleksandr, quoted, 220
Rybinsk Motor Works, 110

Sabirov, Mukhammat, 221
St. Petersburg, 49, 99n14, 112–13, 168, 174; administrative status of, 36–7; as center, 11, 162n10; Staleprokatny Factory, 130–2; status of, 55n18, 56
Sakhalin oblast, 171
Sakha republic, 107, 195–209; bilateral treaty, 48–9
Sakharov, Andrei, 216
Samara oblast, 112
Saratov oblast, 112
secession, right of, 37
segregation, ethnic, in armed forces, 185
self-government, aboriginal, 195–209
self-government, local.
  See government, local
serfdom, abolition of, 23
service sector, 139n20

settlements, aboriginal, 195–209
Shabanova, M. A., 185–6
Shabanova village, 186–91
Shaimiev, Mintimir, 219; quoted, 229–30
Shakhrai, Sergei, 97
share sales, as method of privatization, 108–10
Sheremet'ev, E. M., 95
Shoikhet, Yuri, 91
Shushkevich, Stanislav, 237
Siberia, 170; Armenians in, 183–92; eastern, 150–2, 195–209; population of, 157; southern, 154–7; western, 183–92
Siberian Agreement, 98n9, 127
Sievers, Jacob, 18
Slider, Darrell, 6, 242
"Small-Numbered Peoples of the North," 196, 210n6
"Small Peoples of the North," 200
Smirnyagin, L., quoted, 176
Smolensk oblast, 171
Sobchak, Anatoly, 113
social exchanges, and enforcement, 14
social networks, village, 188–189
social perceptions, village, 189–91
social services, 119–20. *See also* neopaternalism
socioeconomic sectors, 6
Sokolov, M. P., quoted, 198
Solnick, Steven, 8n5
Solzhenitsyn, Aleksandr, 115n6
Soskovets, Oleg, 109
South, shift toward, 146
soviets, as local governments, 88
Special Councils, creation of, 25
specialization, regional, 128, 130
special treatment, regional, 50
species, endangered, 151
Staleprokatny Factory (St. Petersburg), 130–2
Stalin, Joseph, and Tatars, 214
standard of living, regional views of, 71, 73–5

state, 12; "despotic," 17–18; growth of, 19, 22–4; power of, 46
statebuilding, and aboriginal peoples, 200
State Committee on Property (GKI), 107–8; Federal Bankruptcy Agency, 110
statehood, Tatar, 214
State Program of Economic and Social Progress (Tatarstan), 225
states, federal, powers of, 46–7
statistics, vital, 166, 168, 171
Stavrakis, Peter J., 242
Stavropol krai, 98n9; electoral attitudes in, 70–8
steel industry, 156
steelworkers, 125
stereotyping, ethnic, 185–6
Stoner-Weiss, Kathryn, 8n5
subsidies, 85–6; for coal mining, 156; for enterprises, 105, 110, 112; Tatarstan and, 225
suburbanization, 149
suicide, 168–9
Sukiasian, Grachuk, 186–91; quoted, 190
Supreme Court of the Russian Federation, 95
Supreme Soviet Committee for Local Soviet Affairs and the Development of Local Self-Government, 88
Supreme Soviet Committee on Local Self-Government, 95
Sverdlovsk oblast, 49–50, 107, 112

Taimyr autonomous okrug, 45
takeovers, "hostile," 110
Tambov oblast, 51
Tatar autonomous republic, 214
Tatar Public Center, 217
Tatars, 213–14
Tatarstan, 38, 63–4, 213–31; bilateral treaty, 48–9, 221–3; "Declaration of State Sovereignty," 218, 220; economy of, 215, 221; image of, 225; interethnic relations in, 215; Investment-Financial Corporation, 111; natural resources of, 221; oil industry in, 215, 221; "post-sovereignization," 221–3; "pre-sovereignization," 216–18; privatization in, 107; "reorientation" of, 215–16; "sovereignization," 218–21
Tatarstan model, 213–31; evolution of, 217
taxation: under Constitution of 1993, 46; regions and, 86, 89; republics and, 48–9; Tatarstan and, 224–5
taxes: nonpayment of, 224–5; and preindustrial state power, 18–19
technology, and power of state, 12–13, 25
territorial principle, 35–7
territories. See krais
tiger, Siberian, 151
Tilly, Charles, quoted, 196, 210n9
Tokkinsky Evenk, 195–209
Tokkinsky raion, 201
Tokkinsky Village Soviet, 201
Tomsk oblast, 51, 169
trade union federation, 118; identity crisis in, 125. See also Federatsiya Nezavisimaya Profsoyuzov Rossii (FNPR)
trade unions, 119–21, 128–35; alternative, 119; independent, 138n7, 143–4n77; local-national relations in, 131–6; neopaternalism and, 123–6; official, 124–5; traditional, 124–5, 129. See also branch unionism; names of unions
Trans-Siberian Railway, 150
trilateral treaty, 49
Tripartite Commission, 118
Tula, 132–4
Tulachermet Concern (Tula), 132–4
Tuleev, Aman, 117n54
Tuva republic, 170–1

Tver oblast, 51
Tyansky soviet, 197
Tyanya (eastern Siberia), 195–209
typology of regions, 57–70; and electoral attitudes, 70–8
Tyumen oblast, 155

Udmurtia, 107; bilateral treaty, 48–9; privatization in, 111–12
Uglich, 95–6
unconstitutionality, in regional charters, 48
unemployment, 65, 185, 193n10
Union of Soviet Socialist Republics, as federal system, 35–7
Union Treaty (1991), 236–7
United Nations Development Program, 152
Urals Factories FPG, 111–12
Urban, Michael, 8n5
Ust-Ordinsk Buryat autonomous okrug, 56n24
Ust-Ordinsk Buryat autonomous region, 49

value-added tax, 86
village elders, 94
villagization, 202
Vladimir oblast, 94, 112, 171
Vlasov, Yuri, 94
Volga-Vyatka Central Region, 171
Volgograd oblast, 171
Vorkuta, 163n36
voting behavior. *See* attitudes, electoral; behavior, political
voucher auctions, 126

waste management, 148–9, 154
water supply, 171
West, distrust of, 3–4
workers, 130, 141n39, 183–92; and enterprise ownership, 123–4; neopaternalism and, 119–20
World Health Organization, 167
World War I, centralization and, 24–6

Yabloko bloc, 62
Yakovlev, Vladimir, 56n23
Yakut ASSR, 200–2, 211n22
Yakut people, 199
Yakutsk, 197
Yamal-Nenets autonomous okrug, 45, 155
Yaroslavl oblast, 51, 170
Yekaterinburg, 174
Yeltsin, Boris: and adoption of 1993 Constitution, 39–40; centralizing tendency, 240–1; and dissolution, 237–8; and federal relations, 85–6; and Mukha, 98n9; and privatization in Moscow, 107–8; and regional power, 83; and selection of governors, 50; in Tatarstan, 218
Young, John, 6

Zapsib Metallurgical Combinat, 134
Zaria collective farm, 186–91
Zatitsky, Eduard, 131
Zorkin, Valery, 220
Zyuganov, Gennady, 74–7, 229